PUTTING TEETH IN THE TIGER: IMPROVING THE EFFECTIVENESS OF ARMS EMBARGOES

Contributions to
CONFLICT MANAGEMENT, PEACE ECONOMICS AND DEVELOPMENT VOLUME 10

SERIES EDITOR
MANAS CHATTERJI

BOOKS IN THE SERIES

Eurasia: A New Peace Agenda, edited by M. D. Intriligator

Cultural Differences between the Military and Parent Society in Democratic Countries, edited by G. Caforio

Managing Conflict in Economic Convergence of Regions in Greater Europe, edited by F. Carluer

Military Missions and Their Implications Reconsidered: The Aftermath of September 11th, edited by G. Caforio and G. Kuemmel

Conflict and Peace in South Asia, edited by M. Chatterji and B. M. Jain

War, Peace, and Security, edited by Jacques Fontanel and Manas Chatterji

Armed Forces and Conflict Resolution, edited by G. Caforio, G. Kümmel and B. Purkayastha

Regional Development and Conflict Management: A Case for Brazil, by Raphael Bar-El

Crisis, Complexity and Conflict, by I. J. Azis

Putting Teeth in the Tiger: Improving the Effectiveness of Arms Embargoes, edited by Michael Brzoska and George A. Lopez

Peace Science: Theory and Cases, by P. Gangopadhyay and M. Chatterji (Forthcoming)

Advances in Military Sociology: Essays in Honor of Charles C. Moskos (Two Volume Set), edited by Giuseppe Caforio (Forthcoming)

Crisis Management and Regional Cooperation, by I. J. Azis (Forthcoming)

Contributions to
CONFLICT MANAGEMENT, PEACE ECONOMICS
AND DEVELOPMENT VOLUME 10

PUTTING TEETH IN THE TIGER: IMPROVING THE EFFECTIVENESS OF ARMS EMBARGOES

MICHAEL BRZOSKA

GEORGE A. LOPEZ

Emerald

United Kingdom – North America – Japan
India – Malaysia – China

Emerald Group Publishing Limited
Howard House, Wagon Lane, Bingley BD16 1WA, UK

First edition 2009

British Library Cataloguing in Publication Data
A catalogue record for this book is available from the British Library

ISBN: 978-1-84855-202-9
ISSN: 1572-8323 (Series)

Awarded in recognition of
Emerald's production
department's adherence to
quality systems and processes
when preparing scholarly
journals for print

INVESTOR IN PEOPLE

CONTENTS

LIST OF TABLES   *vii*

LIST OF CONTRIBUTORS   *ix*

FOREWORD   *xi*

INTRODUCTION   *xiii*

CHAPTER 1   A FRAMEWORK FOR THE ANALYSIS
OF THE EFFECTIVENESS OF ARMS EMBARGOES
    Michael Brzoska   *1*

CHAPTER 2   THE UNPRECEDENTED
EMBARGO: THE UN ARMS SANCTIONS
AGAINST IRAQ, 1990–2004
    Oldrich Bures and George A. Lopez   *29*

CHAPTER 3   THE CHALLENGE OF MEASURING
SUCCESS: YUGOSLAVIA'S SANCTIONS DECADE
(1991–2001)
    Wolf-Christian Paes   *55*

CHAPTER 4   US MEASURES AGAINST
PAKISTAN'S NUCLEAR POLICIES, 1990–2001
    Sumita Kumar   *81*

CHAPTER 5   TIGHTENING THE SCREWS IN WEST
AFRICAN ARMS EMBARGOES
    Maraike Wenzel and Sami Faltas   *101*

CHAPTER 6   FROM FAILURE TO SUCCESS:
THE IMPACT OF SANCTIONS ON ANGOLA'S
CIVIL WAR
    Wolf-Christian Paes   *137*

CHAPTER 7   UN ARMS EMBARGOES IN THE
GREAT LAKES, 1994–2004
    Marc von Boemcken   *163*

CHAPTER 8   ARMS EMBARGOES AGAINST
ERITREA AND ETHIOPIA
    Marc von Boemcken   *189*

CHAPTER 9   A QUANTITATIVE ANALYSIS
OF ARMS EMBARGOES
    Michael Brzoska   *205*

CHAPTER 10   PUTTING TEETH IN THE
TIGER: POLICY CONCLUSIONS FOR
EFFECTIVE ARMS EMBARGOES
    Michael Brzoska and George A. Lopez   *243*

ABOUT THE AUTHORS   *255*

LIST OF TABLES

Table 5.1   Timeline for Sanctions on Liberia   109
Table 5.2   Timeline of Sierra Leone Sanctions   111
Table 9.1   Average Scores of Dependent and Independent
             Variables.   208
Table 9.2   Ranking of the Most Successful Arms Embargoes . . .   209
Table 9.3   Average Success Rates of Arms Embargoes
             by Initiator   211
Table 9.4   Average Success Rates of Arms Embargoes
             by Sanctions Objective   213
Table 9.5   Average Success Rates of Arms Embargoes
             by Sanctions Type   214
Table 9.6   Average Success Rates of Arms Embargoes
             by Type of Target   215
Table 9.7   Average Success Rates of Arms Embargoes
             by Time Period   216
Table 9.8   Average Success Rates of Arms Embargoes
             by Year of Sanction Case Began   216
Table 9.9   Average Success Rates of Arms Embargoes
             by Their Duration   217
Table 9.10   Statistically Significant Correlation Coefficients   218
Table A1   List of Arms Embargo Cases   238

LIST OF CONTRIBUTORS

Marc von Boemcken	Bonn International Center for Conversion, Bonn, Germany
Michael Brzoska	Institute for Peace Research and Security Studies at the University of Hamburg, Hamburg, Germany
Oldrich Bures	Metropolitan University Prague, Prague, The Czech Republic
Sami Faltas	Centre for European Security Studies, University of Groningen, Groningen, The Netherlands
Sumita Kumar	Institute for Defence Studies and Analyses, New Delhi, India
George A. Lopez	Kroc Institute for International Peace Studies at the University of Notre Dame, Notre Dame, IN, USA
Wolf-Christian Paes	Bonn International Center for Conversion, Bonn, Germany
Maraike Wenzel	Freelance Journalist in Cologne, Germany, Specializing on International Affairs

FOREWORD

International sanctions by organizations like the United Nations or European Union and individual countries, such as the United States, have become a useful tool of foreign policy. It is needed to prevent the target countries from threatening the economic or political interest of the sanctioning organization and their allies. Sanctions are also applied on moral and ideological ground like supporting human rights and freedom, trade policies and patent violations, protectionist policies, etc. However, it is widely believed that the sanctions are not effective. Some of the sanctions are also costly for the organization implementing the sanctions and the target countries can always go around the sanctions and are successful in getting sources of supply.

An often-imposed sanction is the armed embargo. There have been many studies on sanctions, but few on the topic of arms embargo. The evidence in the literature, however, is that arms embargo does not have any impact on the target countries. Most of the conclusions in those studies were drawn on anecdotes without making any scientific analysis using analytical techniques. It is true that arms embargo itself may not be effective, but it may be very helpful in the broader foreign policy objectives. Sanctions and its effectiveness can also be studied in the framework of Public Choice theory taking into consideration of maximization of the choices of decision makers. It can be also related to domestic policies of sanctioning countries.

Manas Chatterji
Series Editor
May, 2009

INTRODUCTION

THE IMPLEMENTATION OF ARMS EMBARGOES: ANALYTICAL FOUNDATIONS FOR IMPROVING THEIR EFFECTIVENESS

Collective sanctions have long been a contested instrument of international politics, especially since 1990, when United States and large power use of the technique increased to the point where Richard Haass declared that a "sanctions epidemic" had emerged (Haass & O'Sullivan, 1999). Regional bodies, most notably by the European Union (EU), paralleled this trend through a dramatic increase in their own resort to sanctions (Kreutz, 2005). The imposition of sanctions by the United Nations (UN) reached the point that, in comparison to pre-1989 behavior, the 1990s were labeled "the sanctions decade" (Cortright & Lopez, 2000).

Yet, coercive sanctions under UN sponsorship were not new tools of statecraft. They are specifically mentioned in Chapter VII of the Charter of the UN as one of the two instruments available to enforce international peace and security. However, the rate of "success" of sanctions, if measured by changes in the behavior of targets, has been low. The imposition of sanctions often led to condemnation of their comprehensive economic effect on humanitarian grounds (Gordon, 1999). This critique was most pronounced in the cases of Iraq and Haiti the early 1990s and has instigated the search for "smart" sanctions (Carnegie Commission on Preventing Deadly Conflict, 1997; Pape, 1997; Elliott, 1998; Doxey, 1999; Cortright & Lopez, 2002a, 2002b; Wallensteen, 2002; Wallensteen & Staibano, 2005).

Arms embargoes comprise one of the major "targeted" or "smart" sanctions with discernible effects on the targets, while projecting as little damage as possible on the wider society. (Cortright & Lopez, 2000, 2002a, 2002b; Fruchart, Holtom, Wezeman, Strandow, & Wallensteen, 2007). The embargoes of arms occupy a preferred position among "smart" sanctions in that, on the one hand, they are an established and frequently used form of sanctions and provide a mechanism by which nations may respond to crisis by "doing something" while, on the other hand, such embargoes seldom impose unusual costs on the imposer. However, arms embargoes often rely on a number of factors for their success.

As is the case with trade sanctions, arms embargoes have often been assessed an apparent low rate of success, yet remain a widely used form of international sanctions. In fact, 19 of the 20 UN sanction regimes mandated by 2005 were arms embargoes, or had such an embargo as an element in the sanction package (see list in concluding chapter). In addition to sanctions mandated by the UN, the United States, the EU, and its applicant states – all powerful players in the international arms market – have announced the termination of arms sales and deliveries vis-à-vis notorious violators of international law and human rights.[1] Through 1987–2006, the period under investigation in this volume, the EU has imposed arms embargoes in 24 separate cases. The United States has halted arms deliveries to at least 35 countries in the past decade (see Appendix 3 of Chapter 9). While arms embargoes have been especially popular as an instrument employed to stifle and stop wars, they were also used as a reaction to gross violations of human rights, as a means of counter-terrorism and to foster democratization.

The policy and scholarly literature on arms embargoes has identified a number of factors that reduce their effectiveness. Among these are the limited participation of suppliers in arms embargoes, especially members of the permanent five (P5) of the UN Security Council. A recent study illustrates the problem by documenting that at the point of passing the last 21 multilateral arms embargoes, in 9 cases one or more P5 members had already established on-going military support for one of the parties about to be targets of the embargo. (Fruchart et al., 2007). Analysts in the non-governmental organization (NGO) community (e.g., Amnesty International, 2006) have regularly documented lack of overall enforcement, while scholars have examined in some detail problems of implementation on the ground in supplier countries; weak border control by neighboring countries; and, the emergence of gray and black arms markets (Brzoska, 1991; Brzoska & Pearson, 1994; Knight, 1998; Carnegie Commission on Preventing Deadly Conflict, 1997; Cortright & Lopez, 2000; Bondi, 2001). Some analysts have argued that UN embargoes imposed in civil war conditions have actually increased the havoc such wars generate and more attention much be devoted to target selection and the logic of engagement with parties affected (Tierney, 2005). On the contrary, recent work indicates that under certain conditions, as when arms embargoes are combined with UN peace-keeping focus, the success of an embargo increases (Fruchart et al., 2007). The varied problems of implementation of arms embargoes have attracted close attention and led to an increased interest in improving their efficacy (Cortright & Lopez, 2000, 2002a, 2002b; Tostensen & Bull, 2002; Brzoska, 2003).

Consistent with these concerns, the German government sponsored a series of meetings among international experts to collect and ventilate proposals on how to improve arms embargoes and travel sanctions. The entire process, which brought together academics and government experts from a large number of countries, was organized by the Bonn International Center for Conversion (Brzoska, 2000, 2001). The academics and government experts involved in the "Bonn-Berlin" process focused on the improvement of legal and practical sanctions mechanisms. The Swedish government later asked the Department for Peace and Conflict Studies at the University of Uppsala to conduct a similar exercise focusing on the implementation of sanctions, including arms embargoes (Wallensteen, Staibano, & Eriksson, 2002; Wallensteen & Staibano, 2005; Strandow, 2006; Fruchart et al., 2007). These interactions between academics and government experts proved useful in assisting governments and the UN with the implementation of embargoes.

Beginning with the 1996 arms embargo against groups connected to the former government of Rwanda, the UN now regularly monitors arms embargoes through expert groups (Berman, 2001). One result is that a number of countries often named in connection with arms embargo violations in the 1990s, such as Bulgaria, have improved their export control systems.[2] But the changes that have been instituted thus far fall short of the measures suggested in the Bonn-Berlin and Stockholm Processes as well as recommendations made as a result of various case studies by the various monitoring bodies (Cortright & Lopez, 2002a, 2002b; Wallensteen & Staibano, 2005).

TOWARD A NEW FRAMEWORK AND MORE NUANCED CRITERIA

Considering the frequent use of arms embargoes at the national, regional, and international level, there has been relatively little systematic investigation of the conditions for their success or failure, or in distinguishing among the various problems related to arms embargoes. The available literature, taking its cue from the more general sanctions assessments (Hufbauer, Schott, & Elliot, 1990; Pape, 1997), often assumes that arms embargoes do not work (Control Arms, 2006; Vines, 2007; Yidhego, 2007). And some condemn the arms embargoes as doing additional harm when they ban weapons coming into a conflict with discriminating between those who are law and norm violators and those who are attempting to defend themselves as victims (Tierney, 2005). However, the perception of widespread ineffectiveness is mostly based on loose analyses of singular cases and a failure to appreciate fully both the dynamics of the arms market and the different goals for arms embargoes. The lack of good studies on arms embargo implementation is partly due to the complexities of studying the subject. Thus, the recent Uppsala-SIPRI study, which has combined on-site analysis in Liberia and Sierra Leone with more traditional expert interviews and data gathering, may be one model for more detailed future research (Holtom, 2007a, 2007b; Fruchart et al., 2007).

However, there remains a great deal of information available on arms flows in general, and, therefore, more systematic scrutiny of arms embargoes is possible. Consequently, however useful suggestions for improving arms embargo regimes, such as those made in the Bonn-Berlin and Stockholm Processes of sanctions reform, may be, they may lack as broad and systematic a basis for their recommendations as they might otherwise have. To undertake a more systematic study proves useful due to the described gap between the popularity of arms embargoes and the generally accepted problems of implementation. This book is designed to provide a better basis for arms embargo implementation through analyzing past experiences on the basis of an analytical framework of incentives and disincentives for effective arms embargo implementation and the examination of a number of case studies that attempt to employ this framework.

Our framework begins with the stipulation that arms embargo design and implementation are the result of complex decision-making by senders and recipients. Without the decision by senders, there can, by definition, be no arms embargoes. Therefore, sender decision-making is a crucial element of the analysis of arms embargoes. At the same time, recipients are also very important. They can dramatically influence the effectiveness of arms embargoes through a variety of countermeasures. The central research question of the volume then is under what conditions have arms embargoes been successful in the past? Our working research hypothesis is that successful sanction regimes depend to an important extent on understanding and affecting incentives and disincentives in the target as well as arms supplier countries. In only rare cases have incentives and disincentives been examined regarding arms embargoes (Cortright & Lopez, 2005).

A precondition for the study of the success of arms embargoes is to refine the measure of their effectiveness. In both public perception and academic study, high standards of success dominate the field. Studies see arms embargoes as having failed when arms continue to be delivered to targeted states or groups, and the targeted policies are not changed. As pointed out by David A. Baldwin (Baldwin, 1985, 2000; see also Drezner, 2000), however, such strong criteria are not concomitant with political decision-making over sanctions. Real politics is based on cost-benefit considerations of sanctions, as well as the policy alternatives available. Academics have also tended to limit their research on the effectiveness of sanctions, including arms embargoes, to the examination of select variables, such as changes in targeted policies, instead of considering a broader spectrum of success.

Until recently, this narrow academic approach has consistently been based on the dominant studies of the Institute of International Economics (Hufbauer et al., 1990). Their much quoted conclusion on pre-1990s sanctions is that the instrument can only be considered "effective" in about one-third of the cases. These authors focused on economic indicators for effectiveness.[3] For arms embargoes, the criterion of success most often used is whether arms reach the target after the imposition of an embargo. This criterion will most likely never be met as long as there remain gray and black markets for arms. More subtle measures could be connected to changes in the conduct of war, getting opponents to the negotiating table or to an increase in the price of weapons. In essence, what has not been examined is the success of the arms embargoes in effecting the unacceptable status quo.

One insight present in the literature that can be considered helpful deals with dependence on arms transfers (Catrina, 1988; Krause, 1992; Brzoska & Pearson, 1994) and public goods theory (Kaempfer & Lowenberg, 1999). In dependency analysis, however, experts should also explore the broader set of factors set out above in our analytical framework, distinguishing between effects on sets of domestic actors and their reactions. A discussion concerning levels of "effectiveness," both with respect to the various types of effects and regarding the various actors, is an overarching theme of this book. Public goods theory asserts that arms embargoes get more efficient with the number of suppliers that cooperate. However, implementation becomes more difficult to monitor as the number of participants increases. As expanding participation in arms embargoes incurs transaction costs, the incentive for a free ride is high due to strong competition and increasing prices on the black market. It seems useful to investigate whether UN arms embargoes that bind all arms suppliers are more effective than those imposed by regional groups of important suppliers, such as the EU, or a single important supplier, such as the United States. Thus, the existing theory that more participants increase the effectiveness of the embargo may be offset by the fact that multilateral sanctions are more difficult to enforce.

An important but unexplored parallel question is which actors among the supplier states are adhering to, or "championing," arms embargoes and what induces states to implement them effectively. Some suppliers have greater implementation costs, in both economic and political terms, than others. In some countries where arms industries are an important source of employment, strong lobbying groups can be affected by a decision to stop arms exports. They may lobby the government to adopt a loose interpretation of an arms embargo. Illegal activity in defiance of an arms embargo will often be stimulated by the higher margins of trade to embargoed states. Lobbying and black market behavior on the supply side are almost as difficult to observe as are their results in targeted regions. However, the experience of research on recent embargo cases reveals that the synthesis of information available in the news media, special journals, and official reports yields necessary, relevant data. The data will never be perfect, yet it is often sufficient to judge trends with a reasonable degree of accuracy. The recent Uppsala-SIPRI collaborative documentation substantiates this (Fruchart et al., 2007).

Clearly, social scientists should adhere to the highest standards of measurement accuracy and data reliability. This is what makes the transfer of arms across malleable borders through gray and black markets a notoriously difficult subject of research. There is a lack of reliable official data cross-nationally or in time-series, and international sources can only partly fill the gap. However, as pointed out in Brzoska and Pearson (1994, Chapter 2), much information can be gleaned from looking at event sources such as regional newspapers and specialized arms trade journals. The data situation has improved somewhat lately, especially in the field of small arms. Major research efforts are underway to collect data on transfers of small arms and light weapons (see the website of the relevant NGO, www.iansa.org), and a good part of this research is related to efforts to improve the control of small arms and light weapons since the late 1990s (see, e.g., Small Arms Survey, 2005) as well as the UN monitoring groups mentioned earlier.

One major difficulty in studying the success of sanctions, including arms embargoes, is insulating the effects of sanctions from other policies at work in a targeted country. The Serbian or Iraqi economies, for instance, were just damaged not only by the international sanctions but also by the economic policies and war machines of their leaders. Their leaders were able to stay in place for so long, not just despite the sanctions, but, to some extent, because of the sanctions. The imposition of sanctions, including arms embargoes, leads to countermeasures by targeted states or groups, many of which were studied in the Stockholm Process. One of these countermeasures is to create alternate ways of supplies, such as for arms. These and related factors comprise another essential factor to study.

THE ORGANIZATION OF THIS BOOK

The chapters in this study examine a number of elements that are central to shaping the effectiveness of arms embargoes as we have discussed them earlier. These include actual arms transfer relations, including options for the substitution of these relations with other means of supply such as domestic production; causes for the implementation of the arms embargoes; type and nature of the sanctioned behavior; decision-making within the targeted country or group; effects on targeted countries; identification of domestic actors in the target country that gain or lose from the sanctions; as well as the implementation of arms embargoes by embargoing states. The case studies describe patterns in arms transfers and embargo-busting, causes for arms embargoes, and their effects in targeted countries and supplier implementation.

Much of the analysis undertaken in the case study chapters is framed by the measures of effectiveness developed in the next chapter and the identification of major variables hypothesized to influence arms embargo success. The methodology proposed here follows the tradition of focused and structured case studies (George, 1979). The case studies were selected to provide a broad range of situations, with respect to sanction objectives, length of the sanctions period, the sender of sanctions, type of target, scope of the sanctions, and geographical location of the sanctions episode. To a great extent, the "bias" of the chapters is toward United Nations Security Council embargoes, but other important cases, such as the US measures against Pakistan for a decade, are included as well. The chapter authors draw from wide ranging sources of both a global and local format, relying on our own analysis of available data, information, and previous analyses to generate our discussions and findings.

In Chapter 1, Michael Brzoska builds from the existing scholarly claims of the strengths and weaknesses of arms embargoes and from the various structural attempts at reforming arms embargo design and implementation to pose the challenge of what it means to evaluate the effectiveness of such measures. Drawing from the literature and analysis of arms flows and arms trade, he sketches a series of multi-leveled goals that can be employed in scrutinizing arms embargoes. These categories and concerns form the framework, which is used in varied ways in the case studies that follow.

In Chapter 2, Oldrich Bures and George A. Lopez examine anew the often analyzed case of the arms embargo against Iraq. Their contribution to our knowledge base is the examination of the flow of a vast array of conventional weaponry that was one aim of the Hussein regime in its quest to evade the strictly enforced sanctions. Their analysis shows that more than in most sanctions episodes, the unreliability of the black market and the strength of the monitoring and interdiction system made it impossible for the Iraqis to acquire any integrated weapons systems. At the same time, a potpourri of weapons, ammunition, and explosive materials did enter the country, which, when combined with the inability of the American armed forces to control weapons depots and ammunition caches around Iraq following their invasion of spring 2003, led these very same materials to arm the insurgency that exacts such high costs from the US forces in the following years.

In Chapter 3, Wolf-Christian Paes provides a thorough examination of the decade long and diverse embargo experience of the international community in its attempts to control arms flowing into the wars in Yugoslavia. Paes examines the complexities and often contradictory dictates of the arms embargoes placed against all parties from 1991 to 1995 and discusses the difficult issue that the war's imbalances and inequities of parties and purposes imposed on those who wanted to hold to a universal embargo. Paes also shows convincingly that the 1992–1995 embargo against Serbia and Montenegro was successful in various ways, while the final phase of sanctions during the Kosovo crisis in 1998 was much less successful. In Chapter 4 Sumita Kumar deals with one of the more confounding cases of arms sanctions in scrutinizing the saga of US measures designed to deny nuclear development to Pakistan during the 1990s. Kumar deftly shows that the dramatic inconsistency of US goals, its use of coercive instruments, and the US failure to appreciate the constellation of motivations guiding Pakistan and other actors in the region contributed to sanctions failure.

The next four chapters in the book examine the weighty complexities of imposing and enforcing arms embargoes in Africa's worst cases of internal wars. In Chapter 5, Mareike Wenzel and Sami Faltas document thoroughly the intertwined nature of the wars and sanctions in Liberia and Sierra Leone. Their analysis of the role of Charles Taylor's sanctions busting systems as well as the lack of enforcement by a myriad of regional and global actors makes this an exceedingly important chapter in the book. They give serious assessment to the utility and effectiveness of the secondary sanctions imposed in this case and show that while these embargoes were imposed too late into the warring situation to change the intensity of the war, once enforced more steadfastly by outside parties, the embargoes played a clear, albeit limited role, in bringing the wars to an end.

In Chapter 6, Wolf-Christian Paes examines the UN's first case of sanctions against a non-state actor in the form of the arms embargo imposed against the UNITA faction in the Angola civil war in 1993. He details the haphazard monitoring and enforcement that plagued this case for much of the 1990s and explores the factors that led to increasingly effective sanctions when UN commitment to use the embargo as leverage for peace solidified. Marc von Boemcken authors Chapters 7 and 8 covering the embargoes on the Great Lakes (1994–2004) and the Eritrean-Ethiopian conflict respectively. In the former, he dissects the very difficult cases of Rwanda and the Democratic Republic of Congo. The initial response of any analyst is that these two brutal tragedies are the ultimate case studies for rejecting any utility to either arms embargoes or the reach of the UN as a peace-building agency. Von Boemcken does not spare any of the international or nation-state actors their distinct culpability in misreading the seriousness of the violence in each instance and in imposing measures that were far too little in scope and much too late to make a difference during the periods of horrific violence on the 1990s. He ends, however, with a tone of cautious optimism as he finds the newer embargoes of this decade more focused, better enforced, and more tied to other regional and international efforts to achieve peace. In Chapter 8, he explores the unique case of threats, imposition, and declining relevance that has been the history of sanctions on Eritrea and Ethiopia. The chapter is especially helpful in tracing the varied external actors, including members of the P5, who provided massive arms to the region during the 1990s, and who then were quickly ready to resupply these nations after the embargo ended in 2001.

We complement these cases with an additional analytical and comparative study in Brzoska's Chapter 9 in which he provides a quantitative analysis of the effectiveness of arms embargoes using clusters of variables identified in the theoretical framework. This chapter reveals a more generalized pattern across a larger number of diverse cases that also appears in the individual cases that preceded it. To wit, the more multilateral the structure of imposing sanctions, the more tied such measures are to monitoring and enforcement, and the more adaptability of the embargo to changing conditions in the situation and target, the more likely that the arms sanctions will attain some level of success.

The results of the case studies and the data comparison of Chapter 9 serve as the basis for a final chapter outlining policy conclusions and recommendations in Chapter 10. Here, we outline suggestions for how arms embargoes might be improved over time by paying greater attention both to the lessons of recent cases and to the array of factors that we discuss as more nuanced in dealing with arms flows than have been related to sanctions in previous studies.

NOTES

1. In addition to "official" sanctions agreed upon formally within the processes of its Common Foreign and Security Policy, the EU member countries can coordinate a de facto stop of arms transfers. In 1998, the EU governments agreed to a code of conduct on arms exports, which among other things, aimed at curbing the supply of lethal equipment to authoritarian regimes that are likely to use them for internal repression or external aggression'. Similarly, the United States has had de facto stops of the delivery military equipment and training without formally referencing these as arms embargoes. Various Acts include arms embargo elements or denial of export licenses on specified grounds, such as the Export-Import Act, the Arms Export Control Act, the International Emergency Economic Powers Act, and others.

2. The Swedish Peace Research Institute SIPRI documents changes in export control systems. On Bulgaria, see http://projects.sipri.se/expcon/natexpcon/Bulgaria/bul_ch.htm

3. For studies on the effects of sanctions in terms of goal achievement (leaving effects on the population aside), see Baldwin (1985, 1998), Leyton-Brown (1987), Nincic and Wallensteen (1983), Hufbauer et al. (1990), van Bergeijk (1994, 1999), and van Bergeijk and van Marrewijk (1995). For a more positive assessment of the effects of sanctions, see Crawford and Klotz (1999). Kaempfer and Lowenberg show in contrast to Hufbauer et al. that "sanctions that create minimal economic hardship can still generate political change": sanctions impact the utility of the ruling as well as the opposition group in the target country in such a way that their interest in maintaining or opposing the policy of misconduct is altered (Kaempfer & Lowenberg, 1988, p. 786; 1999).

REFERENCES

Amnesty International (2006). UN arms embargoes: An over of the last ten years. Control Arms Briefing Note, 16 March, 6pp.

Baldwin, D. A. (1985). *Economic statecraft*. Princeton, NJ: Princeton University Press.

Baldwin, D. A. (1998). Evaluating economic sanctions. *International Security, 23*(2 Fall), 189–194.

Baldwin, D. A. (2000). The sanctions debate and the logic of choice. *International Security, 24*(3), 80–107.

Berman, E. (2001). Sanctions against the genocidaires: Experiences of the 1998 UN international commission of inquiry. In: M. Brzoska (Ed.), *Smart sanctions, the next step: Arms embargoes and travel sanctions*. Baden-Baden: Nomos.

Bondi, L. (2001). Arms embargoes: In name only. In: M. Brzoska (Ed.), *Smart sanctions: The next steps – The debate on arms embargoes and travel sanctions within the 'Bonn-Berlin-Process'*. Baden-Baden: Nomos Verlagsgesellschaft.

Brzoska, M. (1991). Arming South Africa in the shadow of the UN arms embargo. *Defence Analysis*, 7(1), 21–38.

Brzoska, M. (Ed.) (2000). *Design and implementation of arms embargoes and travel and aviation related sanctions – Results of the 'Bonn-Berlin Process'*. Bonn: BICC.

Brzoska, M. (Ed.) (2001). *Smart sanctions: The next steps – The debate on arms embargoes and travel sanctions within the 'Bonn-Berlin-Process'*. Baden-Baden: Nomos Verlagsgesellschaft.

Brzoska, M. (2003). From dumb to smart? Recent reforms of UN sanctions. *Global Governance*, 9(4), 107–119.

Brzoska, M., & Pearson, F. (1994). *Armaments and warfare*. Columbia, SC: University of South Carolina Press.

Carnegie Commission on Preventing Deadly Conflict. (1997). *Preventing deadly conflict*. New York: Carnegie Corporation.

Catrina, C. (1988). *Arms transfers and dependence*. London: Taylor & Francis.

Control Arms. (2006). *UN arms embargoes: An overview of the last ten years*. London: Control Arms.

Cortright, D., & Lopez, G. A. (2000). *The sanctions decade. Assessing UN strategies in the 1990s*. Boulder, CO: Lynne Rienner.

Cortright, D., & Lopez, G. A. (Eds). (2002a). *Smart sanctions: Targeting economic statecraft*. Lanham, MD: Rowman and Littlefield.

Cortright, D., & Lopez, G. A. (2002b). *Sanctions and the search for security: Challenges to UN action*. Boulder, CO: Lynne Rienner.

Cortright, D., & Lopez, G. A. (2005). Bombs, carrots and sticks: The use of incentives and sanctions. *Arms Control Today*, 35(2 March), 19–24.

Crawford, N. C., & Klotz, A. (Eds). (1999). *How sanctions work. Lessons from South Africa*. New York: St. Martin's Press.

Doxey, M. (1999). *United Nations sanctions. Current policy issues*. Canada: Centre for Foreign Policy Studies, Dalhousie University.

Drezner, D. (2000). *The sanctions paradox*. Cambridge, MA: Cambridge University Press.

Elliott, K. A. (1998). The sanctions glass: Half full or completely empty? *International Security*, 23(1), 50–65.

Fruchart, D., Holtom, P., Wezeman, S. T., Strandow, D., & Wallensteen, P. (2007). *United Nations arms embargoes. Their impact on flows and target behaviour*. Stockholm and Uppsala: SIPRI and Department of Peace and Conflict Studies.

George, A. L. (1979). Case studies and theory development: The method of structured, focused comparison. In: P. G. Lauren (Ed.), *Diplomacy: New approaches in history, theory and policy* (pp. 43–68). New York: Free Press.

Gordon, J. (1999). A peaceful, silent, deadly remedy: The ethics of economic sanctions. *Ethics and International Affairs*, 13(1), 123–142.

Haass, R. N., & O'Sullivan, M. L. (Eds). (1999). *Economic sanctions and American diplomacy*. New York: Council on Foreign Relations.

Holtom, P. (2007a). *United Nations arms embargoes. Their impact on flows and target behaviour. Case study: Liberia, 1992–2006*. Stockholm and Uppsala: SIPRI and Department of Peace and Conflict Studies.

Holtom, P. (2007b). *United Nations arms embargoes. Their impact on flows and target behaviour. Case study: Sierra Leone, 1997–present.* Stockholm and Uppsala: SIPRI and Department of Peace and Conflict Studies.

Hufbauer, G. C., Schott, J. J., & Elliott, K. A (1990). *Economic sanctions reconsidered: History and current policy* (2nd ed.). Washington, DC: Institute for International Economics.

Kaempfer, W., & Lowenberg, A. D. (1999). Unilateral versus multilateral international sanctions: A public choice perspective. *International Studies Quarterly, 43*(1), 37–58.

Knight, W. A. (1998). *The United Nations and arms embargo verification.* Lewiston, Queenston, Lampeter: The Edwin Mellen Press.

Krause, K. (1992). *Arms and the state.* Cambridge, MA: Cambridge University Press.

Kreutz, J. (2005). *The European Union's sanctions policy.* BICC Paper. Bonn: BICC.

Leyton-Brown, D. (1987). *The utility of international economic sanctions.* New York: St. Martin's Press.

Nincic, M., & Wallensteen, P. (1983). *Dilemmas of economic coercion. Sanctions in world politics.* New York: Praeger Publishers.

Pape, R. A. (1997). Why economic sanctions do not work. *International Security, 22*(2), 90–136.

Small Arms Survey. (2005). *Small arms survey 2005.* Oxford: Oxford University Press.

Strandow, D. (2006). *Sanctions and civil war. Targeted measures for conflict resolution.* Uppsala: Department of Peace and Conflict Studies.

Tierney, D. (2005). Irrelevant or malevolent? UN arms embargoes in civil wars. *Review of International Studies, 31*(4), 645–664.

Tostensen, A., & Bull, B. (2002). Are smart sanctions feasible? *World Politics, 54*(3), 373–403.

van Bergeijk, P. A. G. (1994). *Economic diplomacy, trade and commercial policy. Positive and negative sanctions in a new world order.* Aldershot: Edward Elgar.

van Bergeijk, P. A. G. (1999). Economic sanctions, autocracy, democracy and success. In: W. J. G. van Genugten & J. de Groot (Eds), *Effects and effectiveness of UN-sanctions, especially in the field of human rights.* Groningen, the Netherlands: Intersentia.

van Bergeijk, P. A. G., & van Marrewijk, C. (1995). Why do sanctions need time to work? Adjustment, learning and anticipation. *Economic Modeling, 12*(2), 75–86.

Vines, A. (2007). Can UN arms embargoes in Africa be effective? *International Affairs, 83*(6), 1107–1122.

Wallensteen, P., & Staibano, C. (Eds). (2005). *International sanctions: Between words and wars in the global system.* New York: Frank Cass.

Wallensteen, P., Staibano, C., & Eriksson, M. (Eds). (2002). *Making targeted sanctions effective. Guidelines for the implementation of UN policy options.* Uppsala: Department of Peace and Conflict Studies.

Yidhego, Z. W. (2007). The role of the Security Council arms embargoes in stemming destabilizing transfers of small arms and light weapons (SALW): Recent developments and challenges. *Netherlands International Law Review, 54*(2), 115–132.

Michael Brzoska
George A. Lopez
Editors

CHAPTER 1

A FRAMEWORK FOR THE ANALYSIS OF THE EFFECTIVENESS OF ARMS EMBARGOES

Michael Brzoska

Arms embargoes have been heavily utilized in the past 10–15 years by international governmental organizations and individual countries alike. The United Nations (UN) has regulated the flow of arms in 19 of the last 20 embargoes from 1990 until 2005. Similarly, the European Union (EU), the United States, and other nations have lists of countries to which they will not sell arms. Yet, despite the apparent popularity of arms embargoes, there is a political undertone about their futility and significant amount of scholarly literature criticizing their level of effectiveness. This apparent paradox illustrates that though arms embargoes have proliferated over the past decade, there is speculation surrounding their success.

The objective of this chapter is to provide a framework for the analysis of arms embargoes, specifically to determine what dictates whether they are deemed successful or failures. I aim to identify several key components of arms embargoes such as the willingness and capability of actors implementing the embargoes, the process of such an embargo implementation, and the reaction of those targeted by the embargo. These variables – which are hypothesized to be important in assessing the success of arms embargoes – need to be specified adequately. The following analysis is

Putting Teeth in the Tiger: Improving the Effectiveness of Arms Embargoes
Contributions to Conflict Management, Peace Economics and Development, Volume 10, 1–27
Copyright © 2009 by Emerald Group Publishing Limited
ISSN: 1572-8323/doi:10.1108/S1572-8323(2009)0000010005

therefore structured to produce a list of variables, which can be found at the conclusion of the chapter that can guide empirical analysis. In addition to providing a set of standards by which to assess arms embargoes, I also hope to come up with a more salient definition of what constitutes an effective arms embargo.

I begin the chapter by differentiating, by broadening the perspective on arms embargoes beyond a simple understanding of stopping the flow of arms to a particular target. Such a view is valid for an outside observer of the behavior of governments espousing to implement an arms embargo, but it is too simple for understanding the issues of why arms embargoes operate the way they do or for how they can be improved. It underestimates the complexity of decision-making on arms embargoes. The inconsistency between the popularity of sanctions with policy-makers and their perceived ineffectiveness has been called the "sanctions paradox" (Baldwin, 1997; Drezner, 1999). At the heart of this paradox lie conflicting views about what constitutes a successful sanctions regime. Arms embargoes are clearly a class of sanctions marked by this paradox. Exploring the "arms embargo paradox" is critical to the analysis of arms embargo implementation.

I then analyze theoretical perspectives on how an arms embargo can be effective. I contrast models of arms embargoes implementation. The first, dominant in the literature, is a top-down model. The second model is bottom-up. It is process-oriented and predominantly concerned with arms transfer control policies as the primary element in arms embargoes. This model has its roots in the literature on arms transfers. Each model has its weak and strong points. Supplier behavior in arms embargoes need to be explained by integrating both models. Such integration also opens up new avenues for thinking about ways to improve the effectiveness of arms embargoes. In the final part of the text, variables for the analysis of arms embargoes are deducted from the earlier discussion.

THE ARMS EMBARGO PARADOX

The popularity of arms embargoes makes sense on the one hand but can be puzzling on the other. Since arms are a type of good often linked directly to war and peace as one of the central objects of international politics, stemming the flow of arms to a country or group accused of acting against international peace and security is a logical response. However, while this reaction is frequent, it is not generally regarded as being effective. In fact, arms embargoes have a reputation of not functioning well. One can find many references, in academic literature and policy papers alike, which state that arms embargoes "do not work" that they are "ineffective" or that they are "not worth the paper they are printed on." The paradox that sanctions are deemed to be of little consequence but are still popular among policy-makers (Baldwin, 1997) is particularly striking.

Academic studies on arms sanctions generally confirm the bad reputation of arms embargoes. Studies on the Tripartite Agreement on the Middle East or the arms embargo against South Africa found many violations of the embargoes and concluded that they had not been properly implemented (Harkavy, 1975; Wulf, 1986; Landgren, 1989; but see also Brzoska, 1991). More recent analysis of the various cases of UN arms embargoes of the 1990s come to similarly sobering conclusions (Cortright & Lopez, 2000, 2002; Bondi, 2002).

Some analysts maintain that the perceived failure of arms embargoes as a structural phenomenon in a market where illegal dealers will substitute law-abiding arms suppliers (Sampson, 1978) while a majority sees limitations in the design and execution of arms sanctions that can be overcome if sufficient political will is mustered (Ohlson, 1987). The experience beyond arms embargoes, such as with the COMECON (Stent, 1985) during the Cold War, or export control regimes in the fields of nuclear, biological, and chemical weapons (Speier, Chow, & Starr, 2001; Beck, 2003) suggest that it is possible to successfully restrict the export of weapons, while acknowledging that no regime is watertight. It is important to analyze the shortcoming of arms embargo implementation to improve their effectiveness.

The overwhelmingly negative perception on the effectiveness of arms embargoes does not seem to deter governments from deliberately restricting arms sales and from invoking arms embargoes. Why is that so? Are arms embargoes so frequent because it is cheap for governments to invoke them? Or are governments full of good will but overwhelmed by the difficulties to design and implement them well? Or are there problems with the prevailing view of arms embargoes as ineffective?

The literature on the sanctions paradox has shown that it is useful to distinguish between various types of sanctions success (Baldwin, 1997). Sanctions may already be successful in the view of those deciding on them, if their political capital is rising because of that decision. The symbolism of invoking an embargo may suffice to improve the standing of decision-makers in the eye of their political constituents or the outside world. Outside analysts, however, will generally have a different view and judge success by actual changes in the targeted policies.

The standards invoked in much of the sanctions literature are high: sanctions are measured by their success in changing the policies of the targeted government or group within a country. The literature on arms embargoes is often less demanding. Here, the criterion of success is often of whether arms flows are stopped or continue to reach the target.

The high standards in the sanctions literature are easily justified by the rhetoric of those deciding on the imposition of sanctions. Few, if any, arms embargoes have been justified as purely symbolic measures. Rather, at a minimum, they are qualified as measures to stop the flow of arms from the country imposing the arms embargo to the target. At maximum, arms embargoes are claimed to change the behavior of a target, in particular to stop it from continuing to fight a war that the sanctions sender wants to end. Still, it would be analytically somewhat naïve to judge arms embargo effectiveness by targeted policy change alone. Decision-making on arms embargoes in implementing countries is obviously more complex than implied in an approach that only allows targeted policy change as a measure of success.

THE EFFECTIVENESS OF ARMS EMBARGOES: OBJECTIVES AND CRITERIA

What makes an arms embargo effective? How can effective implementation of an arms embargo be measured? Effectiveness is frequently defined as the degree of attainment of an objective. The definition of the objectives is thus crucial to the measurement of effectiveness.

In the academic literature on sanctions, the clear and simple objective of targeted policy change dominates (Hufbauer, Schott, & Elliott, 1990; Drezner, 1999). It is also often found in discussions focusing on sanctions policy (Cortright & Lopez, 2000, 2002) as well as in official policy statements justifying sanctions. Such statements typically stigmatize the objectionable behavior and list the changes expected from the target. There is widespread agreement that the core objective of sanctions, including arms embargoes, is targeted policy change. Sanctions, in the general opinion of academics and policy-makers, should be about influencing the behavior of targets. Since policy change in the targeted state is considered the first objective of sanctions, the attainment of that goal we will call "level I effectiveness."

However, achieving policy change through sanctions is a very difficult criterion to attain. Even when arms flows are effectively stopped, there may be no change in the policy of the targeted state because arms imports are not needed or can be substituted by domestic production. More fundamentally, the decision-makers of the targeted state or group have control over whether the objective is met. Furthermore, it is difficult to decipher whether and to what degree sanctions were responsible for policy change.

The analysis of the effectiveness of sanctions has traditionally had a second focus, namely, the degree of the implementation of the sanctions. In the case of arms embargoes, the related objective is the degree to which deliveries of weapons to the target are stopped. In arms embargoes, it is particularly appealing to define their effectiveness in terms of the flow of weapons reaching the targeted states or groups. This criterion of arms embargo success has been used in much of the literature on multilateral arms embargoes, as well as some of the sanction literature when looking at arms embargoes. In the latter, the denial of arms to the target is often put on an equal footing with the objective of targeted policy change, and sometimes, it is even seen as more important. This objective is attractive as it is fairly easy to observe and measure. It is particularly transparent when the targets are at war. Stopping the arms flows can be seen as an objective in itself, to reduce the level of violence on the ground or even help to bring a conflict to an end. When effectiveness is measured by the reduction of arms flows, it also becomes less dependent on the behavior of the targets than on the behavior of the state or body imposing the embargo. This is here called the "level II of objective" of arms embargoes.

Though the reduction of arms flows is primarily controlled by suppliers, level II objectives are not easily obtained. Any given state only has direct control over its national arms exports and can, at best, only indirectly influence the arms export policies of other governments. A government can thus assure that no arms are exported from its territory to the target but cannot guarantee that no arms reach the target (except in the case that it is the only arms supplier and no others will step in). It is necessary to cooperate with other potential arms suppliers to reach level II effectiveness.

However, level II and level I objectives may not be linked this way. The complete denial of arms deliveries is not the only way through which level I objectives can be reached. A partial denial of arms shipments may, for instance, raise the costs of procurement, thus influencing decision-makers in the targeted state or group. A partial denial may also lead to a shift in suppliers that may force targets to integrate new types of weapon systems or increases domestic arms production, which also can increase costs.

Literature discussing sanctions in broader contexts lists additional objectives such as deflecting criticism by domestic and other audiences regarding a crisis situation. Similarly, the literature on international organizations has produced broad lists of objectives against which to measure the effectiveness of internationally imposed sanction regimes (Young, 1999).

A more limited objective than policy change or to stop all or most deliveries of arms to a target is dissociation from the policies of a target. Governments can have many motives to seek to signal dissociation with a target's policies, such as seeing them as a threat to peace and security or to satisfy domestic lobbying groups. Arms transfer relationships, which have been called "diplomacy writ large" are generally seen as signaling political collusion between supplier and recipient (Pierre, 1982). Even though a good part of the arms trade is dominated by commercial considerations, most governments do operate control systems where political criteria are crucial for the licensing process. Arms export restrictions are therefore among the first and most obvious ways to signal criticism of the policies of a potential recipient of weapons, with dissociation requiring the total end of arms flows.

As arms exports are controlled by national governments, dissociation through an arms embargo is thus a matter of national policy. Dissociation is already achieved when arms flows from a particular country to the target are stopped. A government can claim success when no arms transfers are reaching the target from its jurisdiction.

Obviously, the effects of a unilateral arms embargo on a target will not be as strong as a total weapons ban on the target. The latter, level II effectiveness, cannot be attained by one supplier as long as other suppliers are able to be involved. While this will generally be the case, a supplier with a large market share and the power to influence the policies of other states has a good chance to reduce arms flows to a target. The same kind of argument applies to targeted policy change. It seems unlikely that a target will be pressured by dissociation by one supplier. However, if the supplier is a powerful country, this expression of dissatisfaction may have more effect on decision -making than the reduction of arms imports to a trickle. For states that control only small shares of the arms markets, multilateral action is inevitable if the goal is to have an effect on arms flows to the target Also, dissociation will be even more credible if other governments are willing to stop supplying weapons as well. This places a new focus on the cooperation of states and international bodies in implementing the next arms embargo.

This dissociation can be extended. Governments may not be primarily interested in achieving policy objectives (level I) or to stop the flow of arms (level II) but rather in exploiting their support of an arms embargo for other purposes. The discussion of the "arms embargo paradox" can easily be extended to illustrate the intricate ways in which decisions on implementing arms embargoes is linked to and effects desired outcomes. This leads to a spectrum of possibilities by which decision-makers may assess arms embargo success and failure, including the following:

1. *Dissociation from the target*: Decision-makers may not care whether weapons are reaching the target or not and are also not primarily concerned with policy change in the target. Rather they are directing the arms embargo toward other actors such as third-party countries or domestic audiences, whom they want to convince that they are not supporting the target's policies. To be credible, however, it is important that there are no arms flowing from the sender to the target. The priority in arms embargo implementation in this scenario is to prevent arms from one's own territory from reaching the targeted state. The change of policies by the target would be nice to achieve. However, the more realistic objective of success of an arms embargo is not to be implicated in supplying arms to the target.
2. *Efficiency as primary objective*: Decision-making on sanctions, including their implementation, may be guided by a cost-benefit analysis rather than attainment of certain levels of policy output. Measures to reduce arms supplies to a target are comparatively easy to implement nationally. It can be very difficult to achieve a complete end to arms imports by a target, unless there is full-scale cooperation by other arms suppliers and countries surrounding a target. The benefit of achieving the desired policy change in the target may be sufficient to justify the expenditure of a certain level of effort in implementing and managing a major reduction of arms exports to the target. However, it may not be beneficial to attempt the much larger operation that is needed to stop all arms flows to the target, efforts that include convincing other suppliers to also stop arms flows, monitoring of borders, and so on. As a result, effectiveness measured by the degree of achieving the given objective, such as policy change in the target, may be low. But efficiency – measured in terms of the relations between effectiveness and the costs to achieve that level of effectiveness – may be high.
3. *The costs of alternative measures*: Cost-benefit considerations are particularly important in selecting a particular policy measure. Some

policies that can be assumed to induce change in the target's policies include comprehensive economic sanctions and military interventions. Military interventions are generally seen as more effective than arms embargoes in terms of targeted policy change. The cost, however, both for implementers and in terms of destruction in the target, is likely to be much higher. Comprehensive economic sanctions are also generally assumed to be more effective in achieving targeted policy change than arms embargoes. But they have had high humanitarian costs in the target where they were adopted in the recent past, which was the case in Iraq, the Former Republic of Yugoslavia, and Haiti (Weiss et al., 1997).

4. *Closing implementation gaps*: Even when the standard of effectiveness, such as targeted policy change, is high, but the prospects of cutting all arms flows to a target are low, implementation and the continuation of an arms embargo may be attractive beyond the immediate lack of a policy alternative. The effectiveness of implementation may increase over time; more countries may adopt strong policies to stop arms flows, implementing countries may get better at closing loopholes, and so on. Such cumulative improvement in implementation will not only raise the prospects of the desired policy change, it may also be helpful in creating and strengthening formal and informal structures and institutions to make future arms embargoes more effective. The UN sanctions reform process, initiated in the second half of the 1990s, was partially aimed at providing a platform for increasingly identifying and closing implementation gaps.

The abovementioned points of analysis help to explain the apparent paradox that lies in the popularity of arms embargoes and their perceived failure. Arms embargoes may be "effective" for actors for reasons other than changing the policies of the target, which is the most demanding criterion used in many studies. Arms embargoes may serve the interests of actors even without a high degree of effectiveness in changing targeted policies.

The satisfaction of governments in arms embargo implementation constitutes a third level of effectiveness that can be measured in an arms embargo. The analysis of the motivations of arms embargo implementers, beyond those of achieving effects "on the ground" in the targeted states or groups, can reveal new and more realistic ways to improve the actual implementation of arms embargoes. The challenge for policy analysis aimed at strengthening the effectiveness of arms embargoes is to find ways to link such actor behavior to an improvement in the overall implementation of arms embargoes.

MOTIVES AND MEASURES

One important element in the agenda of the analysis of arms embargoes is to link the actual implementation (and "disemplementation") patterns of arms embargoes with the motivations and objectives on the one hand and capabilities of those charged with implementing arms embargoes, that is, national governments, on the other hand. States control arms exports and shipments in their territories. There are also arms embargoes negotiated in multilateral organizations. Of course, motivations and objectives, as well as actual capabilities for control over arms shipments, are influenced by actors other than national governments. These include sub-national interest groups and private economic actors such as arms producers and arms dealers. Often, it is not easy to judge whether violations of arms embargoes stem from a neglect of governments to implement available instruments of control or from a lack of such instruments. Unfortunately, it is often also difficult to be sure about the true motives of governments to initiate or participate in an arms embargo, which may range from dissociation from a target to quickly attaining policy change in the target. Actual motives may clearly differ from pronounced objectives.

Because of these difficulties in analyzing motives and capabilities, many studies of arms embargo focus on the actual implementation of transfer bans. In a way, whether weapons actually flow to a target is a test for the confluence of willingness and capability. If there are no arms deliveries to a target, both willingness and capability to enforce an arms embargo are strong. The problems start, however, when embargoes are not well implemented. This makes it unclear whether this is the result of a lack of political will by suppliers and surrounding states or a lack of capability by some important actors. The predominant early analysis of the failure of arms embargoes focused on the willingness of sender governments to enforce them (Harkavy, 1975; Krause, 1995) or on changes in the policies of the targeted entity (Cortright & Lopez, 2000). The prescription derived from this analysis was that states need to become more serious about enforcement.

After the end of the Cold War, the capability of states to actually control arms transfers to and from their territories has received more attention. The end of the Cold War has brought about a glut in used weapons, often not well controlled (BICC, 1997). States in Eastern Europe with large arms industries, as well as African states that neighbor a number of the recent targets of arms embargoes, have poor arms transfer control capabilities. Thus, they have difficulties in implementing arms embargoes, even if their willingness is high. However, other states have begun to strengthen these states' capacities by providing assistance for border monitoring.

In addition to sender willingness and capability, target behavior is obviously another element in making arms embargoes effective. Governments or groups targeted by arms embargoes can adapt to the reduced flow of arms. They may be impressed more by the political consensus behind an arms embargo than by the actual denial of weapons. Arms embargoes may also affect the allocation and distribution of resources in a target – more money may be spent on arms imports while individuals involved in illegal arms deals may make fortunes, legally or illegally.

MODELS OF ARMS EMBARGO IMPLEMENTATION

Most analyses of arms embargoes are limited to pointing out the lack of willingness and capabilities of those states implementing arms embargoes as a means of discussing the failures of arms embargoes. Though the analysis of the lack of implementation of arms embargoes is crucial, a sole focus on the "disimplementers" can overlook important aspects of arms embargo implementation. While many states will only focus on the effectiveness of their own national arms restrictions, others are trying to broaden restrictions on problem states. The differences between an analytical approach solely looking at national implementation and one also looking at the dynamics of successive international broadening of arms embargo implementation will be analyzed in this section.

There are basically two models for arms embargo implementation. One assumes that those who participate in an arms embargo have both the political will to execute it and the resources to implement its restrictions. The other model does not presume each participant has the will to implement the embargo. Rather, it focuses on the process of broadening restrictions on arms flows to particular targets.

The Top-Down Model of Arms Embargo Implementation

A simple, top-down model of the implementation of an arms embargo runs like this:

1. Ultimate objective is policy change in the target (level I).
2. The denial of weapons is the instrument to reach the level I objective (level II).

3. National governments have to stop all arms exports from their borders to achieve the level II objective. Level III objectives of sender satisfaction are of no independent interest since they are linked to the level I objective by definition.
4. Multilateral organizations, such as the UN, can support implementation of arms embargoes through monitoring, naming and shaming, and other instruments available to them.

In this simple model, a decision to find a policy objectionable, and the desire to change it, is at the beginning of the arms embargo. The denial of the supply of weapons is then seen as an instrument to bring such change about. Arms are used as an instrument because the assumption is that arms are important and that changes in the transfer of arms influence the policies of targets. The goal is to limit the targeted states' and groups' military capabilities and to impede their capacity to wage war. Targeted states and groups fear such weakening of their military capabilities and thus adjust their behavior in such a way as to get the restrictions lifted (or not applied in the first case).

Utilizing this simple model illustrates why the effectiveness of arms embargoes is low. There are many factors that affect the success of this model. For example:

1. The link between effectiveness on level II (a halt of all arms deliveries) and effectiveness on level I (attain policy change) is weak. Targets may not be very impacted by the denial of weapons. They may be able to continue their policies without fresh deliveries of arms. They may also adopt a number of countermeasures (discussed in more detail later) such as domestic arms production or a change in their military tactics.
2. States may not cooperate to achieve an overall low level of deliveries to the target. Governments may not be willing to implement arms embargoes for several reasons, the most important of which is that they do not share the policy objectives of a particular arms embargo and do not want to dissociate themselves from the target. There are various types of arms embargoes, ranging from unilateral to global. The UN Security Council has the power to decide on mandatory global arms embargoes. A decision of the Security Council is binding for all member states and customarily also accepted by non-members. However, decisions in the UN Security Council are only made by a few member states: the 5 permanent members and 10 elected members. The majority of member states are not directly involved in the decision-making. Obviously, there

are discussions among states before decision-making in the UN Security Council, including lobbying of members of the Security Council. Still, in the end, it is a few member states who decide. Member states are obliged to implement Security Council decisions, but they may do so with little willingness.

3. States may have difficulties in controlling arms exports from their territories. Arms are generally produced and sold by private actors, or government-owned facilities that operate on an independent commercial basis. The first precondition for the control over arms transfers thus is the control of the central government over these private actors. Even when governments are willing to control arms exports, their capabilities to do so may be limited. Control over the export of weapons located in a country requires an efficient bureaucracy, which is not prone to corruption, a good border control system and a legal regime that provides efficient punishment in cases of violations. The capability of governments to control arms transfers has always been limited. Obviously, there are differences with respect to types of weapons. Large conventional weapons, such as tanks, are much easier to control than small arms and ammunition. One reason is physical: small arms are much easier to conceal than large conventional weapons. Another reason is legal: in many countries, the production of large conventional weapons is strictly controlled, and ownership limited to the armed forces. The production of small arms, on the contrary, is often under less scrutiny and ownership allowed by a number of government forces, and sometimes even of private actors. The global capacity to control arms exports has eroded in the 1990s. The end of authoritarian powerful bureaucracies in the former socialist countries, in particular, has weakened the control over arms exports from those states. Formerly, direct control of the state over production and export of arms gave little room for activities not directly ordered by the central government. Now, much of arms production is organized on a commercial basis. Instruments of control, such as control bureaucracies, border controls and legal regimes are weak.

This basic top-down model best fits the case of an arms embargo that is initiated, for instance, by the UN, in response to some policy found objectionable by a large number of arms suppliers and other states in a position to stop the flow of arms. A case in point would be the Iraq embargo of August 1990.

Bottom-Up Rather than Top-Down?

The top-down model is in line with the idea of an embargo being implemented in response to a particularly event or objectionable behavior. However, there are few cases where arms embargoes have been initiated this way. More often, arms embargoes were brought about slowly and over time in situations where arms suppliers had already stopped their deliveries and now where interested in internationalizing their behavior (through multilateral arms embargoes) or making their restrictions widely known (through the announcement of a unilateral arms embargo). The bottom-up model of arms embargoes seems, in many cases, to fit reality better because it takes into account the domestic policies of targeted states. The following sections address "normal" arms transfer policies to make this point more clear.

The Nature of Arms Deliveries

Arms continue to be regarded as special products in international trade, as symbols and means of violence and power. It is important to register all four of these words in our mind. Arms deliveries have a material and a symbolic element, which overlap but do not coincide. The delivery of military goods that are insignificant with respect to their contribution to the fighting power of the recipient may have large symbolic value. An example would be the sale of a few machine guns from a European country to Cuba. On the contrary, the sale of very significant amounts of weaponry may carry low symbolic value. An example of this case would be the sale of a large number of machine guns to the US armed forces from a European country.

Arms transfers did not always have this symbolic value. There were periods, for instance during the late 19th century, when arms producers would freely sell to all interested parties. Observers did not generally connect political symbolism with these sales. In fact, neutrality, as for instance codified in the Hague Convention of 1909, requires governments to refrain from sales of arms, not private actors. However, since the end of World War I, arms transfers have increasingly come under government control (MacNeill, 1982; Harkavy, 1975; Krause, 1995). It can be argued whether governmental oversight over arms sales has become a legal obligation, but there is a general presumption that such controls should occur. Conversely, if governments do not exercise such control, this is seen as a symbol that they connive in certain arms deals.

The dual importance of arms in material and symbolic terms is one important facet of the trade in arms, the other is a dual effect on the use of force. Arms transfers increase the capability of the recipient to inflict casualties and their capacity to force their will on others. There is, even if often only marginal, an absolute increase in power. At the same time, arms transfers will also have an effect on the relative power among organized groups willing to use violence to address differences in interest and status. The balance of power is altered, if only marginally in many arms transfers. The absolute and the relative changes in the capability to exert force are predominantly linked to the material side of arms transfers, though they also have relevance for the symbolic side. Political support can be registered in absolute terms as well as in relation to opposing groups.

The delivery of weapons is regarded, in the perspective discussed here, as a political act, an act of support for the recipient. This occurs even if those responsible for the delivery are not politically motivated but only have their material interests in mind. The support is, as the weapons themselves, material and symbolic at the same time. This generally recognized interpretation of arms deliveries puts pressure on governments to exert control over the arms that are delivered from their territories. The costs of not doing so are potentially high. Such costs include the support of organized groups who are willing to use force against the country of origin of the weapons, but also the political costs of being seen to support organized groups that are seen as hostile by others. In addition to these costs that follow from the effect of arms to raise the power of particular groups, there may also be costs connected to their effects on the overall level of force. Governments may have to share in the costs of humanitarian action after wars, and general publics may be opposed to deliveries where there is the danger that they are used. Recent history shows unused or excess arms reappear in later conflicts elsewhere.

Denials of Arms
Because of the material and symbolic value of arms, denial of the sales of weapons is a frequent phenomenon. Obviously, there are differences among various governments. A number of categorizations among groups of arms suppliers can be found in the literature (Harkavy, 1975; Laurance, 1992; Krause, 1995). One of the earliest classifications, made in the late 1960s by researchers working at the Stockholm International Peace Research Institute, has survived most critiques. (SIPRI, 1973). They distinguished between hegemonic suppliers, at that time predominantly the United States and the Soviet Union, but to a lesser extent also regional powers such as China, who used arms deliveries aggressively to separate friends and opponents. Those considered to be on the enemy side would not receive arms.

First, a striking example was the reversal of sides in the Ogaden War of 1977/1978 between Somalia and Ethiopia. The Soviets had built up the Somali forces through large deliveries of weapons during the 1970s. They denied several requests for weapon deliveries from the Dergue who had taken power in Ethiopia in 1974. In early 1998, however, in the middle of the war, the Soviet Union changed course and massively supported Ethiopia, at the same time stopping deliveries to Somalia. The leadership in Moscow saw more potential in an alliance with the Ethiopian government; it felt betrayed by the Somali leadership, which had started the Ogaden War against Soviet advice. The United States, on the contrary, which had been the major supplier of Ethiopia until the coup d'etat in Addis in 1974, began to support Somalia in 1978 (Brzoska & Pearson, 1994).

A second group of governments were classified as primarily motivated by economic motives. These suppliers would be more willing to sell to clients regardless of their political orientation but still be very aware of the political consequences in the world of international politics. Denials would be more exceptional than among the hegemonic suppliers. An example of such behavior was the French denial of arms deliveries to Israel after 1967, which was strongly motivated by economic interests including in selling arms in the Arab world.

The third group distinguished by the SIPRI researchers was the "restrainers." The governments of these countries were highly sensitive to the accusation that arms deliveries would bring misery to recipient countries and would thus deny arms sales to regions at war or where the danger of war was high. The group of "restrainers" is particularly prone to deny arms sales, but cases of denials are likely and have occurred among all arms suppliers. The reasons to deny arms differ. They include the use of power politics, economic interests, and a wish to contain the use of violence in general. As outlined earlier, the material aspects of these causes are supplemented by the symbolic aspects – governments want to be perceived in various ways through their denial politics.

Arms Embargoes in the Bottom-Up Model
A typical case of an arms embargo envisaged in the bottom-up model has as its origin in restrictions on arms sales by individual suppliers in the run-up to a crisis. Suppliers tighten these controls as the crisis intensifies and more suppliers apply restrictions. At some point, individual governments may announce the total derail of sales and deliveries as an arms embargo. Alternatively, or in addition, they may seek allies for a multilateral arms embargo.

The starting point in this model deals with concerns in individual countries that find expression in national arms export policies. The primary objective at this initial level, called level III in the discussion earlier, is to be perceived as working toward an arms embargo. There are many motives behind this objective. They will generally include the wish to signal discontent with the policies of actors producing the crisis.

Actually halting all arms exports under the national government's jurisdiction is one way signal ones intention. However, there will be incentives for governments to try to get others to stop their flows, too, or even to wait with stopping domestic flows before others have implemented sanctions, too. These incentives include the following:

1. Putting more pressure on the target. The standard reasoning in the top-down model applies here too. Level I objectives are more likely to be reached with a high effectiveness of level II objective that, in turn, requires cooperation among suppliers of arms.
2. Convincing domestic audiences and other actors that a government is serious about measures against a country or group of countries.
3. Reducing internal pressure on governments from domestic arms suppliers. When arms sales and deliveries are stopped, producers and sellers lose business. It makes it more difficult to argue for cutting the arms trade if deliveries from other countries are not stopped.

Governments of countries exercising restraint will thus have objectives in addition to influencing the policies of the target. In particular, these include getting other countries to follow its policies. To achieve a multilateral agreement on an arms embargo, and get it to be implemented, is likely to be a negotiating process between initiating, willing, and reluctant parties. In the EU, all member states have to be convinced. In the case of a UN arms embargo, a majority of the members of the Security Council, including all permanent members, need to formally agree to an embargo, and a larger number of suppliers and other states capable of controlling the flow of arms to a target need to cooperate actually implement it.

What will these negotiations entail? One important element is to what extent the level I objective is shared. A common level I objective will make the imposition of joint action more likely. But there are also possibilities to link policies to bring states "on board." Governments interested in building a coalition of support for arms embargoes may also provide incentives for other states to join in, such as an offer to share costs.

Negotiations about a multilateral approach to arms embargoes may lead to the need for initiating states to redefine level I objectives so that they are acceptable to a larger group of countries. Because of this and the costs to convince others, a state may decide not to multilateralize its action because it foresees that the cost of joint action will be higher than its benefits from achieving joint action.

COMPARING THE TOP-DOWN
AND THE BOTTOM-UP MODELS

The differences between the top-down and the bottom-up models are pronounced with respect to multilateral arms embargoes:

1. The bottom-up model suggests that it is important to examine the process behind a multilateral approach to arms embargoes. Who are the initial supporters? Who has to be convinced, by arguments, compensations, or other means? How strong is resistance? Compromises are likely, particularly when the severity of the crisis is not evident to all.
2. Level I objectives may be a compromise and may not reflect the true motives and objections of governments implementing an arms embargo.
3. It also suggests that it is important to know who is maintaining the arms embargo. The compromise worked out at the time of imposing the arms embargo is threatened by the interests of those who would gain from delivering arms and are less interested in achieving the agreed level I objective. A strong power committed to maintaining an arms embargo will likely increase its level II effectiveness.

The bottom-up model questions the assumption often made in the literature that multilateral embargoes are superior to unilateral embargoes. Level II effectiveness certainly requires multilateral action in a world of many arms suppliers. However, multilateral arms embargoes based on a wide range of level III objectives and interests in achieving them may have even less level II effectiveness than a unilateral embargo by an important arms supplier. The bottom-up model certainly explains better than the top-down model the apparent "sanctions happiness" when it comes to multilateral arms embargoes in the 1990s. In almost any international crisis, at least some governments can be counted upon to be interested in imposing multilateral arms embargoes, to multilateralize their own behavior. They will be successful in getting an arms embargo decision, if there is little resistance from others. However, that will not guarantee lively enforcement, and thus level II effectiveness, particularly if there is no strong power supporting the maintenance of the arms embargo.

The bottom-up model seems to provide a good explanation as to why there are many arms embargoes that are not well implemented. It also implies some prescriptions for the improvement of level I and level II effectiveness of arms embargoes. However, there are some assumptions in the model, which limit its value for prescription, such as governments being in full control over arms exports from their territories. Also, by focusing on the senders of an arms embargo, adaptation by targets is ignored.

JOINING THE TWO MODELS THROUGH AN ANALYSIS OF ARMS EMBARGO OBJECTIVE LEVELS

The top-down model emphasizes the capability of senders to implement embargoes and the effects that implementation has on targets. The bottom-up model emphasizes the willingness of senders and the process of the coordination of their actions. The bottom-up model illustrates why sanctions frequently come about but seldom are effective. The top-down model indicates how an arms embargo can be effective beyond level III. A combination of the two models seems to be most promising for analysis for effectiveness in the broader understanding outlined earlier.

Analysis needs to be informed by the motives of supplier governments and those capable of stopping arms deliveries. The willingness and capabilities of these countries are crucial for bringing about effectiveness at level II. In addition, if an arms embargo is supported by a coalition of countries, the process of organizing action of the multilateral organization becomes an important element of analysis. In addition, the multilateral organization itself can become an actor that puts pressure on or provides incentives for states to implement an arms embargo.

Even successful implementation at level II, or by an important supplier at level III, may prove too little to move a target to change policies at level I. It may have little effect on the pursuit of the sanctioned policy and be largely irrelevant for other policy goals of the target.

The denial of weapons may also carry low costs to the target because it can adapt to the arms embargo.

1. The target can reduce the dependence of the incriminated policy on arms imports (level I).

2. The target can try to entice individual governments to cooperate with it (level II) or to find substate actors who are willing to break national laws and deliver arms illegally (level III).
3. A number of unintended effects have occurred in recent embargo cases. One is the growth of black market activities in the target. Similarly, rising costs of armaments through embargoes require increases in income to pay for them. Therefore, exports, particularly of marketable commodities, will have to rise. The adaptive measures by the target will likely have distribution effects – some persons or groups will lose financially while others gain. But there may also be similar political effects, leading to changes in the political leadership that again may or may not help those initiating the sanctions in reaching the strong political objective. Side effects of arms embargoes can increase or reduce level I effectiveness.

MEASURES OF EFFECTIVENESS

Level III Effectiveness

As argued earlier, arms embargoes will generally begin with unilateral action by individual states. Any country can declare an arms embargo on another country. However, if this embargo is ignored by other arms exporters, the effect on the flow of arms to the targeted group or states is not likely to be strong. The question then becomes how to involve others in the implementation of arms embargoes. This capability lies mostly with global powers. An arms embargo by a major power, such as the United States, is likely to also influence the arms export policies of other states, such as its allies.

How can *level III effectiveness* be measured? The simplest would be by the expressed satisfaction of sender government with the operation of an arms embargo. However, as the discussion on the arms embargo paradox indicates, governments are not necessarily giving clear messages of their views on arms embargoes. While they may publicly adhere to high goals, they may in fact be content with an imperfect implementation, particularly in view of the costs of better implementation. A more difficult assessment of sender satisfaction would therefore have to weigh actual behavior, that is, efforts to change the situation, against national interest in achieving level I objectives. If there is little activity in terms for trying to improve embargo implementation, this can either be an expression of satisfaction with the current situation or of little political interest in achieving level I effectiveness.

Level II Effectiveness

Level III objectives, while important for states as the main actors in arms embargo implementation, are setting the stage for what is in much of the arms embargo literature perceived as the "real" objectives as arms embargoes. As policy change (level I) is difficult to measure, level II objectives are the preferred measure of the effectiveness of arms embargoes. Embargoed states or groups generally shift arms procurement to clandestine markets. Information about the effectiveness of arms embargoes is therefore often difficult to obtain. However, much can be pulled together from a variety of sources.

As outlined earlier, analysis of the instruments level II should extend beyond the questions whether arms "get through" and also include questions regarding the costs for imported arms and whether the financing of imports takes different forms after the imposition of an arms embargo. In the case where the targeted group or state is involved in a war, changes in the way the armed forces are operating may also be an effect of arms embargoes.

Level II effectiveness can be analyzed broadly, including as indicators:

1. *Level of imports of arms*: Constant level of imports, significantly lower level of imports, almost no imports, rising imports.
2. *Supplier structure*: Change in the patterns of supply, identification of post-embargo suppliers versus pre-embargo suppliers.
3. *Composition of imports*: No change in types of weapons transferred; less sophisticated weapons transferred.
4. *Transfer mode of arms*: Unchanged; changed with increased importance of brokers and middlemen.
5. *Funding mode of arms imports*: Importance of purchases on credit versus deliveries paid for in cash and kind.
6. *Costs of weapons procurement*: Cost of imported higher, costs of domestic production higher.
7. *Change in conduct of war*: Different types of weapon used, different tactics.

Level II effectiveness is shaped by both recipient and supplier behavior. Recipients will be able to manipulate suppliers and use loopholes in implementation by arms producers. However, recipients need to have the financial means to do so.

Level I Objectives

Policy change is the ultimate objective of embargo implementation. However, it is often difficult to study. Causes of political behavior are often hard to distinguish and identify. Outcomes, which are easier to measure, may be the result of various factors, of which an arms embargo may or may not be one. Targets themselves cannot be trusted to provide a truthful picture of the reasons for policy change or resistance to it. And outside observers often disagree, when they have access to relevant information, which is seldom the case.

Despite these conceptual difficulties, it is important to study and analyze whether and how the target changes policies under an arms embargo. The most important policy to scrutinize is, of course, the one targeted by the arms embargo. However, the objectives of arms embargoes may not be fully clear. Also, there may be other policy changes that, while not directly aimed for through an arms embargo, are important for the initiators of the sanctions. Level I effectiveness can thus have a number of dimensions: policy change in targeted country after imposition of sanctions; change in the conduct of sanctioned policy, for instance, different types of warfare; and preparedness to discuss contentious issues/vacillation on policy or hardening of political position.

HYPOTHESIS ABOUT FACTORS INFLUENCING EFFECTIVENESS

Effectiveness will be influenced by a number of factors, sketched in the preceding discussion. These are grouped here into seven clusters of hypothesis.

Cost Benefit Calculations in Target

A first group of factors refers to the importance of the sanctioned policies to the target on the one hand and the importance of arms deliveries to the target on the other. If the targeted policy is of high importance to the target, it is less likely to yield, making it less likely that level I effectiveness can be achieved. A high degree of dependence on arms imports, on the contrary, will increase the likelihood of achieving level I effectiveness. A strong relation between the sanctioned behavior and arms imports will also increase level I effectiveness.

Decision-Making Structure in Target

A second group of factors reflects type and structure of decision-making power in the target, who is making decisions and under what conditions. Arms embargoes may also have effects on the composition of the leadership, for instance, strengthening groups that gain materially from arms embargo busting. Judging by result from the general sanctions literature on policy changes for different kind of political regimes (Drezner, 1999; Doxey, 1999), level I effectiveness will likely rise with participatory decision-making. Single person dictatorships are less likely to change policies than are more open political processes. A related hypothesis is that the symbolic dimension of arms embargo will be important – whether the arms embargo has been touted as a major injustice or more or less taken as minor reaction by the international community. On the contrary, if the target can see that the arms embargo is embedded in other policies by those states initiating and implementing it, such as diplomatic relations, trade patterns, and possibly also other sanctions, it has a higher probability of level I effectiveness.

Evasion Capacity/Activity of Targets

Because target states or groups may have alternatives to arms imports, particularly domestic arms projection, we can speculate that a domestic arms industry capable of producing weapons in quantity and quality sufficient to substitute for the loss of arms imports will lower the likelihood of level I effectiveness. Related to this is the issue of lead times. Another factor shaping level I effectiveness can be the time between first signs that there might be an embargo and the actual implementation of an arms embargo. The longer the lead time to an arms embargo, the lower the probability of level I effectiveness. Level I effectiveness is also lower when the target is able to reorganize its arms supply away from states with strong enforcement capabilities to others with more limited implementation.

Multilateralization of Arms Embargo

It is important who is initiating the arms. While a dominant supplier to a target may obtain some degree of level II effectiveness by itself, in general, suppliers will seek multilateralization of an arms embargo. Economic suppliers who lose business through national decisions are particularly likely to seek to try to multilateralize their own decisions.

The chance for successful embargo implementation grows when the group of initiators includes governments that have strong influence over other states that do not strongly share the level I objective. The chances of successful multilateral implementation of an arms embargo further grow when the level I objective is important not only to the initiators of the arms embargo but also other states. A shared, strong level I objective leads to strong embargo implementation.

Initiators and early supporters may also be able to use incentives, policy links, or other instruments to bring reluctant states to multilateralize. One such way is to support arms embargo implementation by other states. But states may also use coercive measures such as denial of arms transfers to those delivering weapons. Level II effectiveness becomes more likely when initiators and supporters of an arms embargo are willing to support implementation in other states, cajole them into enforcement, and offer them incentives in case of effective national implementation

Implementation of Arms Embargo

On the supplier side, an important factor discussed in the arms embargo literature are the willingness and capabilities of arms suppliers and neighboring states to prevent weapons to get to the target. More concretely, level II effectiveness is dependent on no or few states with the capability to do so counteracting the embargo. When looking at level II effectiveness, therefore, an important focus is on those states allowing, or not stopping, the delivery of arms. Each individual state responsible for disemplementation of an arms embargo should be involved in the analysis of level II effectiveness. Important questions to ask are whether the state lacks willingness or capability to enforce the arms embargo or possibly both.

Suppliers, and transit states, need to be willing and capable of implementing arms embargoes to achieve the level II objective. If the target is of the impression that some suppliers do not abide by an arms embargo, or cannot bring private actors to stop arms deliveries, and if neighboring states have weak enforcement mechanism, this is likely to additionally affect level I effectiveness. On the contrary, if strong pressure is supplied by major states on such potential or actual "sanction busters," this will enhance the probability of success.

A related factor is the support multilateral organization can give to embargo implementation. At the UN, for instance, sanction committees can be more or less active, the UN Security Council can frequently discuss an arms embargo or widely ignore it. The UN Security Council can also institute expert panels to investigate arms embargo violations and name and shame violates. For instance, extensive monitoring of arms embargoes can also be surmised to increase the chances that a target will see an embargo as threat to its position and change policies to avoid or reverse a sanctions decision. Level II effectiveness will increase with an active role of multilateral organizations that employs mechanisms like that used more recently at the UN in the case of UN arms embargoes and especially in commodity embargoes (Cortright & Lopez, 2000, pp. 181–221).

Countermeasures by Targets

A major factor shaping level II effectiveness is the financial capability of recipient states to import arms, including under difficult conditions, which is when new suppliers have to be found and prices rise. A high level of international trade will allow targets to meet rising weapon import prices and hide arms imports among general, civilian trade. Alternatively, the target's availability of resources that can be easily marketed internationally decreases the likelihood of level II embargo effectiveness. As most of the arms deals under an embargo will likely be done in black or gray markets, the existence of black and gray market ties between the target and the outside world will lower level II effectiveness.

Importance of Embargo Objectives for Initiators

The importance of a level I objective to supplier and transit states would seem to be a prime factor for deciding how much to invest into making an arms embargo effective on level II and, to the extent that this can be influenced from the outside, level I. On the contrary, low interest in the policy goal of an embargo may have the effect that satisfaction with the embargo, level III effectiveness comes without much success on level I or II. The simple fact that there is an official arms embargo may for instance be sufficient to calm domestic audiences and foreign governments who pressure "to do something" about a target state or group's policies.

The importance of level I objectives to a supplier or transit state's government will depend on both domestic and foreign policy interest and considerations. Domestic lobbying groups pro and contra an arms embargo are likely to try to influence decision-making by the government, as will foreign governments (see under multilateralization).

Another group of factors that can shape effectiveness on all levels is the status of arms suppliers who cut off their deliveries. In addition to the material effect on procurement, arms embargoes are political signals that aim to influence decision-making in the targeted state or group. Taking a cue from the general sanctions literature, it is likely that an ending of the arms relationship by states that were considered allies will have a higher probability of level I effectiveness than action by "commercial" suppliers (Hufbauer et al., 1990). A recursive political significance exists in almost all arms transfer relationships; however, while it is central to hegemonic supplier client relations, it is a side effect for commercial suppliers.

OUTLOOK

The framework developed here guides the country case studies included in this book. In addition, there is a quantitative analysis in Chapter 9 of all cases since the early 1990s of UN arms embargoes, EU arms embargoes, and US arms embargoes, using the framework discussed earlier. The objective of the quantitative chapter is to provide a comparative perspective on the importance of factors mentioned earlier as shaping success in arms embargo implementation.

The selection of cases for empirical study follows standard patterns of comparative analysis. First, the universe of possible cases for study are UN arms embargoes, EU arms embargoes, and US arms embargoes. The UN, through the UN charter, provides a natural forum for multilateralization of arms embargoes. However, this is a weak forum. The EU is a much stronger institution, but with only few members. The United States is by far the largest arms exporter in the world and has a variety of means at its disposal to informally multilateralize arms embargoes. And in some cases, as illustrated in Chapter 4 on Pakistan, it will and will not use such means.

A second criterion is to include cases with diverse political backgrounds, level I objectives, and prior arms transfer patterns. The UN arms embargoes against African states, and groups have been analyzed as failures because of the weak, or non-existent, enforcement capabilities of neighboring states. The number of African cases to be included in the qualitative analysis is small compared to the number of possible cases.

The goal of this study is to find ways to improve the effectiveness of arms embargoes on level I. The framework suggested is based on a broad perspective on how such improvements could come about, including improved multilateralization of arms embargoes, national capabilities for implementation, and improved matching between desired policy changes and arms embargoes.

REFERENCES

Baldwin, D. (1997). The sanctions debate and the logic of choice. *International Security, 24*(3), 80–110.

Beck, M. D. (Ed.) (2003). *To supply or to deny. Comparing nonproliferation export controls in five key countries*. Amsterdam: Kluver.

BICC – Bonn International Center for Conversion. (1997). *Conversion survey 1997*. Oxford: Oxford University Press.

Bondi, L. (2002). Arms embargoes. In name only? In: D. Cortright & G. Lopez (Eds), *Smart sanctions: Targeting economic statecraft* (pp. 125–144). Lanham, MD: Rowman & Littlefield.

Brzoska, M. (1991). Arming South Africa in the shadow of the UN arms embargo, in: *Defense Analysis*, Vol. 7, no. 1, 1991, pp. 21–38.

Brzoska, M., & Pearson, F. (1994). *Armaments and warfare*. Columbia, SC: University of South Carolina Press.

Cortright, D., & Lopez, G. (2000). *The sanctions decade: Assessing UN strategies for the 1990s*. Boulder, CO: Lynne Rienner.

Cortright, D., & Lopez, G. A., with Gerber, L. (2002). *Sanctions and the search for security*. Boulder: Lynne Rienner.

Doxey, M. (1999). *United Nations sanctions. Current policy issues*. Canada: Centre for Foreign Policy Studies, Dalhousie University.

Drezner, D. W. (1999). *The sanctions paradox: Economic statecraft and international relations*. Cambridge: Cambridge University Press.

Harkavy, R. (1975). *The arms trade and international systems*. Cambridge, MA: Ballinger.

Hufbauer, G. C., Schott, J. J., & Elliott, K. A. (1990). *Economic sanctions reconsidered* (2nd ed.). Washington: Institute for International Economics.

Krause, K. (1995). *Arms and the state*. Cambridge, UK: Cambridge University Press.

Landgren, S. (1989). *Embargo disimplemented*. Oxford, UK: Oxford University Press.

Laurance, E. (1992). *The international arms trade*. New York: Simon and Schuster.

MacNeill, W. (1982). *The pursuit of power*. London: Blackwell.

Ohlson, T. (1987). *Arms transfer limitations*. Oxford: Oxford University Press.

Pierre, A. (1982). *The global politics of arms sales*. Princeton: Princeton University Press.

Sampson, A. (1978). *The arms bazaar*. New York: Bantam Books.

SIPRI. (1973). *The arms trade with the third world*. Stockholm: Almquist and Wicksell.

Speier, R. H., Chow, B. G., & Starr, S. R. (2001). *Nonproliferation sanctions*. Santa Barbara: RAND.

Stent, A. (1985). *Economic relations with the Soviet Union: American and West German perspectives.* Boulder, CO: Westview Press.

Weiss, T., Cortright, D., Lopez, G. A., & Minear, L. (1997). *Civilian pain and political gain.* Boulder, CO: Rowman and Littlefield.

Wulf, H. (1986). Arms embargoes. In: S. Deger & R. West (Eds), *Security and development.* New York, NY: St. Martin's Press.

Young, O. (1999). *The effectiveness of international environmental regimes.* Cambridge, MA: MIT Press.

CHAPTER 2

THE UNPRECEDENTED EMBARGO: THE UN ARMS SANCTIONS AGAINST IRAQ, 1990–2004 ☆

Oldrich Bures and George A. Lopez

INTRODUCTION

Following Iraq's invasion of Kuwait in August 1990, the international community took vigorous, unprecedented steps to curb Saddam Hussein's military ambitions. The central component of these actions was a set of comprehensive arms, aviation, maritime, and economic sanctions, each imposed by the United Nations Security Council (UNSC). When the multinational coalition forces ousted Iraq from Kuwait the following year, the UNSC made these sanctions and embargoes a component of the armistice agreement. Over time, these sanctions were subsequently used as leverage to press for Iraqi compliance with relevant UNSC resolutions calling for Iraqi disarmament.[1]

Although the embargo methods used against the Hussein regime remained strongly enforced, the rhetoric and rationale for the arms sanctions varied over time. It began, as ironic as it might seem, because an arms embargo was critical for enforcing and attaining disarmament. By

☆This chapter consciously examines the UN embargo through the full period of its legal identity, which continued past the US invasion of March 2003 until 2006.

Putting Teeth in the Tiger: Improving the Effectiveness of Arms Embargoes
Contributions to Conflict Management, Peace Economics and Development, Volume 10, 29–53
ISSN: 1572-8323/doi:10.1108/S1572-8323(2009)0000010006

1997, the United States equated the idea of "regime change in Iraq" to the continuation of sanctions, even though this was not spelled out in the original UNSC Resolutions 661 and 687. For a brief moment, the Bush government sought serious reform of sanctions, but then lost enthusiasm in this approach as long as Saddam Hussein remained in power. After more than 12 years of sanctions passed without bringing about a regime change in Baghdad, a US-led invasion of Iraq in March 2003 quickly swept Saddam Hussein from power. Shortly thereafter, Washington called for, and eventually obtained, the UNSC's lifting of the sanctions. While all of these developments were crucial milestones in the history of the entire Iraqi sanctions regime, they are not the primary objects of analysis in this chapter. They are, therefore, discussed only briefly to put the Iraqi arms embargo in the proper historical and political context.

SANCTIONS REGIME OVERVIEW

The UNSC imposed comprehensive mandatory sanctions against Iraq just four days after its invasion of Kuwait. Security Council Resolution (SCR) 661 suspended all international flights to Iraq, froze Iraqi government financial assets, banned all international trade with Iraq, prohibited all financial transactions, imposed an oil and arms embargo, and created a sanctions committee to oversee the entire regime. Several weeks later, the UNSC adopted resolution 670, which added aviation and maritime sanctions to the regime. In April 1991, the Gulf War cease-fire resolution, SCR 687 (paragraphs 8–13), spelled out a set of eight specific conditions for lifting of the sanctions stipulated in SCR 661. Notwithstanding the continuing divisions among the permanent members of the Council, widespread public concern for humanitarian suffering in Iraq, and Saddam's elaborate and multi-pronged efforts to subvert sanctions compliance, the Council did not lift the majority of sanctions until May 22, 2003, after the United States ousted Saddam Hussein's regime.

Certain arms embargo provisions of SCR 661 were lifted in June 2004 by passage of SCR 1546, which declared that "the prohibitions related to the sale or supply to Iraq of arms and related materiel under previous resolutions shall not apply to arms or related materiel required by the Government of Iraq or the multinational force" to serve the purpose of "developing effective Iraqi police, border enforcement, and ... other Iraqi ministries, for the maintenance of law, order, and security, including combating terrorism." At the same time, SCR 1546 formally kept most other provisions of the sanction regime in place, noting that the aforementioned exceptions do not affect "the prohibitions on or obligations of States related to items specified in paragraphs 8 and 12 of resolution 687 (1991) on 3 April 1991 or activities described in paragraph 3 (f) of resolution 707 (1991) on 15 August 1991."

The new Iraq's United Nations (UN) ambassador Samir Sumaidaie recently urged the Security Council to lift the arms embargo and economic restrictions it imposed on Saddam Hussein's government, calling them "shackles and burdens" on Iraq's fledgling democracy. He noted that Iraq's new transitional government wants the UNSC to end the use of Iraqi oil revenue to pay UN weapons inspectors and to dismantle other legal and bureaucratic restrictions "which have outlived their relevance" (Lederer, 2005). As of April 2005, however, the core of the Iraqi sanctions regime still remains de jure in place and all Iraqi imports are still formally subject to inspection.

THE EMBARGO'S SECURITY COUNCIL HISTORY

To implement the non-nuclear provisions of resolution 687, the Security Council created the United Nations Special Commission (UNSCOM). UNSCOM formally came into being on April 19, 1991, when the Secretary-General appointed Ambassador Rolf Ekéus (Sweden) as the Executive Chairman of the Special Commission. On May 1, 1991, the Secretary-General appointed 20 other members of the Commission, from Australia, Austria, Belgium, Canada, China, the Czech Republic, Finland, France, Germany, Indonesia, Italy, Japan, the Netherlands, Nigeria, Norway, Poland, the Russian Federation, the United Kingdom, the United States, and Venezuela (UN Special Commission, 1999).

UNSCOM's mandate included multiple functions: to carry out immediate on-site inspections of Iraq's biological, chemical, and missile capabilities; to take possession for the destruction, removal, or rendering harmless of all chemical and biological weapons and all stocks of agents and all related sub-systems and components and all research, development, support, and manufacturing facilities; to supervise the destruction by Iraq of all its ballistic missiles with a range greater than 150 km and related major parts and repair and production facilities; and to monitor and verify Iraq's compliance with its undertaking not to use, develop, construct, or acquire any of the items specified above. Under Resolution 687, UNSCOM also was to assist the Director General of the International Atomic Energy Agency (IAEA), which was to undertake activities similar to those of the Commission, but specifically in the nuclear field. Further, UNSCOM could designate for inspection any additional site necessary for ensuring the fulfillment of the mandates given to the Commission and the IAEA (UN Special Commission, 1999).

Through an exchange of letters in May 1991 involving the Secretary-General of the United Nations, the Executive Chairman of UNSCOM, and the Minister for Foreign Affairs of Iraq, Iraq agreed to allow free access and diplomatic immunity to members of UNSCOM, the IAEA, specialized agencies of the United Nations system, and technical experts and specialists in Iraq for the purposes of fulfilling the mandate. In practice, however, a "combination of continued Iraqi truculence and US inflexibility led to a number of crises between UNSCOM and Iraq" (Cortright & Lopez, 2002, p. 26). The most serious came in the fall of 1998, which led to US bombing in November, 1998, and led to the complete collapse of the weapons inspection process by December.

The monitoring of the sanctions regime was revived and adjusted by UNSCR 1284, adopted on December 17, 1999. The resolution established a new United Nations Monitoring, Verification and Inspection Commission (UNMOVIC), outlined the procedures for the completion of the verification process, and declared the Council's intention to suspend sanctions for renewable 120-day periods if Iraq cooperated with UNMOVIC and IAEA. Under the leadership of Swedish diplomat Hans Blix, UMNOVIC assembled a new team of weapons inspectors that were to return to Iraq and pick up where UNSCOM had concluded its work. Iraq, however, steadfastly refused to accept the UNMOVIC mission and demanded an immediate end to sanctions. The stalemate continued and no UN weapons inspections occurred in Iraq until November 2002, when Iraq conceded to the provisions of UNSCR 1441, which afforded Iraq "a final opportunity to comply with its disarmament obligations under relevant resolutions of the Council" (paragraph 2).

An enhanced inspection regime was assembled and UMMOVIC inspectors returned to Iraq. In December 2002, Iraq finally provided UNMOVIC and the IAEA in Baghdad with a declaration of its weapons programs and with a list of personnel associated with its weapons programs, as required by SCR 1441. The Iraqi concessions, however, fell short of convincing the Bush administration that Iraq's willingness to disarm was sincere. By the end of 2002, the United States lost its remaining faith in the sanctions regime's efficacy and opted for forced removal of the Hussein regime. When it became apparent that a US-led invasion to Iraq was inevitable, UNMOVIC inspectors withdrew from Iraq on March 18, 2003 (UNMOVIC, 2003).

Because UNSCR 1546 formally kept most provisions of the sanction regime in place, both UNMOVIC and IAEA inspectors were still formally mandated to continue their work in Iraq after the US invasion. In practice, however, US officials have repeatedly denied UN inspectors' requests to return to Iraq because of "logistics and timing." The spokesman for the US mission to the UN also stated that since the United States and the United Kingdom were taking the lead in searching for the arms, "there was really no reason" to allow the inspectors back (Stockman & Bender, 2004).

In the second half of 2004, however, a number of US and international newspapers reported on the apparent inability of US forces to secure the Iraqi weapons production facilities from widespread looting. An *Associated Press* review of official reporting, for example, stated that

All the world now knows that Iraq had no threatening "WMD" programs. But two years after U.S. teams began their futile hunt for weapons of mass destruction, Iraq has something else: a landscape of ruined military plants and of unanswered questions and loose ends, some potentially lethal ... Dozens of ballistic missiles are missing in Iraq. Vials of dangerous microbes are unaccounted for. Sensitive sites, once under U.N. seal, stand gutted today, their arms-making gear hauled off by looters, or by arms-makers. (Hanley, 2005)

After the disappearance of 380 tons of explosives from the Al Qaqaa facility, the issue of looted Iraqi weapon facilities even became a hot topic in the US presidential election campaigns, with the Democratic challenger John F. Kerry accusing the Bush administration of allowing the explosives to fall into the hands of insurgents (Vieth & Gold, 2004).

The controversy of the Al Qaqaa munitions erupted months after UNMOVIC presented evidence of widespread looting at many other weapons sites. The chief UN arms inspector suggested that outsiders are seeing only a "sliver" of the mess inside Iraq and claimed that satellite images indicate at least 90 sites in the old Iraqi military-industrial complex have been pillaged since March 2003 (Hanley, 2005). This was subsequently also acknowledged by the US Iraq Survey Group, which stated in its 986-page report that "[t]here is nothing but a concrete slab at locations where once stood plants or laboratories" (Duelfer, 2003, 2004a, 2004b). In the summer of 2004, UN inspectors found the first evidence of what had happened – more than 40 missile engines somehow had made their way out of Iraq and into foreign scrap yards, along with four specialized vessels from Iraq's Fallujah chemical plant, which made ingredients for poison gases (Hanley, 2005). UNMOVIC found 20 missile engines in a scrap yard in

Jordan and 22 other missile engines in the Netherlands (Stockman & Bender, 2004).

Somewhat oddly, despite the fact the Bush administration barred the UN and IAEA inspectors from returning to Iraq since their forced departure in March 2003, more than $12 million annually in Iraqi oil money was allocated to the support of UNMOVIC and another $12.3 million should go to the IAEA for nuclear inspectors in the next two years. Not surprisingly, Iraq's UN ambassador soon complained that the two bureaucracies "are doing absolutely nothing that is relevant to Iraq" and argued that the money should be going to the Iraqi people for reconstruction: "We must not be kept waiting (and paying) month after month. Iraq is a fledgling democracy committed to the rule of law, both internationally and domestically. As such, it has the legitimate right to expect to be treated like any other member state" (Lederer, 2005). UNMOVIC was not formally disbanded until June, 2007. As IAEA is a permanent organization, its international work continues but it has not been relevant to Iraq since 2003.

SANCTIONS REGIME MOTIVATION AND OBJECTIVES

Along with the entire sanctions regime, the August 1990 arms embargo against Iraq embodies one of the best examples of a top-down model that was initiated by the UN in response to objectionable policies of one of its member states (MS). After the Iraqi invasion of Kuwait in August 1990, the international community appeared unified in its desire to (1) punish Iraq for its aggression in Kuwait, (2) prevent Iraq from launching a similar aggression in the future, and (3) eliminate its weapons of mass destruction (WMD) programs. These three goals were explicitly spelled out in the relevant UNSC resolutions, thus constituting the official level I objectives of the Iraqi sanctions regime.

Over time, the initial consensus about sanctions objectives eroded. Perhaps most importantly, since the mid-1990s, the Clinton administration repeatedly made it clear that it would block any lifting or serious reforming of sanctions as long as Saddam Hussein remained in power,[2] thus transforming regime change in Iraq into a rationale for the continuation of sanctions. While it is worth noting that none of the original UNSC resolutions contained any regime change provisions and references, the US position was at least partly caused by Iraq's defiance of the UN demands that were spelled out in the relevant UNSC resolutions. Moreover, as documented by Cortright and Lopez, the search for an endgame in Iraq has always been frustrated by differing agendas of the Permanent Five (Cortright & Lopez, 2002). The differences in sanctions objectives and motivations among UN Member States (UNMS) became especially apparent in the late 1990s, in part due to the mounting criticisms that contrasted the sanction regime's harsh impact on the well-being of Iraqi civilians with its ostensibly insufficient pressure on Saddam Hussein and his aids. The UNMS disagreements and differences about the objectives of the sanctions regime complicated the implementation of the sanctions on Iraq in the 1990s. In addition, they caused considerable difficulties when it came to evaluating the sanction regime's effectiveness before the US-led invasion of Iraq in March 2003.

EVALUATING THE ARMS EMBARGO EFFECTIVENESS

A number of objectives and criteria can be used to measure the effectiveness of the arms embargo by focusing on four particular areas of arms capability of the Iraqi regime. These include Iraq's domestic arms production, Iraqi arms imports, Iraqi War Fighting Capacity, and, of course, Iraqi WMD programs. Since the denial of arms to the target is often put on equal footing with the political objectives of the arms embargo, we also explore some of the recent and much debated cases of arms smuggling into Iraq after the arms embargo imposition in 1991.

Domestic Iraqi Arms Production Capacity

Before the first Gulf War, Iraq had a proven capacity to produce certain conventional weapons domestically and seems to have done so at a very high rate. In its report on Iraq's Military Industry, for example, Global Security stated that in the 1970s and 1980s,

> Iraq had developed significant ammunition, small and light arms, and gun barrel production facilities ... Iraq was self-sufficient in small caliber ammunition, artillery shells, aircraft bombs, mortar rounds, rocket-propelled grenades, rockets, tube-launched rockets, mortars, propellant, fuses, and replacement barrels. (Global Security, 2004)

In the 1980s, Iraq also increased its efforts to upgrade and maintain existing tanks and other armored vehicles domestically. The Taji factory complex, for example, had doubled in size by 1985 and included a forge capable of producing 1000 artillery barrels per year and armor maintenance and refit plants for the T-54, T-55, and T-62 tanks in the Iraqi inventory. The complex also included facilities for assembly of the T-72 and would eventually build armor and tank bodies (Timmerman, 1991, p. 209, 323). In addition, under various licenses from the USSR and other Eastern European countries, 30 production lines were put into operation, including a "Yusufiya" howitzer manufacturing plant, an ordnance factory "Hattin" in Iskanderiya, a "Kadysiya" AK rifles manufacturing facility, as well as a tank assembling plant in Taji (Blagov, 2004). Iraq was also a licensed producer of the rocket-propelled grenade-7 (RPG-7), currently one of the most effective weapons employed by insurgents against combat vehicles and helicopters (Grau, 1998). However, Iraq did not attempt to develop significant domestic capabilities to create more sophisticated armaments and relied heavily on foreign technical support teams even for servicing its imported weaponry, such as its French and Russian aircrafts (Cordesman, 1998). Global Security reporters also noted that "[p]rior to 1991, production of defense articles was largely oriented on prototypes and prestige projects" (Global Security, 2004).

There is, nevertheless, little doubt that by 1990, Iraq's military industry was enormous: it employed more workers than the well-known Israeli defense industries, and the military-industrial labor force constituted at least 40 percent or more of Iraq's total industrial employees (Hoyt, 1998). Between 1985 and 1989, Iraq spent $14.2 billion on industrial technology, almost all of which had military applications (Timmerman, 1991, p. 352). US Senator John McCain provided even higher numbers, arguing that Iraq spent $27 billion on weapons technology and industrial supplies from 1980 to 1990 (Hoyt, 1998).

Timothy D. Hoyt suggested that the Iraqi emphasis on developing a sufficient domestic conventional weapons and ammunition capacity in the 1980s was a consequence of two factors. First, there was the negative experience with the Soviet arms embargo during the struggle with the Kurds in 1974–1975. According to Saddam Hussein, the situation then "became extremely dangerous [because] our material and essential munitions cruelly began to run out" (cited in Hoyt, 1998). Consequentially, Iraq subsequently took steps to stockpile munitions, by diversifying its arms purchases and building up its indigenous production capacity. Second, Iraqi conventional military operations relied on high firepower and attrition as a key to their success. High-firepower strategies, obviously, require large amounts of ammunition. During the Iraq–Iran war, analysts reported that Iraqi gunners routinely fired as much ammunition in a single day as US Army planners estimated would be fired in an entire week of high intensity conflict by US Army artillery. Thus, as Hoyt argued, the high-firepower strategy of the Iraqi army became another "major incentive for the development of Iraq's arm industry."

The first Gulf War inflicted considerable damage to the previously booming Iraqi arms industry, but the indigenous arms production capacity was probably not nearly as crippled as some Western analysts had hoped and predicted. Although the lack of reliable data renders all post-1990 assessments of Iraqi domestic arms production capacity speculative, several sources suggested that by 1993, Iraq had regained significant military-industrial capability. None of the outside assessments, however, were as optimistic as the former Iraqi Prime Minister Muhammad al-Zubaydi, who claimed in August 1992 that 87% of Iraq's military infrastructure was again operational (Global Security, 2004).

While we will probably never discover to what extent Iraq managed to revive its pre-1990 domestic arms production capacities, we now know that the sanctions regime, and its arms embargo provisions in particular, prevented Saddam from expanding and upgrading it, keeping Saddam's military expenditures at extremely low levels. This is no small achievement given that that after 1990, the Iraqi government clearly emphasized "guns over butter" – even at the cost of a devastating cut in per capita incomes. Moreover, none of the traditional Iraqi arms license and technology suppliers made official contracts with Saddam's regime after 1991, thus forcing it to turn to the highly unreliable and several times more expensive black market sources. While it is likely that Iraq was able to produce some weapons domestically after the imposition of the arms embargo in 1991, neither their quantity nor their quality was sufficient to rebuild the Iraqi army. As a consequence, it is possible to conclude that regardless of the actual level of resurrection of its domestic, pre-1990 arms production capacity, Iraq was heavily hit by the arms embargo provisions of the comprehensive sanctions regime.

Iraqi Arms Imports

Before the imposition of the arms embargo in 1991, Iraq was a major importer of weapons. Perhaps most importantly, since it did not have the ability to produce advanced weapons systems domestically, Iraq relied on imports for almost all of its heavy military equipment. With plenty of funds generated from its growing oil export industry, Iraq never had problem with finding arms suppliers before its invasion of Kuwait in 1990. Arms sales to Iraq represented a lucrative opportunity, especially for Russia and other Warsaw Pact countries that were looking to sell off heavy military equipment. Between 1958 and 1990, for example, Moscow alone earned $ 30.5 million in contracts with Baghdad (Zaitseg & Litovkin, 2004). However, as Shawn Macomber (2004, p. 15) pointed out, many other countries, including the United States, exported significant amounts of arms to Iraq before the first Gulf War:

> If supplying munitions to Saddam were and Olympic sport Russia would have walked away with the gold, China the silver, and France the bronze. But Australia, Brazil, Bulgaria, Canada, Germany, North Korea, Singapore, South Africa, and, yes, even the United States, along with many others, would all have been in the game – directly or indirectly, depending on whether you chose to believe the alibi.

In other words, both before and after the Gulf War, Iraq was an import-dependent country when it came to sustaining its ability to procure and use advanced military technology. As a consequence, in 1991, many analysts assumed that Iraq would be a good target for an arms embargo.

With the benefit of hindsight, it is possible to say that these assumptions largely proved to be well founded. No government was willing to openly ignore the prohibition on selling arms to Iraq after the imposition of arms embargo in August 1990, although the recent report, the *Duelfer Report*, maintains that "the Governments of Syria, Belarus, North Korea, former Federal Republic of Yugoslavia, Yemen, and possibly Russia directly supported or endorsed private company efforts to aid Iraq with conventional arms procurement, in breach of UN sanctions" (Duelfer, 2003, p. 93). In either case, due to the UN arms embargo, Iraq accumulated an enormous arms import deficit. Although numerous private actors were at certain times willing to risk international displeasure by smuggling arms to Iraq and Saddam proved quite capable in launching elaborate and multipronged embargo busting schemes (Duelfer, 2003), the quantity, quality, and diversity of equipment that Iraq obtained through black market and embargo busting transactions was insufficient when it came to rebuilding and upgrading its military. As Cordesman noted in 1998,

> Iraq's past pattern of arms imports makes it highly dependent on access to a wide range of suppliers – particularly Western Europe and Russia. Even if one nation should resume supply, Iraq could not rebuild its military machine without broad access to such

suppliers and would be forced to convert a substantial amount of its order of battle to whatever supplier(s) were willing to sell. (Cordesman, 1998)

In short, the arms embargo denied Iraq the access to large quantities of advanced weapons from major arms producers that were instrumental in its pre-Gulf War military build-up. Thus, although apparently ineffective in weakening Saddam Hussein's regime internally, the arms embargo was effective in curbing Iraqi military capabilities. A good example in this regard was the decline in the war-fighting capabilities of the Iraqi Air Forces and the Iraqi Navy.

Iraqi War Fighting Capability

After seeing how devastating American/allied air power was in the first Gulf War, Iraq was anxious to upgrade its air defenses. The embargo, however, choked off its access to the highly sophisticated technology that would have been needed to combat the overwhelming superiority of American air power. In addition, the arms embargo hampered the Iraqi Air Force's ability to keep its existing planes operational. Although some spare parts may have been smuggled in from Serbia and North Korea, Iraqi planes did not oppose the coalition invasion. By 2003, Iraq had only a few long-range bombers left out of its vast pre-Gulf War stock (CNN, 2003).

The Iraqi Navy was never a terribly potent force to begin with but after the first Gulf War it was depleted even further. A 2003 CNN.com special report summed up Iraq's naval capacity after the Gulf War and the decade of sanctions as follows:

All that remains are mostly the Sawari class of inshore patrol boats, according to Jane's Sentinel, a risk-assessment publication. Two Assad class corvettes are moored at La Spezia, Italy, but they are unlikely to be returned due to the U.N. arms embargo, the publication says. US Central Command estimates that Iraq's navy has 21 ships (including the presidential yacht) but says most of those are not operational. (CNN, 2003)

Because of the constraints imposed by the sanctions regime, Saddam Hussein did not even attempt any major efforts to upgrade the Iraqi Navy. As a consequence, it was not powerful enough to present a credible threat to a large and modern US fleet and lacked big, power-projecting ships that could threaten its neighbors. In fact, its strength was dwarfed by the fleets of regional rivals like Iran and Saudi Arabia (Cordesman, 1998, p. 72).

Even worse from the Iraqi perspective, they had just learned through painful experience in the first Gulf War that its military was not sufficiently technologically advanced to compete with the world's most advanced armed forces, particularly American air power. According to the 1998 Center for Strategic and International Studies (CSIS) Military Balance in the Middle East, Iraq would need to spend sums approaching $ 20 billion to merely rebuild its force structure to the pre-Gulf War strength. Major modernization efforts to counter US standards of capability would add at least $ 10 billion each in a number of key areas such as land-based air defense, air defense, air and missile strike capabilities, armored modernization, modernization of other land weapons, and reconstitution of the Iraqi Navy (Cordesman, 1998, p. 6). Even if these estimates were substantially exaggerated, it is clear that even the $11 billion that Iraq allegedly generated from 1990 till 2003 through various sanction-busting schemes was woefully insufficient when it came to rebuilding and upgrading the Iraqi forces. While sanction-busting allowed Iraq to maintain a military that was numerically large and quite capable in curbing domestic dissent, Iraqi armed forces were completely outclassed when the US-led coalition invaded in March 2003. In conclusion, although Iraqi armed forces were sufficient to maintain internal order and menace weaker neighbors like Kuwait, after 1990, thanks to the arms embargo and other UN sanctions, they remained unable to withstand a high-tech, combined-arms onslaught by a first-world army.

Iraqi Long-Range Delivery Systems and WMD Production Programs

Since the early 1970s, Iraq had consistently sought to acquire an effective long-range weapons delivery capability. By 1991, Baghdad had purchased the missiles and infrastructure that would form the basis for nearly all of its future missile system developments. The Gulf War and subsequent UN inspections, however, brought many of Iraq's delivery system programs to a complete halt at least until 1996, when proceeds from illegal oil sales spurred a period of increased activity in delivery systems development. According to the Duelfer Report,

> Iraq's ballistic missile programs experienced rapid advancement compared to the previous five years of stunted development and concerned new ideas for longer range missiles, some based on old concepts. Given the ever-decreasing effectiveness of sanctions, Iraq was able to consider bolder steps in areas where it still had technical difficulties. (Duelfer, 2004a)

Yet at the same time, the report noted that "[i]f the sanctions regime remained strictly enforced, there would have been little or no effort by Iraq to address these shortfalls" (Duelfer, 2004a). Moreover, there is some evidence that even with lower enforcement levels and despite the 1998 Iraqi decision to cease all cooperation with UNSCOM and IAEA, UN sanctions were not rendered completely redundant after 1996.

The Al-Samoud 2 missile program provides a good illustration of how even imperfect sanctions and aborted inspections hampered Hussein's ability to upgrade his long-range delivery missile programs. After the first Gulf War, Iraq invested a significant amount of money and effort in its attempts to develop and upgrade the Al-Samoud 2 missile, which was based on the Soviet Volga/SA-2, designed back in the 1970s. Iraqi engineers hoped to convert a surface-to-air missile to a longer ranged surface-to-surface missile by adding engines to it. Their efforts yielded some success – in test flights, the Al Samoud exceeded the 93 mile maximum range restriction that the UN had placed in Iraq. In early 2003, however, the UNSC declared the missile illegal and ordered some 76 missiles already produced to be destroyed. Before the US-led coalition invaded Iraq in March, UN inspectors had overseen the destruction of 70 missiles, leaving Iraq with little to show for years of expensive development (UNMOVIC, 2003).

Finally, although Saddam's alleged possession of WMDs was one of the key justifications for the US-led invasion of Iraq in March 2003, it was the WMD realm where UN sanctions and UN disarmament verification missions eventually proved to have been most effective. Iraq had made significant investments in its WMD programs before the first Gulf War; nevertheless, primarily due to the UN sanctions and inspections, Iraq's ability to reconstitute these programs progressively decayed after 1991. This was confirmed in the findings of the *Duelfer Report*, which reached the following conclusions regarding the Iraqi WMDs:

- "While a small number of old, abandoned chemical munitions have been discovered, ISG judges that Iraq unilaterally destroyed its undeclared chemical weapons stockpile in 1991. There are no credible indications that Baghdad resumed production of chemical munitions thereafter ... The crippling of Iraq's CW infrastructure by the war, and the subsequent destruction and UN monitoring of much of the remaining materials and equipment limited Iraq's ability to rebuild or restart a CW program" (Duelfer, 2004b, p. 12).
- "The advent of postwar UN inspections posed serious problems for Iraq ... ISG's investigation found no evidence that Iraq continued to hide

BW weapons after the unilateral destruction of 1991 was complete, and ISG judges that most of the documents and materials hidden by the Special Republican Guard from 1991 until 1995 were indeed surrendered to the UN. However, Iraq continued to conceal documents from 1998 until 2003"(Duelfer, 2004b, p. 53).

• "Initially, Saddam chose to conceal his nuclear program in its entirety, as he did with Iraq's BW program. Aggressive UN inspections after Desert Storm forced Saddam to admit the existence of the program and destroy or surrender components of the program ... Iraq Survey Group (ISG) discovered further evidence of the maturity and significance of the pre-1991 Iraqi Nuclear Program but found that Iraq's ability to reconstitute a nuclear weapons program progressively decayed after that date" (Duelfer, 2004a, p. 1).

Thus, after the US invasion, it was obvious that UN efforts crippled Iraq's WMD programs more than many people suspected just a few years ago. In fact, taking into account that Saddam Hussein consistently assigned a high value to the WMD programs,[3] it is possible to claim that the combination of sanctions and inspections was extraordinarily effective in de facto shutting down the extensive pre-1991 Iraqi WMD programs (Lopez & Cortright, 2004).

Arms Smuggling

Though the facts are far from complete, it is certain that Iraq was able to obtain some arms in spite of the embargo. As diligently documented in the Duelfer Report, the embargo against Iraq was hardly an impermeable barrier, and various unscrupulous entities, occasionally acting with the knowledge of certain UN MS governments, were at times wiling and able to supply Saddam Hussein with some of the military equipment he sought. The examples below represent but a small selection of those cases of arms smuggling and embargo busting that had come to light long before the Duelfer Report was published in late September 2004. In addition to providing an illustrative overview of the numerous arms embargo violations, they also demonstrate the inefficiencies [from an Iraqi perspective] of black market transactions as well as the low reliability of sources that Iraq was forced to turn to for weapons purchases because of the UN arms embargo restrictions. Thus, to the extent to which an arms embargo is meant to dramatically increase the exchange costs for a target doing business, this embargo was rather successful.

In April 2002, the *Los Angeles Times* produced one of the most extensive investigations of how arms slipped into Iraq in spite of the sanctions. In "Banned Arms Flowed Into Iraq Through Syrian Firm," *Times* reporters Bob Drogin and Jeffrey Fleishman (2003) detail how the Syrian firm SES International Corp. served as a middleman, receiving arms shipments destined for Iraq and then smuggling them across the border. In particular, they uncovered documents showing that Evax, a Polish company, signed four contracts with Iraq and successfully shipped up to 380 surface-to-air Volga/SA-2 missile engines to Baghdad through Syria. They were subsequently used as engines in the Al Samoud 2 missile program.

Drogin and Fleishman also documented that two North Korean officials met the head of Al Bashair at SES offices in Damascus a month before the war to discuss Iraq's payment of $10 million for "major components" for ballistic missiles. US intelligence agencies were unaware of the deal at the time, or of a meeting 10 months earlier in which Iraqi officials authorized a $1.9-million down payment to Pyongyang through SES. In the end, the missiles were not delivered and Baghdad had lost its payment.

In another case uncovered by the *Los Angles Times* reporters, Slovenia's STO Ravne company, then a state-owned entity, shipped 20 large battle tank barrels identified as "steel tubes" to SES in February 2002. The next month, Slovenia's Defense Ministry blocked the company from exporting 50 more tank barrels to Syria. Overall, STO Ravne's secret contract called for delivering 175 tank barrels to Iraq. Last but not least, Drogin and Fleishman alleged that South Korea's Armitel Co. Ltd. shipped $8 million of sophisticated telecommunications equipment for what Iraqi documents described as "air defense."

In September 2002, Balkans-based North Atlantic Treaty Organization (NATO) peacekeepers obtained evidence that a state-owned Yugoslav company was party to an illegal deal to sell weapons components and repair services to Iraq. The raid on Orao, a Bosnian aviation company, discovered that Orao had a contract and documentation for an $ 8.5 million deal to repair and upgrade Iraqi Mig fighter aircraft engines. In response, the Yugoslav government dismissed several officials, including a deputy defense minister and the head of the state-owned company, and announced it was opening an investigation. Several Republika Srpska officials were also forced to step down, including Mirko Sarovic, the incumbent chairman of Bosnia's three-member presidency, who resigned because he knew about and failed to stop the transaction (CBSNEWS.com, 2003).

The US government announced in September 2002 that it had authenticated a tape recording in which President Leonid Kuchma of the Ukraine is heard to personally authorize a deal, worth $100 million, to supply sophisticated radar to Iraq through a Jordanian intermediary. President Kuchma has denied this accusation, rejected the tape as false, and stated that in any case the radar system was never supplied to Iraq (Human Rights Watch, 2002).

Also in September 2002, Russia's Millenium Company Ltd. signed an $8.8 million contract to supply mostly American-made communications and surveillance equipment to Iraq. The company's general manager in Moscow later wrote several documents suggesting "the preparation of a sham contract" to deceive UN weapons inspectors (Drogin and Fleishman). This sale has caused substantial amount of friction between the US and the Russian Governments. The United States alleges that although the equipment, which included night-vision goggles and jamming equipment that were troublesome to US forces, was sold by private companies, the Russian government should have been more vigilant (Richter & Murphy, 2004).

In October 2002, reports surfaced that the United States suspected Yugoslavia of selling missile technology to Libya, likely for Iraq. Yugoslav academics acknowledged having traveled to Iraq but denied US assertions that they provided missile technology (Williams & Wood, 2002, p. A26). Also in October 2002, a Tonga-registered ship intercepted off Croatia's coast was found to contain more than 200 tons of suspicious cargo, identified by the Croatian authorities as an explosive material used in the production of rockets and other munitions. Croatian police sources indicated they believed the cargo was destined for Iraq. The ship had originally departed from a Yugoslav port (CBSNEWS.com, 2003).

In the same month, Bulgarian armored personnel carrier parts were intercepted in Syria, on route to Iraq. The Bulgarian government scrambled to resolve the scandal before the NATO summit, firing the chief executive of the state-owned company that produced and shipped the parts. Other evidence suggests Bulgaria shipped parts and engines for T-55 and T-72 tanks to Iraq (Beckett, 2002). In November 2002, authorities in Bulgaria announced that they had detected a scheme to illegally export spare parts for armored personnel carriers but a consignment falsely labeled as "farm machinery" had already been exported to Syria. A US firm based in Washington was said to be implicated in the deal as well.[4]

The Iraqi military also obtained four optical scanners, which can be adapted to help divert laser-guided missiles. They were sold by the

Massachusetts-based Cambridge Technology Inc. to a student in Canada, who immediately shipped them to Amman, Jordan. He originally told the company he was donating it to an Arab university whose name he claimed not to remember (Macomber, 2004, p. 15). Thus, without the US company's knowledge, the real buyer was the Iraqi military.

According to Iraqi defectors interviewed by the British newspaper, *The Guardian*, sales of anti-aircraft rockets, missiles, and guidance systems for long-range missiles to Iraq had been licensed for export by the Czech Republic to Syria and Yemen, with one defector claiming he oversaw the transfer of the cargo from Syria to Iraq (Borger, 2002). The allegation was hotly denied by Iraqi and Syrian officials. The Czech government, for its part, stated that it had not approved exports of such equipment to Syria or Yemen in 2001 or 2002, nor authorized any re-sale of equipment sold to Syria or Yemen. A senior Czech official, however, told the Boston Globe that a large arms shipment to Yemen in early 2002 roughly matched the description given by Iraqi defectors of the arms cargo headed to Iraq (Whitmore, 2002).

Last but not least, according to a September 2004 article by Shawn Macomber, the US army found post-embargo illegal weapons everywhere in Iraq. The article specifically mentions French bomb fuses from 2001, Ukrainian Cornet anti-tank missiles, cluster bombs that the Russians did not even begin manufacturing until 1993, Russian AA-8 air-to-air missiles, two-axel Urals troops carries, which were not produced before 1995, and so on. While it is unclear how all these weapons got to Iraq, Macomber believes that they were smuggled in through the middlemen from Jordan and Syria, whose governments proved unwilling to halt the illicit weapons trade because of the hundreds of millions of dollars in cut-rate oil flowing from Iraq outside the UN Oil-for-Food program (Macomber, 2004, p. 18).

In summary, the arms embargo was not completely effective in denying Saddam Hussein the opportunity to purchase arms for his military. The aforementioned examples demonstrate vividly that shipments ostensibly destined for Jordan, Syria, Yemen, or other destinations near Iraq could have been smuggled across the border. However, the hodgepodge of suppliers and the irregular nature of the deliveries precluded Iraq from upgrading its war-fighting ability in any meaningful way that would result in it returning to the fighting capacity it had in the late 1980s. On the contrary, in spite of these shortcomings, Iraq's military continued to be one of the largest in the region, and it was perfectly adequate for stifling internal dissent and keeping the Baath Party in power (Hoyt, 1998).

Thus, it is possible to conclude that the combination of a devastating military defeat and immediate, comprehensive sanctions struck the Iraqi military a harsh blow. The comprehensive economic sanctions and intrusive arms inspections worked in concert with the arms embargo to limit Iraq's ability to arm itself. Iraq was able to obtain some conventional arms in spite of the embargo and with oil revenues slowed to a trickle. But Saddam Hussein had only limited funds available, and black market transfers proved to be more expensive and complicated than open purchases. In addition, only a fraction of the arms purchased on the black market actually made it to Iraq. Thus, greater expense and restricted availability significantly limited Iraq's ability to repair or upgrade its damaged military forces.

ENDING THE ARMS EMBARGO AND SECURITY IN POST-SADDAM IRAQ

The post-Saddam era in Iraq represents a unique case study of a highly interesting and important, yet generally understudied aspect of arms embargoes – the impact of their lifting upon the security situation in the target states. The June 2004 partial lifting of the arms embargo went almost unnoticed in the mainstream media, and only few analysts devoted their time to access the wisdom, timing, and repercussions of this important decision. Below we highlight the negative impact of the many conventional weapons that Saddam managed to either produce domestically or import legally before 1990 or smuggle in illegally after this date. This in turn raises some intriguing issues about the effectiveness of arms embargoes in particular and the unintended consequences of legal conventional weapons sales to unscrupulous authoritarian regimes and conflict-ridden countries in general.

When the US-led coalition forces took over Iraq, they found the country awash in arms. The US military estimates there are between 650,000 and one million tons of conventional weapons distributed throughout Iraq (Macomber, 2004, p. 16). While the main bulk of these weapons are pistols, rifles, and AK-47s, substantial amounts of sophisticated Western military hardware have also been found, including shoulder-fired surface-to-air missiles, sea mines, high-tech tracking systems, RPG, and bombs weighing in at hundreds of pounds. To make things even more complicated, as Macomber noted, it was discovered that Saddam Hussein hid stockpiles of weapons in "*highly* inappropriate places," including city playgrounds, soccer stadiums, private houses, schools, and hospitals (original emphasis). These arms were part of the available national cache to dissidents and insurgents as by 2004 occupation forces had managed to secure only 350,000 tons of weapons, with new arms caches being discovered weekly. According to Macomber, a frequent bit of black humor among the US soldiers and governmental officials dealing with this dilemma claimed that "Before the war, Iraq was an ammo dump with a government. Now it's just an ammo dump" (Macomber, 2004, p. 15).

The ready availability of small arms plagued the occupation authorities by providing insurgents the means to arm themselves with ease. Kalashnikov assault rifles and RPG, the weapons of choice for guerrilla fighters around the world, are nowadays common and inexpensive in Iraq as the massive stockpiles of conventional weapons are looted not only by the insurgents waging attacks on coalition forces but also by the cash-strapped Iraqi civilians. According to John Pike, founder of GlobalSecurity.org, this is worrisome because even trivial seepage from stockpile of the size found in Iraq is more than enough to sustain the insurgents:

> The total amount of explosives being used against the coalition is relatively small. The average car or truck bomb takes maybe a quarter of half ton of explosives, ... [less than] one-hundredth of a percent of the total unsecured weapons available. (Macomber, 2004, p. 16)

Macomber surmises that "recriminations over the failure to locate Weapons of Mass Destruction (WMDs) have drowned out the danger posed by massive unguarded stockpiles of conventional weapons" (Macomber, 2004, p. 15). Thus, it was somewhat surprising that only few experts questioned the wisdom of the little publicized June 2004 UNSC decision to partially lift the 14-year old arms embargo on Iraq. Officially, as noted earlier, this was done to enable its government to refurbish its arsenal and take responsibility for its security needs. While this may sound reasonable to the wider public, Frida Berrigan, a senior research associate with the Arms Trade Resource Center, a project of the World Policy Institute, raised the following questions: "How much of this is a photo op? A way to whitewash the occupation by showing the world that we are allowing Iraq to rebuild its army?"(Schaeffer-Duffy, 2004). For her part, Rachel Stohl, a researcher with the Center for Defense Information, believes that importing arms will only exacerbate the security problems posed by the country's already overstocked and unregulated arsenal of small arms: "Obviously countries and defense industries are excited about lifting an arms embargo. But the policy is problematic because there has been no thorough inventory of Iraq's arsenals" (Schaeffer-Duffy, 2004).

Another key problem is that while being free to buy, Iraq is currently unable to pay for its military hardware because it almost entirely relies on US military aid. According to a report in the *The National Interest*, the US Congress has appropriated a little less than $3 billion for Iraq's security needs, $2 billion of which are earmarked for developing the country's new army (Schaeffer-Duffy, 2004). Stohl questions the wisdom of spending so much on replenishing Iraq's heavy conventional weaponry instead of focusing on the reconstruction of the basic civilian infrastructure in the country:

> Do they need to be spending a significant amount of money on new weapons? The threats they are facing are not going to be solved with tanks alone. What are the greatest needs of reconstruction? Is it military goods and services or is it roads and services? (Schaeffer-Duffy, 2004)

Several other analysts also pointed out that Iraq's lack of independent purchasing power has translated into a bias toward American companies for arms deals. *The Asia Times*, for example, recently reported that shortly before its transfer of power to the Iraqi interim government, the Coalition Provisional Authority negotiated contracts for six C-130 Hercules military transport aircraft, 16 Iroquois helicopters, and a squadron of 16 low-flying, light reconnaissance aircraft to be delivered by April 2005 by Lockheed Martin. As Schaeffer-Duffy pointed out, "an ironic detail of the Iraq purchase is that Lockheed Martin products were used during US bombing campaigns of the first Gulf War, which destroyed much of Iraq's air force" (Schaeffer-Duffy, 2004). Cynical though it may be for a company to sell military aircraft to a country after it made a profit building the weapons that destroyed its aircraft, the practice is allegedly commonplace. According to Chatap Pratterjee, an investigative journalist for the online publication *CorpWatch*, "weapons manufacturers will sell to anybody unless there is an arms embargo" (Schaeffer-Duffy, 2004).

As the Iraqi interim government grew more independent and the Pentagon proved unwilling to supply modern US weaponry to the new Iraqi security forces, the Iraqis' arms request aimed at the Russians. In November 2004, the Russian Defense Minister Sergey Ivanov responded that Russia is ready to resume supplies of weapons and military equipment to Iraq, as well as send its technical specialists to teach the Iraqi servicemen how to use Russian weaponry (Ivanov & Terekhov, 2004). Perhaps even more interestingly, in April 2005, *The Washington Times* reported that the

US army "is considering buying a large number of AK-47 assault rifles and other small arms from, of all places, China," which previously tried to arm Saddam Hussein's regime.[5] Privately, one Pentagon official told the reporters that buying Chinese rifles for the Iraqis is "just stupid" for a number of reasons: "One is that Iraq remains awash in weapons, including thousands of new AK-47s, many of which are brand-new and packed in boxes" (Gertz & Scarborough, 2005, p. A6).

The supporters of embargo lifting argued that the new UN provision is a formality because Iraq has technically been open to the arms trade since May 2003, when the country came under the governance of the Coalition Provisional Authority. They also pointed out that arms exports to post-Saddam Iraq came from many non-US companies. In 2004, Russia, Ukraine, the European Union, as well as other major arms exporting countries recently lifted their national restrictions on supplying arms and military hardware to Iraq (Zaitseg & Litovkin, 2004). According to the *Asia Times*, over the past year, Iraq has already purchased 50,000 handguns from the Austrian company Glock, 421 UAZ Hunter jeeps from Russia, millions of dollars worth of armored cars from Brazil and Ukraine, along with AK-47 assault rifles, 9-mm pistols, military vehicles, fire control equipment, and night vision devices from a number of other countries (Schaeffer-Duffy, 2004). In that year, Iraq has also purchased a number of aircrafts, helicopters, and armoured personnel carriers (APCs), and in early 2005, the interim Prime Minister Iyad Allawi even ordered tanks for an entire division of the new Iraqi army (Silverstein & Miller, 2005). According to figures available from SIPRI Arms Transfers database, the total value of arms imports by the new Iraqi government in 2004 amounted to $ 81 million US dollars (SIPRI, 2005).

A number of analysts also suggest that lifting the arms embargo was a natural outcome of Iraq's sovereignty and should not be questioned, especially given the severity of the current insurgency. Cordesman, for example, admits that there are practical obstacles to Iraq's rearmament, including lack of money and the lack of a stable security force to absorb the arms, but he believes the current insurgency necessitates that the new government have access to weapons:

> If you cannot create effective security, you have no chance of creating a national government. For an Iraqi government to succeed it has to take this mission [of security] over. There is no question the insurgents are able to draw from a large cache of weapons left over from Hussein's regime. Suggesting Iraq should remain under an arms embargo is about as relevant as suggesting an arms embargo for the Spanish government when they were fighting the fascists during the Spanish Civil War. (cited by Schaeffer-Duffy, 2004)

On a similar note, Jeremy Binnie, an Iraq analyst with the London defense consultancy Jane's, suggested that "with all these people with RPGs running around," the Iraqi security forces are going to need armor to protect themselves:

> The general idea is that Iraq will not have an offensive capability that its neighbors find threatening. They'll be much lighter, mobile forces that can resist security threats when they arise, not like the previous forces organized to launch heavy armored assaults. (Jim, 2004)

For their part, Iraqi officials argue that Iraq needs a strong military to survive in one of the world's toughest regions and to wean itself from an unpopular dependence on the United States. Ibrahim al-Jaafari, one of Iraq's two incoming vice-presidents, for example, claims that

> We don't want to turn Iraq into an arsenal. We don't want the military to return to a strategy of aggression. But we want Iraq to be strong enough to return assaults from others. There must be an army with reasonable weapons that can make the country safe, so no one can assault it. (Jim, 2004)

When insurgent violence reached epic proportions from 2005 through 2006, virtually no analyst raised the issue of the return of an arms bazaar in Iraq that had marked the 18-month period after the US invasion.

CONCLUSIONS

In combination with other sanctions and intrusive on-site inspections, the UN arms embargo was remarkably successful in curbing the Iraqi access to advanced military technology. As a consequence, Iraq's offensive and war-fighting capabilities were at best stagnant during the years of the embargo. Perhaps most importantly, the sanctions also deprived Saddam of oil export revenues that could be used to purchase arms.[6] The Iraqi military was neither able to upgrade nor modernize through imports and was not able to produce certain weapons domestically. Some arms shipment evaded the embargo net, but many of the smuggled weapons were inferior or outdated, quantities were limited, and delivery was inconsistent. As a consequence, the Iraqi military remained large but had a difficult time maintaining and modernizing its more advanced weapons systems. In addition, the sanctions and inspection system forced Saddam to give up its WMD programs. Moreover, although Iraq's post-1996 attempts at developing indigenous long-range delivery systems delivered some tangible results in the form of the Al Samoud 2 missiles, these were subsequently destroyed under the auspices of UN observers. In these areas, then, the embargo was a demonstrated success.

Regarding the shortcomings of the embargo, some clear differences developed over time among senders regarding level I objectives of the entire sanctions regime. In particular, the United States shifted its goal from disarming Saddam to fostering regime change in Baghdad. In this respect, the arms embargo, as well as all the other UN sanctions, proved to be rather ineffective. The bitter irony of the Iraq case is thus twofold. First, UN sanctions appeared to achieve the original goals of SCR 687 and disarmed Iraq of WMDs and the means of developing them. Secondly, through a war waged to achieve such disarmament, the United States suffered substantially from the shortcoming of the Iraqi sanctions regime in the area of conventional weaponry and its own lack of foresight in securing the tons of weapons caches that existed.

NOTES

1. For a detailed discussion of the synergy between sanctions and the weapons inspection process, see Lopez and Cortright (2004, pp. 90–103).
2. Bill Clinton, for example, stated in November 1997 that "sanctions will be there until the end of time, or as long as [Hussein] lasts." Quoted in Barbara Crossette, "For Iraq: A Dog House with Many Rooms," *New York Times* (New York), 23/11, 1997, A4.
3. The Duelfer Report, for example, stated that "events in the 1980s and early 1990s shaped Saddam's belief in the value of WMD. In Saddam's view, WMD helped to save the Regime multiple times. He believed that during the Iran-Iraq war chemical weapons had halted Iranian ground offensives and that ballistic missile attacks on Tehran had broken its political will. Similarly, during Desert Storm, Saddam believed WMD had deterred Coalition Forces from pressing their attack beyond the goal of freeing Kuwait. WMD had even played a role in crushing the Shi'a revolt in the south following the 1991 cease-fire" (Duelfer, 2003, p. 1).
4. Statement of the Speaker of the Council of Ministers. Available at www.government.bg (retrieved November 13, 2002 & translated by Human Rights Watch, 2002).
5. For example, *The Washington Post* noted that China was caught in 2002 illegally selling Saddam a fiber-optic communications system that was used to network its nationwide air defenses, which tried for years to shoot down patrolling US jets.
6. Revelations generated during the Independent Inquiry Committee (IIC) shows that within the Oil-for-Food program, Hussein probably smuggled $11.8 billion outside of UN approval. The data reveals also $3.75 million was skimmed by Saddam within the direct purview of the program.

ACKNOWLEDGMENT

The authors thanks Benjamin Rooney for researching and writing parts of the arms smuggling section of this chapter.

REFERENCES

Beckett, P. (2002). Backyard bomb business. MODKRAFT.dk, ⟨http://www.modkraft.dk/article.php?sid = 1865⟩, December 13. Accessed in April 2005.

Blagov, S. (2004). Russia fights a battle of words with U.S. Inter Press Service News Agency, ⟨http://www.ipsnews.net/interna.asp?idnews = 17129⟩, March 28.

Bob, D., & Fleishman, J. (2003). Banned arms flowed into Iraq through Syrian firm. *Los Angeles Times*, December 12, Available at ⟨www.latimes.com/news/nationworld/iraq/la-fg-iraqarms30dec30,1,7925533.story?coll = la-home-headlines⟩. Accessed in April 2005.

Borger, J. (2002). Iraq re-arming for war, say defectors-gun-running Baghdad buying up East European weapons. *The Guardian* (London), April 29.

CBSNEWS.com. (2003). Top Bosnian quits over Iraq arms deal. CBSNEWS.com. Available at ⟨http://www.cbsnews.com/stories/2003/04/02/iraq/printable547330.shtml⟩, April 4.

CNN. (2003). Forces: Iraq/Air Force, in Special Report: War on Iraq. CNN. Available at ⟨http://www.cnn.com/SPECIALS/2003/iraq/forces/iraq/air.force/index.html⟩.

Cordesman, A. H. (1998). *Military balance in the Middle East – X: The Northern Gulf: Iraq* (Available at ⟨http://www.csis.org/mideast/reports/mbmeXiraq122898.pdf⟩). Washington: Center for Strategic and International Studies.

Cortright, D., & Lopez, G. A. (2002). *Sanctions and the search for security: Challenges to UN action*. Boulder, CO: Lynne Rienner.

Duelfer, C. (2003). Comprehensive report of the special advisor to the DCI on Iraq's WMD: Volume I. CIA, Available at ⟨http://www.foia.cia.gov/duelfer/Iraqs_WMD_Vol1.pdf⟩.

Duelfer, C. (2004a). Comprehensive report of the special advisor to the DCI on Iraq's WMD: Volume II., CIA, Available at ⟨http://www.foia.cia.gov/duelfer/Iraqs_WMD_Vol2.pdf⟩, September 30.

Duelfer, C. (2004b). Comprehensive report of the special advisor to the DCI on Iraq's WMD: Volume III. CIA, Available at ⟨http://www.foia.cia.gov/duelfer/Iraqs_WMD_Vol3.pdf⟩, September 30.

Gertz, B., & Scarborough, R. (2005). Chinese arms for Iraq? *The Washington Times*, April 15, p. A6.

Global Security. (2004). Iraqi military industry. Global security. Available at ⟨http://www.globalsecurity.org/military/world/iraq/industry.htm⟩, August 9.

Grau, L. W. (1998). A weapon for all seasons: The old but effective RPG-7 promises to haunt the battlefields of tomorrow. Foreign military studies office. Available at ⟨http://fmso.leavenworth.army.mil/fmsopubs/issues/weapon.htm#N_1_⟩. Accessed in April 2005.

Hanley, C. X. (2005). Missiles, microbes, sacked weapon sites: Loose ends proliferate in Iraq. *Associated Press*, March 26.

Hoyt, T. D. (1998). Iraq's military industry: A critical strategic target. *National Security Studies Quarterly*, Available at ⟨http://www.npec-web.org/published/critical.htm⟩, Spring. Accessed in April 2005.

Human Rights Watch. (2002). The NATO summit and arms trade controls in central and Eastern Europe. Available at ⟨http://hrw.org/backgrounder/arms/nato1115-bck.htm⟩, November 15.

Ivanov, V., & Terekhov, A. (2004). Shock, awe and Russian arms. *Nezavisimaya Gazeta*, November 17, p. 250.

Jim, K. (2004). Iraqi military won't get tanks, offensive capabilities. *Associated Press*, June 25.

Lederer, E.M. (2005). Iraq ambassador urges lifting sanctions. *Associated Press Online*, April 12.

Lopez, G. A., & Cortright, D. (2004). Containing Iraq: The sanctions worked. *Foreign Affairs*, *83*(4), 90–104.

Macomber, S. (2004). Weapons of conventional destruction. *The American Spectator*, *37*(3).

Richter, P., & Murphy, K. (2004). Evidence cited of Russian arms in Iraq. *Los Angeles Times*, January 10. Available at ⟨http://www.boston.com/news/world/articles/2004/01/10/evidence_cited_of_russian_arms_in_iraq?mode = PF⟩.

Schaeffer-Duffy, C. (2004). Iraq allowed to rearm. *National Catholic Reporter*, September 10. Available at ⟨http://www.ncronline.org/NCR_Online/archives2/2004c/091004/091004k.php⟩. Accessed in April 2005.

Silverstein, K., & Miller, T. C. (2005). Army ignored broker on arms deal; U.S. General supervised an Iraq contract that a slain American said was tangled in kickbacks. *Los Angeles Times*, 15 March, p. 1.

SIPRI. (2005). Trend-indicator values of transfers of major convential weapons to Iraq 1970–2004. Available at ⟨http://www.sipri.org/contents/armstrad/TIV_imp_IRQ_70-04.pdf⟩.

Stockman, F., & Bender, B. (2004). UN inspectors say entry denied, allegations made on Iraq arms sites. *The Boston Globe*, October 30.

Timmerman, K. (1991). *The death lobby: How the West Armed Iraq*. New York: Houghton & Mifflin.

United Nations Special Commission. (1999). *United Nations Special Commission* (Available at ⟨http://www.un.org/Depts/unscom/General/basicfacts.html⟩). New York: UN.

UNMOVIC. (2003). Thirteenth quarterly report of the Executive Chairman of the United Nations Monitoring, Verification and Inspection Commission in accordance with paragraph 12 of Security Council Resolution 1284 (1999), New York: UN, Available at ⟨http://www.unmovic.org/⟩, May 30

Vieth, W., & Gold, M. (2004). Candidates feud over Iraq arms. *Los Angeles Times*, October 28, p. 1.

Whitmore, B. (2002). Illegal trade: Gun smugglers' trail leads through Prague to Mideast. *Boston Globe* (Boston), October 15.

Williams, D., & Wood, N. (2002). Yugoslavia's arms ties to Iraq draw U.S. scrutiny. *Washington Post Foreign Service*, January 11, p. A26.

Zaitseg, A., & Litovkin, D. (2004). Russian arms permitted to flow to Iraq. *Defense and Security* (Russia), May 14.

CHAPTER 3

THE CHALLENGE OF MEASURING SUCCESS: YUGOSLAVIA'S SANCTIONS DECADE (1991–2001)

Wolf-Christian Paes

The embargoes applied by the international community against the Socialist Federal Republic of Yugoslavia (SFRY) and its constituent republics between September 1991 and September 2001 stand out among the sanctions regimes established during the 1990s for a number of reasons. In many cases, arms and trade embargoes were aimed at countries either already weakened by military defeat (such as Iraq) or decade-long civil wars (Angola and Afghanistan), with all the attendant economic and humanitarian problems. However, the SFRY of the early 1990s was an industrialized country in the heart of the Balkans, self-sufficient in terms of both arms and food production. Unlike most other conflicts during this period, the violent dissolution of Josip Tito's Yugoslavia captivated the attention of the international news media and increased the pressure on foreign governments to act. The sanctions applied by the European Union (EU), the United States of America (US) and the United Nations (UN), combined with the initial reluctance to apply military force, were the most important coercive instrument being used during the first five years of Yugoslavia's sanctions decade. The initial set of sanctions on the delivery of arms and military equipment imposed in September 1991 also stands out among similar cases because this initiative was actively supported by the

Putting Teeth in the Tiger: Improving the Effectiveness of Arms Embargoes
Contributions to Conflict Management, Peace Economics and Development, Volume 10, 55–79
Copyright © 2009 by Emerald Group Publishing Limited
ISSN: 1572-8323/doi:10.1108/S1572-8323(2009)0000010007

diplomatic representative of Yugoslavia at the UN, who aimed to suspend the influx of arms to the break-away republics while retaining most of Yugoslavia's substantial military stocks for Serbia and Montenegro (Kulessa, 1999, p. 45).

One can clearly distinguish between three separate, albeit partially overlapping, periods of international sanctions against Yugoslavia in the period between the break-up of Yugoslavia in 1991 and the regime change in Belgrade in the fall of 2000, which preceded the lifting of the last remaining sanctions in September 2001. The first phase was characterized by an arms embargo against Yugoslavia imposed by the UN Security Council (UNSC) on 25 September 1991, following the adoption of UNSC resolution 713. This move aimed to strengthen similar initiatives by the EC and the US, which had declared unilateral arms embargoes as early as July 1991. Triggered by the fighting between the Yugoslav People's Army (YPA) and militias in the break-away republics of Slovenia and Croatia, the resolution called for an immediate cease-fire and for a return to the negotiation table.

The second distinct phase of international sanctions against Yugoslavia was a comprehensive trade embargo imposed by the UNSC on 30 May 1992, under resolution 757, later expanded by UNSC resolution 787 passed on 15 November 1992. This regime was triggered by the civil war in Bosnia and Herzegovina, and unlike the arms embargo, specifically targeted Serbia and Montenegro, aiming to force Milosevic to make diplomatic concessions. This period came to a close following the signing of the Dayton Peace Accords, and the UN embargo was lifted in 1995, while the US retained an "outer wall" of sanctions banning Serbia and Montenegro from membership in international financial institutions. The sanctions of the European Union also remained in force, but were gradually weakened in the late 1990s as the former Yugoslav republic moved closer to NATO and EU membership. The arms embargo against Slovenia was lifted in August 1998, Montenegro and Kosovo were exempted from the ban in September 1999, and the remaining sanctions against Croatia and the Former Yugoslav Republic of Macedonia was removed in November 2000 (Kreutz, 2006). The third phase was the direct result of intensified fighting in the Serbian province of Kosovo between Serb security forces and Albanian insurgents. UNSC resolution 1160 established a renewed arms embargo against Yugoslavia which remained in place throughout the conflict until a post-Milosevic regime established its power in Belgrade in 2000. The arms embargo was finally lifted on 10 September 2001 with UNSC resolution 1367. By the end of 2004, the only remaining sanctions still in place were EU measures freezing the assets of individuals indicted by the International

Criminal Tribunal on the former Yugoslavia. The EU also adopted a common position on the strict implementation of the EU Code of Conduct on arms sales vis-à-vis the former Yugoslav republics (Kreutz, 2006).

Although the SFRY (and its successor states Serbia and Montenegro) was subject to some form of embargo or other for a decade between 1991 and 2001, the impact of the instruments applied vis-à-vis the regime in Belgrade is difficult to assess. This results partially from the imposing countries' failure to clearly define criteria for success and is also because some of the (explicit and implicit) goals of the instrument were contradictory. The arms embargo was designed to deny the fighting parties' access to external sources for arms, ammunition and other equipment, in a sense trying to starve the civil war. Yet it is widely accepted that the embargo initially benefited the YPA at the expense of Croatian and (particularly) Bosnian Muslim forces (Lukic & Lynch, 1996). The trade embargo imposed a year later against Serbia and Montenegro was designed to hurt the regime in Belgrade by depriving it of the necessary resources to continue the civil war and to force it back to the negotiation table. At the same time the implicit assumption was that the economic hardship caused by the embargo would foster discontent among the Serbian public, thereby creating a climate conducive to regime change (Delevic, 1998). Some observers (Cortright & Lopez, 2000) argue that the economic sanctions played an important role in getting Milosevic's support for the Dayton Peace Accords, a view also expressed by the UNSC's (1996) own assessment of the effectiveness. Other analysts (Woodward, 1995; Licht, 1995) have been more cautious, stressing the fact that Milosevic emerged strengthened rather than weakened from the sanctions period, hinting at the contradiction between the stated goal of changing Belgrade's foreign policy and the (implicit) aim to remove the Milosevic regime from power.

THE ARMS EMBARGO AGAINST SFRY (1991–1996)

The disintegration of the SFRY, which had its roots in the late 1970s and 1980s (Delevic, 1998), started with the decision of the Slovenian and Croat governments in 1990 to seek independence from Belgrade. The event triggering the outbreak of war in Slovenia was the takeover of Yugoslav custom houses by the Slovenia government, which prompted the YPA to intervene militarily, pitting a well-armed conventional army against the security forces of a nascent state, largely consisting of milita-style Territorial Defense Units (Lucic & Lynch, 1996, pp. 183–185). The EC and the United States moved quickly to impose an arms embargo against Yugoslavia following the military escalation of the crisis in June 1991. This was followed by resolution 713 of the UNSC (1991) imposing a "general and complete embargo on the delivery of weapons and military equipment to Yugoslavia" on 25 September 1991. During this early stage of the conflict, there was agreement among the key international actors (USA, Russia and the EU) that the conflict in Yugoslavia had to be contained and that the breakup of the federal republic should be avoided at all costs, not least because it would set a dangerous precedent for other parts of Eastern Europe. Some permanent members of the Security Council (such as France, Russia and the United Kingdom) sympathized with the Serbian position vis-à-vis the break-away republics and while the decision to apply the arms embargo on Yugoslavia as a whole was justified by the fact that none of the republics had been recognized as a subject of international law, policymakers must have been aware that they were putting Slovenia and Croatia at a military disadvantage through this decision (Lucic & Lynch, 1996, pp. 295–300).

The text of the resolution expressed support for the mediation attempts by the EC and the Conference on Security and Cooperation in Europe (CSCE) in Yugoslavia, while calling upon the Secretary-General of the UN to also offer his assistance to the solution of the conflict. Ostensibly, the purpose of the embargo was to "reduce the intensity of the fighting by preventing the influx of arms into the country and thereby avoid a further escalation of war" (Lucic & Lynch, 1996, p. 295). At the same time, the decision to impose an embargo was also aimed to please domestic constituencies particularly in Europe and North America by taking quick diplomatic action in the face of escalating violence, signaling that "the international community rejects the notion that an arms build-up and resort to military force can provide a solution to the Yugoslav crisis" (Lucic & Lynch, 1996, p. 295). Taking these comparatively popular measures allowed European and North American governments to gain some time to ponder the usefulness of military intervention and to try to find a consensus on the future course of both the EC and the UN vis-à-vis Yugoslavia (Calic, 1996, pp. 158–166).

However, most observers (Bondi, 2001, pp. 65–66; Cortright & Lopez, 2000, p. 65; Kulessa, 1999, p. 46) stress the largely symbolic role of the arms embargo during this phase. The limited impact of the sanctions with respect to their stated goal is due to two closely interrelated facts. The most important one was the military balance at the outset of the conflict. The second was the disposition of the defense industry within Yugoslavia. As mentioned earlier, by the summer of 1991, the YPA had been transformed from a federal institution into the de facto military arm of the Serbian (and Montenegrin) leadership. Before the breakup of Yugoslavia, the YPA had numbered some 195,000 soldiers on active duty, while another 510,000 reservists served with the Territorial Defense Units (BICC, 2002, p. 126). According to one estimate (Small Arms Survey, 2001, p. 75), the country had stockpiled a total of 2,330,000 rifles in military depots throughout the territory. The unusually high number of guns in relation to the (military) manpower available was the direct result of the peculiar Yugoslav military doctrine of "general people's resistance" modeled on the World War II guerilla-type arming of the civilian population (Gorjanc, 2000, p. 5). Arms depots were scattered throughout the republics, often located in municipal buildings such as schools, in anticipation of the need to dispense weapons quickly. When the conflict came, the YPA tried but failed to seize these stocks in the break-away republics (with the notable exception of Macedonia), leaving behind substantial amounts of (mostly) small arms and light weapons for the nascent "self-defense units" in Slovenia and Croatia, which were usually organized around the old territorial defense structures. At the same time, Belgrade retained the control of the YPA, armed with a sophisticated arsenal including modern fighter jets, helicopters, large numbers of armored vehicles and artillery units, as well as a modern communication network. In addition to the regular units of the YPA, the Serbian leadership also began to arm Serb civilians living outside of the Republic of Yugoslavia with automatic weapons, thereby forming paramilitary units who fought alongside with the YPA particularly in Croatia and in Bosnia and Herzegovina (Gleny, 1996, p. 77).

The military advantage enjoyed by the government in Belgrade due to the continued loyalty of the YPA was further strengthened through the dislocation of the Yugoslav defense industry. During the 1970s and 1980s, the country had risen to a prominent role as an exporter of arms and military equipment, using its status as a non-aligned country to access markets in the developing world. Weapons manufactured in Yugoslavia were often based on Eastern designs but incorporated Western technologies to enhance performances (Berghezan, 1997, p. 29), making them cheaper than their Western competitors and more reliable than products from the Warsaw Pact countries. Employing some 70,000 people, the Yugoslav defense industry contributed between US$400 million (Brzoska & Ohlson, 1987, p. 111) and US$1 billion (Wattkins, 2001) annually to the country's export earnings. This strong industrial base made Yugoslavia largely self-sufficient with regard to the country's military needs. Geographically, the defense industry was extremely decentralized. Berghezan (1997, p. 29) mentions the making of the M-84 main battle tank, based on the Russian T-72M1, whose components were produced respectively in Bosnia and

Herzegovina (34 percent), Serbia (21 percent), Croatia (21 percent), Slovenia (19 percent), Macedonia (3 percent) and Montenegro (2 percent). The spread of production plants (and the duplication of processes within the system) had been designed in such a way as to allow the continuation of arms manufacturing in the face of an attack by superior enemy forces (and the attendant loss of territory). Following the prevailing strategic doctrine of that time, the defense industry was centered in the Yugoslav "heartlands" of Bosnia and Herzegovina, as well as in Serbia (Wulf, 1993, p. 388). This geographic dispensation meant that Serbia (and the Serb-dominated Republika Srbska in Bosnia and Herzegovina) inherited the bulk of the Yugoslav arms industry at the outset of the conflict.

Given these parameters, it seems fairly obvious that an arms embargo on its own against Yugoslavia was not likely to succeed in bringing forth a peaceful solution to the conflict. This would only have been possible if the sanctions regime had been able to disrupt the supply of arms and ammunition to the warring parties to such an extent that their ability to continue fighting would have been threatened. As mentioned earlier, Yugoslavia's military doctrine for a long time had envisioned a scenario in which the country would have to stand alone over a long period of time and therefore was self-sufficient both with regard to existing stocks and manufacturing capacities. Furthermore, the arms embargo affected the opposing parties differently – whereas the government in Belgrade had inherited both most of Yugoslavia's military and arms industry, the break-away republics of Slovenia and Croatia were initially struggling to arm their self-defense units. The embargo therefore arguably conferred a military advantage to the Serbian side (Woodward, 1995, p. 263), a point not lost on the government in Belgrade, which in a little-remembered diplomatic quirk had actually called for an arms embargo against Yugoslavia at the UNSC through the federal foreign minister (Kulessa, 1999, pp. 45–46).

Given the strategic imbalance at the start of the sanctions period, it does not come as a surprise that most violations recorded were aimed at transporting arms and ammunition to the beleaguered governments of Croatia and Bosnia and Herzegovina, rather than benefiting the government in Belgrade (the conflict in Slovenia had merely lasted ten days, ending with the withdrawal of the YPA). Croatia's position was more favorable in this context as it enjoyed access to numerous ports along the Adriatic coast, shared land borders with Slovenia and Hungary, and received financial and political support from a substantial Croatian Diaspora in Western Europe and in the United States. Furthermore, most of the fighting on Croatian soil was confined to the border regions with Serbia, Montenegro, as well as

Bosnia and Herzegovina, allowing much of the country's industrial base to remain operational. In contrast, the situation of Bosnia and Herzegovina was much more precarious. Whereas Serbs and Croats received military and economic support from their respective "mother countries," Bosnia's Muslim majority population found itself trapped. Without access to the sea and surrounded by Serbia and Montenegro, as well as by Croatia, whose intentions remained unclear for most of the conflict, the forces of the government in Sarajevo were out-gunned nine-to-one by Serbian units (Lucic & Lynch, 1996, p. 246). In September 1992, it was estimated that the Bosnian forces possessed two tanks and two armored personnel carriers (APCs), whereas "the Serb army in Bosnia had 300 tanks, 200 APCs, 800 artillery units and 40 aircraft. A later estimate, in June 1993, speculated that the arms captured by the Bosnians included up to 40 tanks and 30 APCs, together with a large number of light artillery pieces; the Croat forces in Bosnia were thought to have roughly 50 tanks and more than 100 artillery pieces" (Malcolm, 1994, p. 243).

Croatia received arms shipments from numerous sources during the course of the conflict. Some of the clandestine deals preceded the outbreak of violence between Croatia and the YPA by several months. This includes the import of surplus AK-47 assault rifles produced by the German Democratic Republic (GDR) through the Budapest-based brokering firm Technika Foreign Trade in October 1990. It is believed that some 20,000–60,000 assault rifles were shipped to Zagreb during this phase, and some observers have suggested that this was partly the result of deliberately less than stringent controls on the part of the German authorities (Berghezan, 1997, p. 8). Another important supplier in the months preceding the outbreak of violence was the Christian militias in Lebanon. The "Forces Libanaises" sold arms, ammunition, land mines and other military equipment made redundant by the end of the civil war in Beirut for about US$100 million to the government in Zagreb (*International Herald Tribune*, 2 July 1991), allegedly partly financed through a loan of the Vatican Bank (Berghezan, 1997, p. 8). Following the imposition of the arms embargo, Croatia imported weapons from South Africa, mostly R-4 assault rifles produced by state-owned Armscor. As South Africa itself was subject to an arms embargo at that time, the shipments were directed through other African states to obscure their origins (Berghezan, 1997, p. 9). In one documented case, a Boeing 707 was chartered to fly a cargo of weapons from Mambastho in the South African "homeland" of Bobhutatswana via Entebbe (Uganda) to Zagreb (*New African*, November 1991). As far as heavy weapons are concerned, some sources have suggested that Germany's Federal Intelligence

Service ("Bundesnachrichtendienst") continued to supply T-55 tanks as well as dismantled MiG fighter planes from the arsenals of the GDR via Russia, Ukraine and Hungary to the Croatian authorities in violation of the embargo until at least 1993 (Berghezan, 1997, p. 9).

The government of Bosnia and Herzegovina also made an attempt to arm its security apparatus in the anticipation of the war. These imports included the receipt of a cargo of Heckler & Koch automatic rifles that arrived onboard of an Austrian-registered DC-9 at Sarajevo airport on 7 October 1991 as well as the delivery of several cargoes of arms during 1992 made by Iranian-registered Boeing 747s both directly to Bosnia and via Slovenia and Croatia (Berghezan, 1997, p. 12). Following the outbreak of fighting in Bosnia and Herzegovina in mid-1992 and the closure of the airfield in Sarajevo, the pipeline supplying the armed forces loyal to the government of President Izetbegovic came under attack. Arms coming from a number of Islamic states, including Iran, Pakistan and Malaysia, were flown to Zagreb and transferred by the Croatian authorities to Bosnia and Herzegovina, a complex operation which allowed the Croatian security apparatus to profit handsomely from the trade (Berghezan, 1997, pp. 14–15). The necessary funds for this operation came from both private and government donors in the Islamic world, often channeled through a network of charities closely linked to the government in Sarajevo. One of these charities – "Third World Relief Agency" – collected more than US$350 million in a single account at the First Austrian Bank in Vienna. Founded by a Sudanese diplomat in 1987, senior managers of the agency traveled on diplomatic passports issued by the government of Bosnia and Herzegovina, while maintaining close contacts with radical Islamic groups, including Osama Bin Laden (Berghezan, 1997, pp. 15–16).

Meanwhile, the military capacity of the YPA was not seriously affected by the arms embargo. As mentioned earlier, the Yugoslav defense industry was self-sufficient for the production of arms and ammunition. Whereas a substantial part of the industry had been located in Serbia before the war, the YPA made a conscious (and largely successful) attempt to move strategic production facilities from Croatia and Bosnia and Herzegovina to Serbia before the outbreak of the fighting (Lucic & Lynch, 1996, p. 298). Furthermore, the YPA "had purchased an extra 14,000 tons of weaponry from the Middle East just before the arms embargo came into force" according to Malcolm (1994, p. 243). Despite intensive scrutiny from 1992 onwards, only few cases of violations benefiting the YPA became known. They usually involved individuals rather than foreign states supplying arms and ammunition to Serbia and Montenegro, including a group of Russian officers selling surplus equipment from bases in Germany (*Armed Forces*

Journal, 1 February 1995) as well as three high-ranking Bulgarian officers who allegedly sold US$670,000 worth of military equipment in 1993 (*AFP,* 25 August 1995). Russian weapons were also delivered directly to Bosnian Serbs in violation of the embargo, according to media reports in 1994 "more than 4,000 railway wagons packed with artillery and ammunition" were delivered, with most of the material allegedly coming from Russian bases in Germany (*Jane's Intelligence Review,* May 1996). The scope of these shipments remains doubtful in the light of Serbia's own capacities. So confident was Belgrade of its military strengths that it actually attempted to export weapons (to Somali warlords) in exchange for hard currency while under an arms embargo (Almond, 1994, p. 224).

As the conflict in Bosnia and Herzegovina continued, calls for the lifting of the arms embargo became more urgent, both in Europe and in the United States. The government in Sarajevo argued that it denied the means to exercise its right to self-defense enshrined in Article 51 of the UN (Lucic & Lynch, 1996, p. 296). Whereas the UN General Assembly voted several times in favor of lifting the embargo against Bosnia and Herzegovina, the UNSC and particularly its permanent members Russia, France and Great Britain remained steadfast in support of the embargo, arguing that UN peacekeepers deployed in Bosnia and Herzegovina would be put into additional danger. The embargo was explicitly extended to all successor states through UNSC Resolution 727 in 1992 after the SFRY disappeared as legal entity. Whereas the embargo was not seriously policed until 1992–1993, there can be little doubt that it helped to lock the military imbalance between Belgrade and the governments in Zagreb and Sarajevo into place. As the resolution made no distinction between aggressor and victim, in effect it assisted the former, at least in the view of influential scholars and many policymakers.[1] Robert Jackson (1993, p. 600) noted that it was "a profound injustice to the Bosnian government for the UN to assume a position of neutrality in relation to the warring parties: the Bosnian state was a victim of aggression by the other parties, particularly the Serbs, who should be treated as the parties most responsible for the conflict".

THE TRADE EMBARGO AGAINST SERBIA AND MONTENEGRO (1992–1995)

Whereas the arms embargo targeted all successor states of the SFRY, the trade embargo imposed on 30 May 1992 by the UNSC resolution 757 was aimed exclusively at the two republics of Serbia and Montenegro, which constituted the Federal Republic of Yugoslavia (FRY). In this case, the members of the Security Council aimed to sanction the government in Belgrade and indirectly its allies among the Serb population in Croatia and Bosnia and Herzegovina for their aggression in Bosnia–Herzegovina. Cortright and Lopez (2000, p. 67) note that the UNSC passed resolution 752 just two weeks earlier, calling for an end to hostilities and for the withdrawal of the YPA. The comprehensive embargo imposed pursuant to resolution 757 banned all international trade with FRY, prohibited air travel to and from the FRY and outlawed all financial transactions involving Yugoslavia. All technical and scientific cooperation was to be suspended, as were sports and cultural exchanges. The scope of the sanctions regime was further extended on 17 April 1993 when UNSC resolution 820 froze all financial assets of the FRY abroad and prohibited the transit of vessels owned or registered in FRY. Each tightening of the sanctions regime was preceded by new reports of atrocities committed by Serb forces fighting in Bosnia and Herzegovina, showing both the importance of the instrument as a tool to placate domestic audiences in the West and the fact that the UNSC now squarely placed the blame for the fighting on the government in Belgrade. In the same vein (and unlike in the case of the arms embargo), extensive use was made of the sanctions as a diplomatic tool: Following a "carrot and stick" approach, the implementation of Resolution 820 was delayed for nine days to give the Bosnian Serb authorities sufficient time to endorse the Vance–Owen plan. Despite Milosevic's support for the plan the parliamentary assembly in Pale refused to do so, the UNSC voted to extend the sanctions to the territory controlled by the Bosnian Serbs in UNSC resolution 942. This resolution was passed on 23 September 1994, and on the same day, the UNSC lifted some restrictions on Serbia and Montenegro (UNSC resolution 943), as reward for Belgrade's support to the Vance–Owen plan.

The use of economic sanctions by the UNSC against Serbia and Montenegro was based on a number of assumptions, namely that the Milosevic regime was helping Serbs in Croatia and Bosnia and Herzegovina in their military pursuits. Second, without assistance from Serbia and Montenegro, those campaigns could not be sustained over a long period and therefore would come to an end. Third, it was assumed in New York that the pressure on Serbia would be transferred to the Serbs in Croatia and Bosnia and Herzegovina. And finally the "UN presumed that the dissatisfied people of Serbia would defeat the Milosevic regime (and thereby the primary cause of the war), and the possible danger of conflict spreading would disappear" (Licht, 1995, p. 154). Sanctions were chosen by the international community over military intervention because these measures were more palpable to domestic constituencies. Furthermore, the international community remained divided about the utility of sending combat troops to the Balkans, while the major powers saw no strategic interest at stake, the EC lacked both the military capacity and political cohesion to take more decisive measures (Woodward, 1995, p. 144). Given these constraints, the use of sanctions was seen as an "inexpensive and potentially potent weapon" (Mueller, 1994, p. 363), not necessarily more effective than other instruments, but given the unknown price of military intervention, relatively more useful (Maull, 1991, p. 342; Calic, 1996, p. 168).

Whereas the sanctions were initially largely declaratory and symbolic in nature, an increasing number of reports detailing violations forced the international community to tighten the implementation of the sanctions regime. Realizing that the weak link was likely to be found among Serbia and Montenegro's immediate neighbors, CSCE and EC formed a Sanctions Liaison Group tasked with providing technical assistance. Customs officials were dispatched from October 1992 onwards to Albania, Bulgaria, Croatia, Hungary, Macedonia, Romania and Ukraine. Linked among themselves with a coordinating office in Brussels through satellite communication, these Sanctions Assistance Missions were tasked with the verification of shipping documents. From April 1993, further assistance in the enforcement of the embargo was provided by the Western European Union (WEU), which sent eight patrol vessels with crews to police the Danube, as well as by the North Atlantic Treaty Organization (NATO), which established Operation "Sharp Guard" from June 1993 in collaboration with the WEU at the Adriatic Coast. In this context, 14 nations provided ships and crews for the checking of vessels entering or leaving Yugoslav ports (Cortright & Lopez, 2000, p. 69). The coordinated efforts by the UN, EC, CSCE, WEU and NATO to monitor and enforce the embargo set this example apart from similar attempts elsewhere. Nevertheless, the impact is difficult to measure in quantitative terms. Whereas the United States Department of State (1996, p. 11) reported that Sharp Guard "prevented large merchant vessels from calling at Bar – Serbia's only significant port" and therefore had a significant impact on trade, other observers remain skeptical. Long time gaps between the imposition of sanctions and the implementation of efficient monitoring mechanisms meant for example that NATO and WEU forces "had no authority to stop vessels suspected of breaking sanctions" between May 1992 and June 1993 (WEU, 1993, p. 17). Things were further complicated by a disagreement between some UN member states about what constitutes illegal transshipment of goods. This allowed for the shipment of fuel from Serbia proper to Serbian enclaves in Croatia via areas of Bosnia under the control of Serb forces, despite the embargo imposed by UNSC resolution 924 (Lucic & Lynch, 1996, p. 301).

Despite these loopholes, Yugoslavia's economy went into a sharp decline during the 1990s: Gross Domestic Product (GDP) fell by 30 percent in 1993 compared with the previous year – from US$13.60 billion to US$9.52 billion. Industrial production fell by 40 percent within three months of the imposition of the embargo. Plants either reduced their capacity or closed down completely and by the end of 1993, 1.3 million people were on "paid leave of absence," while another 750,000 were unemployed. For those fortunate enough to remain employed, average salaries had fallen to US$15 per months (Delevic, 1998, pp. 76–80). The government in Belgrade responded by printing money, increasing inflationist tendencies which saw the Yugoslav Dinar being devalued on a daily basis. Inflation rose from an already steep 122 percent in 1991 to 9,000 percent in 1992. By late 1993, inflation had reached 100 trillion percent, the highest rate of inflation recorded since the days of the Weimar Republic (Cortright & Lopez, 2000, p. 73). Shopkeepers changed prices several times daily, while both businesses and consumers abandoned the Yugoslav currency in favor of German Marks (DEM). This development had massive social consequences for large parts of the population, particularly for city dwellers relying on salaried work or on pensions, which lost their value rapidly. Whereas people in rural areas were able to grow and barter agricultural products, the urban lower and middle classes were hit hardest. By the end of 1993, the part of the population classified as poor had grown from 14 to 44 percent (United States Department of State, 1996, pp. 1–2). Although humanitarian goods were exempted from the embargo, the Yugoslav health system suffered massively from the lack of both funds and drugs. Although some observers (Cortright & Lopez, 2000, p. 74) noted that Yugoslavia's endowment of rich agricultural soil helped to avert the humanitarian disasters experienced in other sanctioned countries such as in Iraq, there is no doubt that the most vulnerable parts of the population, the poor, the elderly, the disabled and children experienced extreme hardships.

Although the contraction of the Yugoslav economy coincided with the imposition of the international embargo, these measures were by no means the sole cause of the recession. As a matter of fact, following the comparatively high growth rates of the 1960s and 1970s, all Yugoslav republics had been experiencing a period of economic stagnation before the breakup of the federal state in 1991. As early as 1989, there had been reciprocal boycotts of Serbian and Slovenian goods, triggered by political arguments and by 1991 the republics had begun to print their own money (Delevic, 1998, p. 77). The dissolution of Yugoslavia had a serious impact on economic development in Serbia and Montenegro as well, destroying a common and very integrated market, where many industries relied on inputs from other republics. The internal market had shrunk by 60 percent by the time the FRY was established in 1992 by Serbia and Montenegro, while the number of consumers fell from 24 million to a mere 10.5 million people. Delevic (1998, p. 77) notes that imports from other republics had accounted for 47 percent of the Serbian GDP in 1989 (compared with 27 percent for other countries), whereas exports to other republics accounted for 49 percent of GDP (compared with 20.4 percent for other countries), showing the enormous dependency of the Serbian economy on the common market. Following the war with Slovenia and Croatian in 1991, economic exchange with those countries came to a standstill, whereas the trade with Macedonia and Bosnia and Herzegovina was affected by the creation of new customs barriers. Another factor that had an enormous impact on the economic development was the economic policy of the government in Belgrade. Although the Yugoslav economy continued to contract in the early 1990s, government's expenses kept growing, not least because of the cost of financing military operations in Croatia as well as in Bosnia and Herzegovina. Although public spending stood at 49 percent of GDP in 1990 compared with revenues of 46 percent, spending increased to 63 percent of GDP in 1991, while revenue remained constant. The deficit grew further in 1992 and 1993 when spending rose to 65–70 percent of GDP, while revenue fell to 24 percent in 1992 and 10–11 percent of GDP in 1993 (Delevic, 1998, pp. 77–78). This record deficit of more than 50 percent of GDP was financed through the printing of fresh Dinars, a practice which contributed to the inflation experienced by Yugoslav citizens in 1992–1993. In essence, the government in Belgrade used an "inflation tax" to impoverish the population and to finance the military operations. Another tactic used by the Milosevic regime was to rob the population of their foreign currency savings which amounted to some US$4 billion in 1990. Attracted by the high interest paid on foreign currency accounts by private banks, often owned by close associates of the ruling party, most of this money was lost when two major banks collapsed in December 1993 (Delevic, 1998, p. 80).

The turning point came in the summer of 1994 when Milosevic supported the latest peace initiative and agreed to cut economic and military ties with the Serbs in Bosnia and Herzegovina, in effect putting them under an embargo of his own. Belgrade even agreed to the deployment of UN monitors on the border between Serbia and Bosnia–Herzegovina to verify the implementation of these measures. As a direct reward for this significant shift in Belgrade's position, the UNSC voted to suspend some of the sanctions imposed on Yugoslavia (UNSC resolution 943), while imposing comprehensive sanctions against the Bosnian Serbs on the same day (UNSC resolution 942). Although some analysts have argued that Belgrade's military support for the Serbs in Bosnia and Herzegovina continued clandestinely throughout 1994 (Lucic & Lynch, 1996, p. 301), Milosevic's decision to give in to international demands seems to have been motivated as much by the need to reduce public spending as by the offer to lift some of the sanctions imposed against his country. However, the breakthrough in the search for a negotiated solution for Bosnia and Herzegovina came only in late 1995 after Croatian forces managed to drive Serbian troops out of those parts of Croatia which had been under Serbian control since 1991. Shortly thereafter, Croatian and Bosnian troops also gained ground against the Serbs in Bosnia and Herzegovina, supported by NATO warplanes which operated a massive air campaign in August and September 1995. By the end of this campaign, the share of Bosnia and Herzegovina under Serbian control had shrunk from about 70 percent to 49 percent. On the basis of this new strategic picture, the warring parties agreed to the Dayton Peace Accords, which continue to form the basis of Bosnia and Herzegovina's fragile existence as a multi-ethnic state up to the present day. Following the signing of the accords, the UNSC lifted the arms embargo and the economic sanctions against Yugoslavia.

Many observers seem to agree that the sanctions were "effective in applying pressure on Serbian officials and were key factors in the bargaining process that eventually brought the war in Bosnia to an end" (Cortright & Lopez, 2000, pp. 80–81). Even critics of the sanctions regime such as Milica Delevic (1998, p. 83) admit "that a parallel between the economic deterioration in Yugoslavia and Milosevic's evolvement towards a more cooperative position suggests that sanctions, though helped to a great extent with the pre-existing economic difficulties […], succeeded in making the Serbian President Milosevic abandon the pan-Serbian policy he had been pursuing." This view is also expressed by the official evaluation of the sanctions regime undertaken by the UN, which claims that the embargo was the "single most important reason" for Serbia's policy change vis-à-vis the international community (UNSC, 1996). Although this argument discounts other important developments, which eventually contributed to the resolution of the conflict, such as the need to reduce hyperinflation triggered to a large extent by the cost of supporting military operations, as well as the significant setbacks experienced on the battlefield during the summer of 1995, there seems to be little doubt that the trade embargo had played an important role in "moderating the conduct of Belgrade's most immoderate leadership" (Luttwark, 1995, p. 118). Although the embargo has been criticized for it's humanitarian consequences (Licht, 1995, pp. 156–157) and some (Lucic & Lynch, 1996, p. 300) have even argued that "a professionally conducted military campaign [...] would have had dramatically lower humanitarian costs than sanctions," the fact remains that in the absence of an international consensus on the use of armed forces, the comprehensive embargo was an effective diplomatic weapon in resolving the civil war in Bosnia and Herzegovina.

However, while the sanctions played a role in affecting the regime's behavior, they were markedly less successful in destabilizing Milosevic's grip on power in Serbia and Montenegro. Although this goal was never clearly stated, there was an assumption that the worsening of the economic situation would lead the Serbian population to rebel against its leadership (Licht, 1995, p. 154). On this issue, the sanctions missed their mark completely, if anything the embargo might have even strengthened Milosevic's political power by providing him with a "convenient excuse for whatever was wrong in the country" (Delevic, 1998, p. 84). The government used the embargo to play on the widely held belief that Serbia was being unfairly victimized by an international community, generating a rally "round the flag" effect also observed in other countries under sanctions. As far as Serbia's internal political dynamics were concerned, the political opposition against Milosevic was hit hard by the effectiveness of the embargo. On the one hand, the urban middle class, who had formed the opposition's main support base, suffered more from hyperinflation than rural dwellers. Many members of the intelligentsia left their academic careers behind to engage in petty trading or what was euphemistically called "cross-border retail" (i.e. smuggling) to support their families, while other professionals went into exile. The embargo on cultural and scientific exchange helped to sever important ties between this group and their counterparts elsewhere, while the opposition media suffered from the increasing cost of equipment and newsprint (Cortright & Lopez, 2000, p. 75). Politically, many opponents of Milosevic shared the government's view that Serbia was unfairly singled out as an aggressor among the warring parties on the Balkans, creating rifts among the democratic opposition and leading to a further radicalization of Serbian politics. Woodward (1995, p. 386) argues that the embargo might have increased opposition to Milosevic, but that, in fact, it strengthened hard-line nationalist rather than liberal democrats. From the available sources, it is not clear whether the embargo had any significant impact on the military capacities of the YPA. Given the strong position of the Serbian defense industry, Belgrade was relatively independent of foreign suppliers of spare parts and other materials. In addition, a number of countries such as Greece, Romania and Russia permitted the transshipment of critical resources (in particular fuel), despite the embargo (Lukic & Lynch, 1995, p. 301).

Although many ordinary citizens of Serbia and Montenegro suffered from the effects of the embargo, a small group of well-connected people benefited from the opportunities generated by state-sanctioned embargo busting. Although people from all walks of life engaged in "cross-border retail," most of the activities remained at a fairly minor scale, involving goods smuggled in the trunks of private cars. However, the kingpins of this trade relied on the protection afforded by close links to the regime to amass a fortune. One of the few strategic commodities, which were not produced in sufficient numbers in Serbia and Montenegro, was oil. As a result, the illicit import of oil became a priority for the Milosevic government both to placate domestic consumers and to grease the regime's military machine. As a result, smuggling was not only tolerated but billed as a patriotic act by the government media. Andreas (2005, p. 341) notes that 40 percent of Serbia's petrol stations were owned by companies close to the governing party or to military leaders close to the regime. The difference between a 210-liter barrel of oil purchased at a price of DEM 160–190 in Albania and sold for DEM 300–400 (Hajdinjak, 2002, p. 15) allowed a small group of people to grow very rich indeed. It has been argued by some authors (Andreas, 2005; Pugh & Cooper, 2004) that the emergence of a *nouveau riche* class of government-protected smugglers is one of the most enduring legacies of sanctions against Serbia and Montenegro.

THE ARMS EMBARGO AGAINST SERBIA AND MONTENEGRO (1998–2001)

Following the signing of the Dayton Peace Accords in 1995, the UNSC voted to lift both the arms embargo and the comprehensive package of economic sanctions against Yugoslavia. In contrast, the United States decided to retain an "outer wall" of financial sanctions, barring the government in Belgrade from membership in international financial institutions, such as the World Bank or the International Monetary Fund. These sanctions were intended to force Milosevic to cooperate with the International Tribunal for Former

Yugoslavia and to prevent repression and human rights abuses in Kosovo (Cortright & Lopez, 2000, pp. 81–82). The European Union also imposed a bilateral embargo on arms shipments to all former Yugoslav republics on 26 February 1996. This embargo was justified with the need to protect the security of international forces deployed in Croatia and Bosnia and Herzegovina, as well as with the need to "establish peace and stability for the people of the region." Unlike the UN embargo, which it effectively replaced, the EU embargo was more selective in its application. Whereas blanket embargoes were imposed against Croatia, Bosnia and Herzegovina and the FRY (Serbia and Montenegro), export license applications for transfers to Slovenia and Macedonia were to be considered on a case-by-case basis. The transfer of de-mining equipment was excluded from the embargo on account of the humanitarian threat posed by landmines. However, beyond the declaratory nature of these measures little is known which impact, if any, the embargo had on the transfer of arms and military equipment to the conflict parties in the inter-war period (1995–1997).

In 1997 another crisis manifested itself in Kosovo, a Southern Serbian province mainly populated by ethnic Albanians. Supported by a large and well-organized Diaspora abroad, the Kosovo Liberation Army (KLA) made its first public appearance in Kosovo in November 1997. Organized as a loosely knit guerilla army, the KLA began to attack Serb police posts and refugee camps. Their weaponry originally came from Albania, where the breakdown of popular pyramid schemes in December 1996 led to a political crisis and the disintegration of state authority in most parts of the country. During this anarchic period, government armories and police stations were looted and some 600,000 ended up in the hand of civilians, out of which only a fraction was recovered later on (Heinemann-Grüder & Paes, 2001, p. 13). A large number of these weapons ended up on the regional arms market, where the sudden surge in supply saw prices tumbling to as low as DEM 15 for an automatic gun, rising later to DEM 250 (Reuter & Clewing, 2000, p. 172). The KLA was therefore able to arm itself with Chinese- and Russian-made military weapons at a comparatively low price, particularly as the Serbian security forces were unable to effectively patrol the mountainous border region between Kosovo and Albania. Estimates of the total number of arms available to the insurgents vary, whereas Reuter and Clewing (2000, p. 172) claim that some 100,000 guns were available to the KLA, Troebst (1999, p. 167) claims that their equipment "remained poor and insufficient" throughout the conflict.

The conflict intensified in 1997 and 1998, with the KLA's strength increasing to some 12,000 fighters by the summer of 1998 (Heinemann-Grüder & Paes, 2001, p. 14). It soon became apparent to the KLA's political leadership that international public opinion was their strongest weapon in the fight for secession (Zejnullahu, 2001, p. 59). The government in Belgrade responded to the attacks of the KLA with sweeping anti-terrorist operations, often killing civilians in the process and committing other human rights abuses. By early 1998, UN relief agencies reported some 50,000 to 60,000 displaced Kosovars and the international media was descending on what was seen as "another Bosnia" in the making. It was in this climate of increasing public demands for action that the international community decided to reinstate an arms embargo against Serbia and Montenegro. This proposal was developed by the Contact Group, a policy-making body on Balkan issues consisting of Britain, France, Germany, Italy, Russia and the United States. The idea met considerable opposition from China, which maintained that Kosovo was an internal dispute for the Yugoslav government to settle. The resolution presented a compromise between those countries (like the United States and Britain), which called for stronger action vis-à-vis Belgrade and the more cautious members of the Security Council, including Russia. On 31 March 1998, the UNSC voted (with China abstaining) to adopt resolution 1160, prohibiting all member states from transferring arms or military equipment to Serbia and Montenegro.[2] At the same time, a sanctions commission was reinstated to monitor member state compliance with this regime. In September 1998, the UNSC passed resolution 1199, asking member states to prevent the collection of funds on their territory for the financing of the conflict in Yugoslavia (Cortright & Lopez, 2000, p. 82). Unlike the arms embargo, this measure was directly aimed at the KLA which received most of their funding from the Albanian Diaspora in Germany, Switzerland and the USA (Heinemann-Grüder & Paes, 2001, p. 13). Some of this money came from voluntary contributions, while substantial sums seem to have stemmed from Albanian drug cartels controlling key Central European markets (Reuter & Clewing, 2000, pp. 182–183). Citing secret service sources, German journalist Erich Schmidt-Eenboom (1999, p. 17) claims that the KLA had received some DEM 500 million until March 1999, whereas Yugoslav calculations are even higher. In addition to the action taken by the UNSC, the EU and the United States also decided to tighten the net of sanctions against Serbia and Montenegro. In addition to the arms embargo, measures taken included targeted financial sanctions and travel bans for key members of the Milosevic regime (Cortright & Lopez, 2000, p. 82). Furthermore, the EU imposed an oil embargo against Serbia and Montenegro in 1999, targeting the country's dependence of fuel imports. However, under the "oil for democracy" program, shipments to municipalities controlled by the Serbian opposition were exempted from the embargo. Besides the oil embargo and the freeze of Serbian government assets abroad, no steps were taken to broaden the economic scope of the sanctions. This seems surprising given the fact that the UN's own report on the trade embargo vis-à-vis Yugoslavia between 1992 and 1995 had deemed them effective (UNSC, 1996). The sanctions regime this time also lacked an efficient enforcement component; no attempt was made to set up new Sanctions Assistance Missions on the territory of Serbia's neighbors. Compared with the previous attempts, the final reincarnation of an embargo against Belgrade was largely symbolic in nature, seemingly designed to please domestic constituencies rather than to influence Milosevic's behavior. This led Cortright and Lopez, (2000, p. 82) to state that "the lessons from Bosnia were not applied during the Kosovo crisis."

However, some lessons were clearly drawn from previous experience in the Balkans. Cortright and Lopez, (2000, p. 82) mention that the "decision to impose an arms embargo was curious given the controversy over the earlier embargo during the Bosnia war," as Serbia and Montenegro had retained its military superiority on account of inheriting Yugoslavia's vast defense industry and conventional army. On the other hand, enforcing an embargo against the KLA would have required a large and well-equipped military force deployed in Albania and Macedonia to secure the border with Kosovo. As the sympathies of most of the published opinion in the international community were with the plight of the Albanian population in Kosovo, policymakers were keen to avoid a scenario where an arms embargo could be seen as again aiding the regime in Belgrade. As a result little effort was made to stop financial assistance and military supplies flowing to the KLA, particularly after the United States, in a memorable policy shift, in the summer of 1998, following a meeting of US Special Envoy Richard Holbrook with KLA fighters in Kosovo, recognized the insurgents as "a [political] reality on the ground," rather than as threat to regional security as before (Heinemann-Grüder & Paes, 2001, p. 15). As a result, military planners in Europe and North America started to see the KLA as a potential ally in the conflict with Milosevic and there have been numerous reports about training and material support being provided by Western intelligence services to the KLA in 1998 and 1999 (Walker & Laverty, 2000; Katulis, 2000). Unlike in the case of Bosnia and Herzegovina, the international community quickly settled for a military solution for the Kosovo crisis. Following an intensive aerial campaign against Serb military targets both in Kosovo and in mainland Serbia, international troops under the command of NATO established the Kosovo Protection Force (KFOR). KFOR entered Kosovo on June 12, 1999 without meeting resistance, as the

Serb security forces (alongside of parts of the Serb population) simultaneously withdrew from the territory. Thus, the Kosovo conflict ended after a
relatively short military campaign with the establishment of a de facto
protectorate under the administration of the UN.

The embargo failed to prevent arms and ammunition from reaching the
KLA from Albania and Macedonia. At the same time, the Serbian defense
industry continued to meet the demands of the security forces. Although it
had already been weakened by the economic sanctions imposed against the
FRY between 1992 and 1995, which had made the import of components
more difficult and created substantial hard currency shortages, the military–
industrial complex continued to operate throughout the Kosovo crisis, the
arms embargo and the NATO bombing campaign (*Jane's Defence Weekly*, 5
January 2000). During this period, Belgrade attempted to buy some
sophisticated weapons on the international market, mostly using established
fraternal ties to other Slav nations. This includes rumors about the import of
a small quantity of Russian-made S-300PM surface-to-air-missiles (SAM)
smuggled with a Russian humanitarian convoy in early 1999, just weeks
before the start of the NATO air raids (*Jane's Defence Weekly*, 4 August
1999). However, there are no reports indicating that these missiles, if they
existed at all, ever saw action against the allied aerial forces. Another
unsuccessful attempt to breach the embargo involved surplus MiG-21
fighter aircraft from Kazakhstan. On 19 March 1999, a Russian-registered
cargo plane, transporting the dissembled aircraft, was detained during a fuel
stop in Azerbaijan after the customs authorities grew suspicious about the
shipment. Several months later this incident led to the sacking of
Kazakhstan's defense minister and other senior officials (*Jane's Defence
Weekly*, 18 August 1999).

Following the occupation of Kosovo by international troops, the
embargo remained in place for another two years. This might seem
surprising given the fact that the main reason for the imposition of the UN
arms embargo had been the international desire to protect the Albanian
population from reprisals by Serb security forces according to the text of
UNSC Resolution 1160. This was done in order to keep the pressure on the
Milosevic regime and to prevent the Serb military from re-arming. Towards
these goals, the arms embargo was useless – despite the aerial campaign
against Serbian military installations, the country retained its regional
superiority. The country's defense industry, which had been hit hard by
allied bombs, not only retained sufficient capacity to re-supply the Yugoslav
Army's stocks but actually managed to export weapons during the embargo,
earning much needed hard currency in the process. These weapons often

went to other "pariah" states under UN sanctions, such as Iraq and Liberia, and continued even after the Milosevic had been swept from power on 5 October 2000, raising serious questions on the monitoring of the embargo and on the degree of political control of the new leadership over Serbia's military–industrial complex (ICG, 2002). The extent to which the targeted sanctions and the oil embargo contributed to the political change in Belgrade is also open to debate: The economic crisis experienced by Serbia and Montenegro in the late 1990s was not as severe as the one experienced five years earlier. The mechanics of sanctions busting were established and the country's political leadership had used the period of Milosevic's honeymoon with the international community between 1995 and 1997 to hide their assets abroad. The oil embargo imposed by the EU was largely useless given the fact that non-EU member states continued to provide oil (and gas), often bartered for shipments of grain. Most of this trade was also with other "pariah" states such as Libya, Syria, Iraq (where Serbia participated in the UN's "oil-for-food" program), but also with Russia and Ukraine (ICG, 2000).

CONCLUSIONS

Given the complexity of the sanctions regime imposed against Yugoslavia (and later on Serbia and Montenegro), it is difficult to come to general conclusions as to their effectiveness. The arms embargo imposed on all constituent republics of the SFRY in 1991 and maintained until the Dayton Peace Accords in 1995 was certainly effective in disrupting the flow of arms and ammunition to the conflict zone. However, with hindsight it seems that the embargo was imposed by the international community without due regard to how it would affect the military balance. Given the fact that Serbia and Montenegro retained the bulk of Yugoslavia's military power and industrial strengths, at least initially it hurt the breakaway republics of Croatia and Slovenia, as well as Bosnia and Herzegovina more than it interfered with Belgrade's ability to operate. The international community recognized this imbalance during the civil war in Bosnia and Herzegovina and, after Milosevic was seen as the aggressor by most of the international news media, calls to "lift [the embargo] and strike" became common currency in newspaper editorials in Western Europe and North America. However, the "law of the instrument" prevented the UNSC from changing the scope of the sanctions regime, while the governments in Paris and London cynically argued that excluding the Bosnian forces from the arms embargo would improve their military capabilities and therefore lead to more fighting. Others argued that lifting the sanctions would threaten the security of the international peacekeepers deployed in Croatia, as well as in Bosnia and Herzegovina, an argument which was often viewed as cynical given their inability to stop the fighting.

Despite these concerns, the widely shared perception that the UN embargo prevented the government in Sarajevo from exercising its right under the UN Charter to self-defense against aggression led some governments, particularly in the Islamic world, to openly conduct sanction busting operations. In the case of Croatia, European and North American intelligence services also provided training, arms and other equipment in violation of the embargo. It is doubtful whether the military successes of the Croatian armed forces in the Krajina in early 1995 (which eventually led to the Dayton Peace Process) would have been possible without this support.

In contrast, the comprehensive economic embargo targeting Serbia and Montenegro between 1992 and 1995 was remarkably effective in achieving its stated goal, namely to force the Milosevic government into diplomatic concessions. Whereas the self-congratulatory report of the UN (1996) neglects to mention the role of other contributing factors (the military setbacks in Croatia as well as Bosnia and Herzegovina, and the escalating costs of the war), more critical assessments miss the evidence that points to the conclusion that the embargo contributed to the policy shift in Belgrade. As Serbia and Montenegro were largely self-sufficient with regard to mineral resources and food production, the embargo did not hit the country's war economy directly. However, it did contribute to the development of a deep fiscal and monetary crisis, which forced Milosevic to surrender his pan-Serbian dreams in exchange for retaining power in the heartland. With its comprehensive monitoring mechanism, the use of sanctions assistance missions in neighboring countries, and the joint military efforts of NATO, WEU, EU and OSCE in policing the embargo, could also serve as a role model for the supervision of similar embargoes elsewhere.

The final phase of sanctions against Serbia and Montenegro, imposed in 1998 in response to the Kosovo crisis, was weak in comparison. Given the successes of the previous embargoes, this might come as a surprise. However, it seems that by 1998 the international community had finally decided that the only solution towards sustainable peace in the Balkans lay in the departure of Slobodan Milosevic from the helm of government in Belgrade. Therefore, no serious attempt was made to enforce the arms embargo, knowing fully well that doing so would be very difficult and costly, while hurting mostly the Albanian insurgents, rather than Yugoslavia's military machine. Not only did Western governments do little to stop the flow of money (and recruits) from the Albanian Diaspora to Kosovo, but some intelligence services even provided training and equipment. This development mirrors events in Croatia and Bosnia and Herzegovina three years earlier. Under these circumstances, the sanctions against Serbia and Montenegro became an elaborate charade, designed to please domestic constituencies, while the military leadership was already planning for a "quick-fix" military solution to the Kosovo.

NOTES

1. This triggered a major public debate in the USA as well as within the United Nations. Several times the UN General Assembly voted to lift the embargo against Bosnia and Herzegovina, only to find this decision to be ignored by the UNSC. The US Senate voted to lift the embargo in April 1994. It also denied the government the use of public funds to support the implementation of the UN arms embargo. Whereas President Clinton decided to keep it in force, his administration turned a blind eye towards Iranian arms shipments reaching the Bosnian Muslims via Zagreb (*Jane's Intelligence Review*, December 1997). It was clear to the US administration that it violated its obligations under international law. However, this was considered as the least harmful course of action to the administration's foreign policy in view of a congressional majority favouring arms supplies to Bosnia, even if this meant breaking the UN arms embargo (see answers to Congressman Hamilton by Barbara Larkin, Acting Assistant Secretary of State, Congressional Record, 11 June 1996, p. E1054, http://www.fas.org/irp/congress/1996_cr/h960611a.htm).

2. The embargo's wording thus included transfers to the KLA in Kosovo, but not to the KLA in other countries such as Albania.

REFERENCES

Almond, M. (1994). *Europe's backyard war, the war in the Balkans*. London: Mandarin.
Andreas, P. (2005). Criminalizing consequences of sanctions, embargo busting and it's legacy. *International Studies Quarterly*, *49*(2), 335–360.
Berghezan, G. (1997). *Ex-yougoslavie, L'embargo sur les armes et le réarmement actuel*. Brussels: GRIP.
BICC. (2002). In: *Conversion survey 2002. Global disarmament, demilitarization and demobilization*. Baden-Baden: Nomos Verlagsgesellschaft.
Bondi, L. (2001). Arms embargoes. In: M. Brzoska (Ed.), *Smart sanctions, the next steps – the debate on arms embargoes and travel sanctions within the 'Bonn-Berlin Process'*. Baden-Baden: Nomos Verlagsgesellschaft.
Brzoska, M., & Ohlson, T. (1987). *Arms transfers to the third world, 1971–85*. Oxford: Oxford University Press.

78 WOLF-CHRISTIAN PAES

Calic, M.-J. (1996). *Krieg und Frieden in Bosnien-Herzegovina*. Frankfurt/Main: Suhrkamp Verlag.
Cortright, D., & Lopez, G. A. (2000). *The sanctions decade – assessing UN strategies in the 1990s*. Boulder: Lynne Rienner Publishers.
Delevic, M. (1998). Economic sanctions as a foreign policy tool, the case of Yugoslavia. *International Journal of Peace Studies, 3*(1), 67–89.
Gleny, M. (1996). *The fall of Yugoslavia, the third Balkan war*. New York City: Penguin Books.
Gorjanc, M. (2000). *Small arms and light weapons and national security* (Paper prepared for the Workshop on SALW and the Stability Pact for Southeastern Europe, Ljubljana, 27 January).
Hajdinjak, M. (2002). *Smuggling in southeastern Europe, the Yugoslav wars and the development of regional criminal networks*. Sofia: Center for the Study of Democracy.
Heinemann-Grüder, A., & Paes, W-C. (2001). *Wag the dog, the mobilization and demobilization of the Kosovo liberation army, BICC brief no 20*. Bonn: Bonn International Center for Conversion.
ICG. (2000). *Serbia's grain trade, Milosevic's hidden cash crop*. ICG Balkans Report No. 93. Brussels: International Crisis Group.
ICG. (2002). *Arming Saddam, the Yugoslav connection*. ICG Balkans Report No. 136. Brussels: International Crisis Group.
Jackson, R. (1993). Armed humanitarianism. *International Journal, 48*(3), 579–606.
Katulis, B. (2000). *US diplomacy towards Kosovo, 1989–99*. Woodrow Wilson Case Study No. 2. Princeton: Woodrow Wilson School of Public and International Affairs.
Kreutz, J. (2006). *Hard measures by a soft power? Sanctions policy of the European union 1981–2004*. BICC Paper No. 45. Bonn: Bonn International Center of Conversion.
Kulessa, M. (1999). Sanktionen gegen Jugoslawien. *Internationale Politik, 54*(6), 43–48.
Licht, S. (1995). The use of sanctions in the former Yugoslavia, can they assist in conflict resolution. In: D. Cortright & G. A. Lopez (Eds), *Economic sanctions, panacea or peacebuilding in a post-cold war world*. Westview: Boulder.
Lucic, R., & Lynch, A. (1996). *Europe from the Balkans to the Urals, the disintegration of Yugoslavia and the Soviet Union*. Oxford: Oxford University Press.
Luttwark, E. (1995). Towards post-heroic warfare. *Foreign Affairs, 74*(3), 33–44.
Malcolm, N. (1994). *Bosnia-a short history*. New York: New York University Press.
Maull, H. (1991). Wirtschaftssanktionen als instrument der Außenpolitik. *Jahrbuch für Politik, 1*(2), 341–367.
Mueller, J. (1994). The catastrophe quota, trouble after the cold war. *Journal of Conflict Resolution, 38*(3), 355–376.
Pugh, M., & Cooper, N. (2004). *War economies in a regional context, challenges of transformation*. Boulder: Lynne Rienner.
Reuter, J., & Clewing, K. (Eds). (2000). *Der Kosovo Konflikt – Ursachen, Verlauf, Perspektiven*. Klagenfurt: Wieser Verlag.
Schmidt-Eenboom, E. (1999). UCK – Zur Karriere einer terroristischen Vereinigung. *Wissenschaft & Frieden* (2), 17–19.
Small Arms Survey. (2001). *Small arms survey 2001, profiling the problem*. Oxford: Oxford University Press.
Troebst, S. (1999). The Kosovo war, round one, 1998. *Südosteuropa, 48*(3/4), 156–1990.

United States Department of State. (1996). *UN sanctions against Belgrade, lessons learned for future regimes* (Paper prepared by the Interagency Task Force on Serbian Sanctions, Washington DC).

UNSC. (1991). *Resolution 713 as of 25 September 1991*. New York: United Nations.

UNSC. (1996). *Letter Dated 24 September 1996 from the Chairman of the Security Council Committee established pursuant to Resolution 724 (1991) concerning Yugoslavia addressed to the President of the Security Council*. S/1996/776. New York: United Nations.

Walker, T., & Laverty, A. (2000). CIA Aided Kosovo guerilla army. *Sunday Times*, (12 March).

Wattkins, A. (2001). Yugoslav industry revival, fact … or fiction? *Jane's Defence Weekly*, (25 July).

WEU. (1993). *Lessons drawn from the Yugoslav conflict. Assembly of the Western European Union*. Document 1395. Paris: Western European Union.

Woodward, S. (1995). *Balkan tragedy, chaos and dissolution after the cold war*. Washington DC: Brookings Institution Press.

Wulf, H. (1993). *Arms industry limited*. Oxford: Oxford University Press.

Zejnullahu, S. (2001). *War for Kosova, commander Remi speaks*. Pristina: Zeri.

CHAPTER 4

US MEASURES AGAINST PAKISTAN'S NUCLEAR POLICIES, 1990–2001

Sumita Kumar

INTRODUCTION

Sanctions are normally used as an instrument by one country or an alliance of countries to affect change in the behaviour of another country. As Ian Anthony has noted, "Within the legal code of states, sanctions are that part of a law that inflicts a penalty for its violation. In common usage, international sanctions can be defined as any restriction or condition established for reasons of foreign policy or national security applied to a foreign country or entity by a group of states using substantially equivalent measures" (Anthony, 2002, p. 204). Most analysts would agree that clearly defined goals on the part of the initiator – and outlining a consistent set of policies with respect to such goals – are an important factor in gauging the effectiveness of sanctions at any given time.

Punitive policy measures, including sanctions, have been used by the UN and other actors as a persuasion tactic to bring changes in the nuclear policies of target states and to induce their adherence to the nuclear non-proliferation regime. The use of economic tools has been especially active in South Asia. In the case of Pakistan, sanctions and other punitive policy measures, such as reductions in promised military and economic aid, were

Putting Teeth in the Tiger: Improving the Effectiveness of Arms Embargoes
Contributions to Conflict Management, Peace Economics and Development, Volume 10, 81–100
ISSN: 1572-8323/doi:10.1108/S1572-8323(2009)0000010008

applied by the United States throughout the 1990s and focused primarily on non-proliferation of weapons of mass destruction.

A main feature of such policy measures, particularly notable in the Pakistani case, is their sensitivity to the pursuit of other strategic interests. US punitive policy measures against Pakistan have, from time to time, receded into the background to pave the way for the pursuit of what Washington deemed more important strategic interests. Soon after Soviet troops withdrew from Afghanistan in 1989, Pakistan's strategic relevance to the US was reduced. The US government suspended economic and military assistance to Pakistan in 1990 by withholding the Presidential certification which would have verified the absence of nuclear weapons in Pakistan. Although these sanctions were diluted over a period of time, the Clinton administration again imposed military and economic sanctions on Pakistan in response to its nuclear tests on May 28 and 30, 1998, which effectively dismantled the Pakistani policy of nuclear ambiguity. The October 1999 coup in Pakistan led to the imposition of a new set of measures mandated by US laws that required aid to be cut off to countries where the democratic process had been interrupted. However, in the aftermath of September 11, 2001, it became obvious that Pakistan became a significant frontline state in the coalition against international terrorism in Afghanistan, and a US Presidential Directive issued on September 22, 2001, stated that maintaining sanctions against Pakistan was not in the national security interests of the US (Bush, 2001).

The aim of this chapter is to study the various factors that have influenced the effectiveness of sanctions on Pakistan through the 1990s. A number of critical questions guide this inquiry: What were the varied objectives behind US sanctions on Pakistan, and related policy measures from 1990 to 2001? Was there continuity in the stated and unstated objectives? What kind of impact did sanctions have on Pakistan? Did the sanctions lead to the desired change in behaviour on the part of Pakistan? Why were sanctions lifted after September 2001? Did the US achieve its previously outlined objectives? The above queries need to be examined in detail as well as the intricacies involved in the legal, economic, political and strategic factors that have defined US–Pakistan relations in general and US strategic interests in Pakistan in particular. To address these questions, the following aspects of the sanctions regime will be examined: the evolving US objectives for imposing sanctions, the degree arms transfers to Pakistan were affected as a result of these sanctions, and whether the sanctions achieved the targeted goals outlined at their inception.

US OBJECTIVES: CONSISTENT OR INCONSISTENT?

In the 1980s, the United States moderated its earlier more aggressive response to Pakistan's nuclear program as the containment of the Soviet Union in Afghanistan assumed growing importance due to Cold War imperatives. A striking example occurred in 1981, when the United States offered military and economic aid to Pakistan, despite its clear violation of the Glenn–Symington Amendment in 1979, which called for the suspension of military and economic aid to countries which imported uranium enrichment materials without inspection. In 1981, the US government suspended the application of the uranium-enrichment sanctions provisions of the congressional Glenn–Symington Amendment. The Reagan administration explained the logic of providing increased military and economic assistance to Pakistan by arguing that the restoration of aid would help to promote US objectives of non-proliferation. The aid was meant to improve Pakistan's overall security, which would in turn reduce its motivation for acquiring nuclear arms (Jones, McDonough with Dalton, & Gregory, 1998). The US Congress adopted the Pressler Amendment in 1985 to find a way to weaken the punitive measures legally imposed by the Glenn–Symington Amendment. The Pressler Amendment required an annual presidential certification to the effect that Pakistan "did not possess a nuclear explosive device and that the proposed United States assistance program will significantly reduce the risk that Pakistan will possess a nuclear explosive device" (Foreign Assistance Act of 1961; U.S. Code, Sec. 620E (e), 22 Sec. 2375, 1985, *Ibid.*, p. 140). Economic and military assistance was contingent on this annual Presidential certification. Despite numerous reports about Pakistan's continuing nuclear activities, Presidential certifications continued to allow economic and military assistance to Pakistan.[1]

The substantial military and economic assistance that flowed to Pakistan during the 1980s strengthened the military regime of General Zia-ul-Haq. During this period, the US nuclear policy towards Pakistan officially continued to lay emphasis on prevention, even though it was clear to expert observers that Pakistan was investing heavily in a nuclear weapons program. Thus, the opinion was voiced that the offers of aid had in fact worked as leverage against the non-proliferation efforts of the United States instead of against Pakistan's nuclear-weapons development program (Leventhal, 1987). In addition to the effects of US behaviour on Pakistan itself, this assessment was based on concerns over the credibility of US non-proliferation policy in general, as well as on the fear that Pakistan might decide to share nuclear weapons, or weapons material and technology with other countries or "elements in the Islamic world" in the future (*Ibid.*).[2]

The withdrawal of Soviet troops from Afghanistan enabled the United States to pursue its non-proliferation policy towards Pakistan with renewed vigour. In October 1990, the United States suspended new economic assistance and military sales to Pakistan after the Bush administration was unable to certify that Pakistan did not possess a nuclear explosive device. The reason given for this was that, in late 1989 and early 1990, Pakistan, instead of maintaining a freeze on production, had in fact fabricated cores for several nuclear weapons from pre-existing stocks of weapons-grade uranium (Jones et al., 1998). The Clinton administration's thinking on non-proliferation was enunciated in the April 1993 "Report to Congress on Progress Toward Regional Non-Proliferation in South Asia." The US objective was defined as "first to cap, then over time reduce, and finally eliminate the possession of weapons of mass destruction and their means of delivery" (Lavoy, 1994, p. 93). The United States urged Islamabad to sign the Nuclear Non-Proliferation Treaty (NPT) and to cease production of fissile material for weapons purposes, either unilaterally or on a regional basis. In addition, other states such as Russia, Britain, France, Germany and Japan were encouraged to discuss non-proliferation issues with Pakistan bilaterally (*Ibid.*, pp. 93–94). The US policy of engagement with Pakistan not only was pursued in the hope that it would lead to constructive results in the sphere of non-proliferation but was also meant to further other strategic interests in the South Asian region.

Although the Clinton administration apparently retained the ultimate objective of eliminating nuclear weapons and their delivery systems from South Asia, the emphasis shifted from elimination to a rollback of Pakistan's nuclear weapon program and then to an emphasis on a cap on its nuclear weapons capabilities (*Ibid.*). In 1995, the US Senate passed the Brown Amendment which was a modification of the Pressler Amendment and was supposedly designed to "create incentives for Pakistan to continue the restraints that it had voluntarily imposed on its nuclear program" (Jones et al., 1998, p. 133). This allowed a one-time sale of military equipment and spare parts to Pakistan that had been withheld due to the unilateral military sanctions imposed as a result of the 1985 Pressler Amendment. The interest from Washington concerning Pakistan at this time also centred on the hope that stronger ties between the two countries would help Pakistan evolve into a moderate Islamic democracy. It was also argued that creating positive incentives for Pakistan would engage the region and diffuse the growing sense of isolation to deter an intensification of the country's pursuit of nuclear arms (*Ibid.*, p. 141). Pakistan's position on the Comprehensive Test Ban Treaty (CTBT), one of the key elements to strengthen the nuclear non-proliferation, was that it would become a party to the CTBT only if India joined as well.

During the 1990s, as in the previous decade, numerous reports linked the development of Pakistan's nuclear and missile programs with China. In June 1991, sanctions were imposed against companies and agencies in China and Pakistan implicated in transfers of equipment related to the M-11 missile capable of carrying a nuclear warhead (Monterey Institute, n.d.). However, doubts arose in various quarters about the adequacy of these sanctions in the face of reports about complete M-11 missiles being supplied to Pakistan from China. Although the sanctions against Chinese companies were lifted in 1992, sanctions were again imposed against Chinese and Pakistani entities in August 1993 because of renewed transfers of M-11-related items to Pakistan. Reports about Chinese assistance in Pakistan's efforts to acquire nuclear enrichment technology surfaced from time to time, a prime example being Pakistan's purchase of 5,000 ring magnets from China in 1995. However, Chinese entities escaped sanctions this time. One reason was the United States fear of adverse impacts on US firms doing business in China. The US trade relations were considered to be an important factor for the US reticence in imposing penalties on China, although the United States did pressurize China to stop its nuclear and missile assistance to Pakistan.

In 1998, Pakistan was pressured by the United States not to answer Indian nuclear tests on May 11 and 13, 1998, by testing its own nuclear devices. American diplomacy at this time stressed the economic and military benefits that Pakistan could accrue from the United States by not testing. Members of the US Congress and administration proposed to repeal the Pressler Amendment in an effort to encourage Pakistan not to conduct nuclear tests. Bilateral talks between the United States and Pakistan during this time, focussed on addressing Pakistan's security concerns with the aim of preventing Pakistani tests. At the same time, Japan offered to shift its aid from India to Pakistan if the latter refrained from testing (*Washington Post*, May 20, 1998, p. A21; *International Herald Tribune*, 4 September 1998, p. 8). However, as Pakistan continued with nuclear testing on May 28 and 30, 1998, the attention of the international community focussed on South Asia and the failure of the non-proliferation regime, despite the US policy being shaped to address these concerns.

Even though the nuclear tests by India and Pakistan were widely condemned, there was little support for the imposition of economic sanctions from international bodies such as the UN and European Union. Not only was the lack of consensus evident within the P5, the five permanent members of the UN Security Council (UNSC) regarding the effectiveness of sanctions, but it has also been argued that there was a lack of sufficient legal basis to levy sanctions against India and Pakistan (SIPRI, 1999, pp. 680–681). The United Kingdom and France raised doubts about the efficacy of sanctions as a response. China and Russia refused to support sanctions even though they condemned the tests. States such as Denmark, Japan and Sweden suspended or curtailed development assistance programs to the region (SIPRI, 1999, p. 522). Japan not only froze most developmental aid but also refused to back new loans for Pakistan from international bodies. Japan's actions could have been in response to US urging, as also motivated by its being the largest source of bilateral aid to Pakistan (Asia Society Publications, 1998). The G-8 nations agreed to freeze all non-humanitarian lending by multilateral agencies to Pakistan.

In formulating its response to the nuclear tests by India and Pakistan, the United States drew upon the objectives outlined in several communiqués from the UNSC's five permanent members (P5). (UN SCR communiqué on June 4, 1998, UNSC Resolution 1172 of June 6, and a G-8 foreign ministers communiqué of June 12; Mistry, 1999). The initial reaction of the United States was to impose economic sanctions on India and Pakistan, which was required by Section 102 of the 1994 Arms Export Control Act, known as the Glenn Amendment. The stated objectives of the United States in imposing these sanctions were:

- to send a strong message to would-be nuclear testers;
- to have maximum influence on Indian and Pakistani behaviour;
- to target the governments, rather than the people; and
- to minimise the damage to other US interests.

Further goals were listed as:

- halt further nuclear testing;
- obtaining Indian and Pakistani signatures to the CTBT immediately and without conditions;
- prevent deployment or testing of missiles or nuclear weapons;
- obtain their co-operation at Fissile Material Cut-off Treaty (FMCT) negotiations in Geneva;

- maintain and formalise restraints on sharing sensitive goods and technologies with other countries; and
- reduce bilateral tensions, including Kashmir (Bureau of Economic and Agricultural Affairs, 1998).

The Clinton administration engaged India and Pakistan in high level talks to reduce tension in the region, while advancing non-proliferation measures. As the talks seemed to make some headway, the United States moved to reduce certain economic sanctions and showed more flexibility on the issue of export controls. As the opinion in Congress increasingly veered towards economic sanctions being unsuitable, the Congress passed the Omnibus Appropriations Act in October 1998, which included a section amending US sanctions law (the specific provision being the India-Pakistan Relief Act of 1998, also called the Brownback Amendment). Under this act, the President could waive certain sanctions until October 1999. Hence, on December 1, 1998, President Clinton granted waivers that permitted US loans and investments in India and Pakistan, the use of foreign assistance funds for international military training and education programs, and allowed the US to support the International Monetary Fund's (IMF) program of economic measures with Pakistan (United States Information Agency, 1998). The Brownback II Amendment was passed in October 1999, which extended the previous legislation.

In October 1999, in the aftermath of General Musharraf's takeover, further sanctions were imposed against Pakistan under Section 508 of the 1999 Foreign Operations Appropriations Act, which is applicable to countries where an elected government has been deposed by a military coup (Foreign Appropriations Act, 1999). However, during this period certain measures, such as IMF bail-out packages and rescheduling, were adopted to ensure that Pakistan's economy managed to endure the problems associated with political change. Although the imposition of sanctions in the face of democratic instability appears to highlight the importance of a democratic tradition for the United States, it was immediately ignored in the face of the September 11, 2001, attack on the World Trade Center. As Pakistan extended its support for anti-terrorist measures in Afghanistan, President Bush lifted sanctions imposed on India and Pakistan, in May 1998, in an effort to provide incentives to Pakistan for its continued co-operation through Presidential Determination of September 22, 2001, which stated that sanctions and prohibitions are not in "the national security interests of the United States" (Bush, 2001; Wagner, 2001a).

The fact that sanctions on Pakistan and India were lifted simultaneously was an indicator of Pakistan's renewed strategic importance for the

United States as discussions on sanctions till then had largely focused on lifting sanctions against India. US and Pakistani representatives signed an agreement to reschedule Pakistan's debt to the United States on September 24, 2001. On October 4, 2001, the US Senate Foreign Relations Committee passed a bill, S.1465, which removed impediments on foreign assistance for Pakistan for the next two fiscal years. It was based on the condition that aid was granted as part of the war against international terrorism. The legislation was supposed to serve as a reward for Pakistan choosing to stand with the United States and highlighted the importance of Pakistan as a frontline state in its war against terrorism. The justification given for the waiver was that it would not only be an important factor in the US efforts against international terrorism but also facilitate the transition to demo-cratic rule in Pakistan. However, certain reservations surfaced regarding ending sanctions, as it could lead to a significant new arms relationship with Pakistan. On October 27, 2001, President Bush signed the bill that granted him authority to waive prohibitions on major military sales and economic assistance to Pakistan for two years. This law granted exemptions to sanctions that were imposed due to the October 1999 coup and for defaulting on US loans. After the lifting of these sanctions, Pakistan became free from most US military and all economic sanctions for the first time since 1990 (Wagner, 2001b).

ARMS TRANSFERS TO PAKISTAN: RESORT TO OTHER MEANS

Pakistan–US security relations, including arms transfers, received a new impetus in the early 1980s as relations between the two countries improved. This was due to a reappraisal of Pakistan's strategic worth in the light of its role as a frontline state in the US war against the Soviets in Afghanistan. The first US assistance package, in 1981, amounting to US$3.25 billion over a six-year period, was divided equally between economic assistance and military sales. Military assistance related to foreign military sales credits for acquiring new weapons, military equipment, radar, and communication gear for improving the mobility, efficiency, and strike capability of the three services. From 1983 to 1986, Pakistan also obtained 40 F-16 aircraft costing approximately US$1.1 billion. This amount was paid in cash from its own resources as well as funds provided by some Arab countries, mainly Saudi Arabia. The second US assistance package, from 1987 to 1993, was worth

US$4.02 billion. From this amount, US$1.74 billion was in the form of credits for purchasing new military equipment in artillery, armour, anti-armour, air and naval defence as well as communication. In 1989, the US agreed to supply 60 more F-16 aircraft (Rizvi, 1994).

In June 1990, the United States agreed to the licensed production of spare parts for the F-16 aircraft in Pakistan. Pakistan agreed to a cash payment for the purchase of a second batch of 60 F-16s. However, no aircraft were supplied, because the military sales program was suspended in October 1990. This was done in keeping with the provisions of the Pressler Amendment, which terminated all government-to-government military sales or aid to Pakistan (Rizvi, 1994). Pakistan had also ordered 28 additional F 16 aircraft and certain other military hardware – to be acquired on a government-to-government basis, rather than a commercial one – which became subject to provisions of the Pressler Amendment. Early 1995 was witness to deteriorating relations between Washington and Islamabad over the F-16 issue. Pakistan focussed on the failure of the US government to deliver the 28 F-16s and other military equipment, due to sanctions under the Pressler Amendment, and the fact that the US had not returned the approximately US$1.3 billion Pakistan paid for this equipment. In 1995, legislation was introduced by the Clinton administration to modify the Pressler Amendment so that US $368 million worth of arms contracted before 1990 could be released, and initial cash refund of US$120 million could be provided. Owing to the potential of the F-16s for nuclear delivery capability, it was decided that none of them would be released to Pakistan. Pakistan was to be reimbursed for the purchased F-16s by the funds generated from the resale of the F-16s elsewhere (Jones et al., 1998).

The changes made to the Pressler Amendment were to ensure the end of prohibition on US economic assistance to Pakistan, and on certain military assistance including anti-narcotics, anti-terrorism, peacekeeping and military-to-military contacts. The released military equipment included artillery, P-3C Orion anti-submarine-warfare aircraft, Harpoon anti-ship missiles, and AIM-9L air-to-air missiles, spares and explosives. Although the new F-16s were excluded from the package, spare parts and engine upgrades for Pakistan's existing force of F-16s were included (Jones et al., 1998). In return Pakistan was expected to continue to implement existing restraints on its nuclear program. However, the release of military hardware to Pakistan under the provisions of the Brown Amendment was briefly postponed due to the transfer of ring magnets to Pakistan from China which brought to the fore Pakistan's continuing quest for uranium enrichment.

In April 1997, Pakistan made known its plans to buy 32 Mirage 2000-5 combat aircraft from France to make up for the stalled F-16s (*Reuters*, April 8, 1997). Islamabad also threatened to sue the United States in the US court system if no progress was made on repayment of the US$650 million owed to Pakistan for the undelivered F-16s (*New York Times*, May 24, 1997). In April 1998, the United States apparently offered to resolve the F-16 dispute by reimbursing Pakistan if it agreed to forego the test of its medium range missile, the "Ghauri", but to no avail. These restrictions were not palatable to Pakistan as its efforts to find solutions to its security concerns demanded not only an up-grade of its air fleet but also an effort to modernize its missile forces.

The F-16s were sporadically offered to the Pakistani government as incentives to stop developing its nuclear and missile programs. However, Pakistan's proliferation activities continued, causing Pakistan to look to other sources of procurement. During this period China continued to be Pakistan's main ally and supplier. Although Chinese weapons had the advantage of being cheaper than those of other suppliers, the level of technology they were able to offer was invariably low. According to some reports, Pakistan was interested in acquiring the Chinese combat aircraft, the Super-7, for its second line of defence (SIPRI, 1998). In the late 1990s, Pakistan's production facilities were also facing problems in developing the Al Khalid tank, causing them to turn towards the Chinese Type-85-IIM and the more modern Ukrainian T-80 UD tank (SIPRI, 1998). While France delivered refurbished Mirage-5 combat aircraft to Pakistan in 1999, Pakistan also reportedly assembled Swedish RBS-70 anti-aircraft missiles and placed its first order after a gap of ten years for Bofors spare parts and ammunition for the FH-77B howitzer (SIPRI, 2000). The denial of F-16s had thus affected Pakistan's military capability considerably and made it more dependent on Chinese and French transfers of fighter aircraft. However, French weapons were more expensive and Chinese weapons of a lesser quality. It has been stated that the Chinese combat aircraft, the F-7 MG, could only be used as a "stopgap" (SIPRI, 2000, p. 330). These drawbacks adversely affected Pakistan's military modernization.

Although Pakistan's military capability has been adversely affected by the imposition of sanctions by the United States, its determination to pursue its nuclear weapons and missile development programs persisted. Through the 1970s and 1980s, there were numerous reports on Pakistan's reliance on illegal clandestine imports of sensitive technology for its nuclear weapons program. It depended on smuggling and black market transactions to obtain hardware from Western countries, often violating their export control laws.

Through the 1980s, the Chinese connection with Pakistan's development of nuclear technology became visible. In early 1983, it was reported that China provided Pakistan with sensitive information concerning the design of nuclear weapons (Spector, 1984; *Arms Control Reporter,* January 28, 1983). A report in June 1984 indicated that China had actually given Pakistan the design for the weapon used in China's fourth nuclear test, a low yield uranium device detonated in 1966 (Spector, 1984; *Financial Times*, August 14, 1984).[3] Although the United States had extended aid to Pakistan during the 1980s with the assumption that it would advance US non-proliferation measures, various reports continued to negate this theory. For instance, *Washington Post* correspondent Robert Woodward reported in November 1986 that Pakistan had enriched uranium to 93.5 percent and detonated high explosives to test the triggering device. Nuclear non-proliferation expert Leonard Spector was quoted as saying that if true "it would be the last important step in the Pakistan program" (*Washington Post*, November 4, 1986). In November 1989, Chinese Premier Li Peng announced that China would sell Pakistan a 300-megawatt nuclear power reactor, under a nuclear co-operation agreement, the two states had signed in 1986. The contract for the nuclear power plant was finally signed on December 31, 1991, in Beijing in the presence of Prime Minister Li Peng (Spector with Smith, 1990; Asian Recorder, 1992).

One of the most well-known cases of Chinese assistance to Pakistan in the 1990s was the purchase of 5,000 ring magnets by the A.Q. Khan Research Laboratory in Kahuta, Pakistan. The ring magnets were to be used in gas centrifuges that enrich uranium for weapons. The firm involved, the Chinese National Nuclear Corporation and its predecessor organization, the Second Ministry of Machine Building, was believed to be involved in Beijing's nuclear weapons co-operation with Islamabad for a long time (*International Herald Tribune*, 3 April 1996).[4] This was a blatant violation of the NPT to which China had become a signatory in 1992. Intelligence sources believed that the magnets were used in special suspension bearings at the top of a spinning chamber in the centrifuges. Reportedly, the ring magnets would allow Pakistan to double its capacity to enrich uranium for weapons (*Arms Control Reporter*, February 1996). However, disregarding Pakistan's nuclear inclination and China's supply of ring magnets to Pakistan, the United States confirmed the transfer of US arms worth US$368 million to Pakistan as proposed by the Brown Amendment.

China has also been Pakistan's primary support for developing its missile capability for the delivery of nuclear weapons. On February 11, 1989, Pakistan's Chairman of the Army Staff, General Mirza Aslam Beg, announced that Pakistan had successfully tested two new surface-to-surface ballistic missiles, the Hatf I and the Hatf II (JPRS-TND, 1989 cited in Spector with Smith, 1990).[5] Both these weapons reportedly had payloads of 500 kg, in effect making them powerful enough to carry a relatively crude nuclear warhead. According to the US Arms Control and Disarmament Agency, Pakistan received assistance in developing the missiles from China and West European countries (Spector with Smith, 1990). It received M-11 missiles from China, including key components for the system. In 1991, the United States applied category II sanctions on governmental or government-owned entities in China and Pakistan because China transferred missile-related equipment to Pakistan, although there were doubts that the transfer involved complete M-11 missiles. The transfer also involved mobile launchers for the Chinese M-11 missile. After China agreed to abide by the provisions of the Missile Technology Control Regime (MTCR), the Bush administration waived the sanctions in March 1992 (Jones et al., 1998). In August 1993, the United States again imposed sanctions on Pakistan's Space Agency and on China's Ministry of Aerospace Industries, because of the sale of M-11 components – although it is believed that the transfers of actual missiles may have been involved (Spector, McDonough, & Medeiros, 1995). In July 1995, reports indicated that strong evidence existed of Chinese shipments of complete M-11 missiles. According to US intelligence officials, more than 30 complete missiles had been stored at the Sargodha Air Force Base in Pakistan since 1992 (Jones et al., 1998; *Arms Control Reporter*, November 1995). However, the Clinton administration was not willing to accept the evidence as conclusive or trigger sanctions. According to reports in June 1996, US Intelligence confirmed that Chinese M-11 missiles were in Pakistan and that Pakistani army personnel had been trained by Chinese experts (Jones et al., 1998; *Arms Control Reporter*, June 1996). In August 1996, a National Intelligence Estimate (NIE) further disclosed that Pakistan was building a secret plant to produce medium range missiles with Chinese assistance and that it could begin production of missiles based on the Chinese M-11 (*Arms Control Reporter*, September 1996; Jones et al., 1998). However, none of these incidents of missile transfer from China to Pakistan triggered any sanctions.

The Hatf III, with a range of 600 km and a payload of 500 kg, was test fired in July 1997. The Hatf III was believed to be a derivative of the Chinese M-9 missile. In April 1998, a 1,500-km range (the range demonstrated in the test was 1,100 km) surface-to-surface missile Ghauri or Hatf V was tested by Pakistan. Although Pakistan claimed to have produced this missile indigenously, some US officials suggested that the Ghauri had been transferred from North Korea in 1997. Japan also identified North Korea as the main source of technology for the Ghauri (Smith, 1998; Harney & Bokhari, 1998). The Ghauri II, which was tested in April 1999, is also considered to be a derivative or export version of the Nodong I, developed in North Korea (Kak, 1999). Reportedly, Pakistan had, in return, helped North Korea with its nuclear program. Extensive Pakistani help in nuclear proliferation to a number of countries was confirmed in 2004, although Pakistani authorities claimed that the "father" of the Pakistani nuclear weapons program, A.Q. Khan, had acted independently and without government support (see note 2). Another missile, the Shaheen I, was flight tested on April 15, 1999, and is believed to have been reverse-engineered from the Chinese M-9 missile (SIPRI, 2001). In September 2001, sanctions were imposed on some organizations involved in nuclear weapons production in China and Pakistan as President Bush determined that institutes and enterprises in both countries had engaged in missile technology proliferation activities (Federal Register, 2001).

THE EFFECTS OF SANCTIONS

Although US diplomacy towards Pakistan in the 1980s focused on preventing Pakistan's quest for the development of nuclear weapons, it was not successful in persuading the decision-making elite in Pakistan to stop the drive towards this goal. In fact, Pakistan was doubly benefiting from US policies during this period. Not only was the government in Pakistan able to shore up its conventional military capability thanks to the inflow of military equipment, it was also able to continue on the nuclear track, gambling on the assumption that strategic imperatives would prevent the United States from implementing severe measures. The assumption by Pakistani leadership proved to be largely correct, as the United States turned a virtual blind eye to Pakistan's nuclear weapon development in the 1980s. The inconsistency in the US actions, which began in the late 1970s by terminating aid to Pakistan, only to restore it when it was strategically beneficial, signalled to a weakness in US resolve. General Mirza Aslam Beg later admitted that Pakistan had enriched uranium up to 95 percent and above by 1987. He went on to say that while Pakistan had developed nuclear capability by 1987, it was only in 1990 that US displeasure was made evident (POT, 1993). At the same time, the incentives provided to Pakistan for its support against the Soviets in Afghanistan played a significant role in strengthening the position of the military regime in Pakistan. Thus, the Afghan war during the 1980s may be termed as a golden point in Pakistani diplomacy, which dissuaded the United States from taking stringent measures against Pakistan.

During the 1990s, the impact of sanctions on Pakistan was diluted with the modification of the Pressler Amendment. Even as Pakistan and the United States engaged in a dialogue to promote efforts towards non-proliferation, Pakistan continued to improve its nuclear weapons infra-structure and increase stockpiles of fissile material. It also continued to develop nuclear weapons design and acquire ballistic missiles that primarily acted as viable delivery systems. Political leadership at the time made it quite clear that a roll back of the nuclear program was not an option.[6] A.Q. Khan later revealed that Pakistan continued to produce highly enriched uranium despite the Benazir Bhutto government's 1991 freeze on production of weapon-grade uranium (Iqbal, 1998). The reluctance within Pakistan to reduce its nuclear ambitions was displayed in a report issued by the Pakistani Senate's Foreign Affairs Committee, which urged the government to speed up its nuclear weapons program to make up for the damage done to Pakistan's conventional military forces by US sanctions (*Associated Press*, July 21, 1995).

Pakistan's decision to continue with the nuclear tests in May 1998 further highlighted the inadequacy of US non-proliferation efforts. After the tests, Pakistan announced a unilateral moratorium on nuclear testing. In an effort to get the United States to ease some of the sanctions applied after the nuclear tests, Pakistan was amenable to negotiations with respect to non-proliferation. The Pakistani government showed a certain willingness to adhere to the CTBT as well as support the commencement of negotiations on a "non-discriminatory, universal and effectively verifiable treaty banning the production of fissile material" which would not preclude discussion of existing stockpiles (*Arms Control Today*, June/July 1998). It also committed itself to strengthening controls on the export of nuclear and ballistic missile technology.[7] Speaking at the United Nations on September 23, 1999, the Pakistan Prime Minister Nawaz Sharif expressed willingness to adhere to the CTBT before the Conference of States Parties, which was to take place in September 1999. However, he insisted that "Pakistan's adherence to the Treaty will only take place in conditions free from coercion or pressure" (Diamond, 1998). Prime Minister Nawaz Sharif linked the signing of the CTBT to the lifting of economic sanctions imposed by the United States after the nuclear tests. Sanctions were eventually lifted, but not because of Pakistani cooperation on the non-proliferation front or the re-establishment of a democratically elected government. Instead, it was due to a US strategic decision to seek the support of the Pakistani government vis-à-vis

Afghanistan and the fight against global terrorism. Pakistan again, as in the 1980s, was able to ask for economic and military assistance to be restored.

A major factor that contributed to Pakistan's constant pursuit of nuclear and missile programs was their importance to the military and fragile political leadership in Pakistan. The logic of Pakistan's nuclear program was Indo-centric. By pursuing this program, Pakistan sought to neutralize India's conventional military superiority. The immediate reason for Z. A. Bhutto's decision to go nuclear was Pakistan's defeat in the 1971 Indo-Pakistan War and India's proven conventional military superiority. India demonstrated nuclear weapons capability through its nuclear test in 1974, which further reinforced the Pakistani leadership's resolve to speed up activities in its nuclear program. It may stated however, that Pakistan had conceived its nuclear weapons program in 1972 at a meeting held by then Prime Minister Z. A. Bhutto. Mr. Bhutto also believed that the acquisition of nuclear weapons would help to shift power and influence in Pakistan from the military to civilian rulers, foremost himself (Palit & Namboodiri, 1979). But very soon Bhutto lost power and the military took charge of the nuclear weapons program, almost to the exclusion of the civilian political leadership. Another reason cited for Pakistan's pursuit of nuclear weapons was its aim to reduce dependence on the United States. This is apparently also one of the reasons for China's active support of Pakistan's clandestine nuclear weapon program since the late 1970s. In addition, China also sought to prop up Pakistan as an ally in the region to keep India off balance. In this geo-strategic game, China has been extremely helpful to Pakistan for obvious reasons. Not only did Pakistan get strategic support, through the supply of nuclear material and ballistic missiles and requisite components from China, but the Middle Kingdom was also able to keep its rival, India, at bay, by keeping it entangled in border disputes with itself.

The Pakistani economy has been adversely affected by sanctions. Years of economic mismanagement as well as mounting debt made Pakistan dependent on aid and grants from international financial institutions. Internal political instability has been a factor, which constrained Pakistan's economic growth, deterred investment and exacerbated economic problems like a high debt service burden. Lack of economic infrastructure has affected support for agricultural and industrial expansion. Thus, Pakistan remains heavily dependent on foreign aid, and since 1990, after the withdrawal of most US aid to Pakistan, Japan emerged as Pakistan's largest bilateral donor. Although economic liberalization and deregulation since 1990 signalled that the country was open to foreign investment, the level of

investment remained low due to foreign concerns about inadequate infrastructure, perceptions of political instability and inconsistency in policies.
The situation was aggravated due to the 1998 sanctions. Although the Glenn
Amendment sanctions appear to have had an impact on Pakistan's economy,
the United States was a relatively small provider of aid, trade and investment
for Pakistan even before the Glenn Amendment was triggered.

The bigger impact occurred when Japan, Pakistan's largest trading
partner, joined the other G-7 countries in cutting all aid except humanitarian
aid. After the imposition of economic sanctions, the government of Pakistan
implemented emergency economic measures to fend off an impending
economic crisis (US International Trade Commission, 1999). In July 1998,
Standard and Poor downgraded Pakistan's credit rating and issued a
warning that Pakistan could go bankrupt within two months (*Financial
Times*, July 15, 1998). As Pakistan's economic situation deteriorated, the G-7
agreed to relax their multilateral sanctions to allow the IMF to negotiate a
support program for Pakistan in late 1998. Pakistan's external debt for the
year 1998–1999 stood at US$38 billion. Pakistan obtained relief from the
Paris Club rescheduling in January 1999, January 2001 and December 2001
(Government of Pakistan, 2002).

A concern about the Pakistani economy and expectations of abundant
economic fallout was a significant factor influencing Pakistan's decision to
support the United States in the post-September 11 situation. Although the
United States lifted economic sanctions against Pakistan in September 2001, it
also made trade concessions pertaining to textile imports from Pakistan. The
Pakistan economy benefited from a total of about US$1 billion in economic
aid, mostly from the United States, but also from Japan and the European
Union. There was a new loan from the IMF, a loan extension from China and
other debt rescheduling and write-offs from the Paris Club, the United States
and Canada. According to one report, Pakistan received extraordinary
bilateral assistance in view of its support of the fight against terrorism. This
includes a grant of US$600 million from the United States, US$45 million
from the EU, US$45 million from Japan, US$50 million write-off from the
UK, a DM 100 million social sectors debt swap from Germany and US$340
million debt swap for social sectors from Canada (Government of Pakistan,
n.d.). However, doubts were raised as to whether these packages would be
enough to help Pakistan in the face of its external debt liabilities. Also, the
events of September 11, 2001, and its aftermath, created a difficult investment
climate. Despite getting generous financial assistance from various sources,
Pakistan found it difficult to improve its economic performance. Part of the
failure in this could be attributed to the domestic political situation, which was

mired in the controversial hold of the military, and the inability of the civilian political leadership to stand up and take a front line position in governance.

CONCLUSION

The US policy towards Pakistan, including sanctions and other coercive measures has been marred by inconsistency in its objectives. This inconsistency on the part of the United States has allowed China the scope to pursue its strategic interests in Pakistan, thus achieving the twin objective of having Pakistan as a strategic ally vis-à-vis Central Asia and the Middle East, but more importantly to countervail India. In this connection, the United States, while pursuing its own strategic interests, seems to have miscalculated Pakistan's importance for other actors. Pakistan thus had little difficulty in compensating for the interim loss of the United States as an arms supplier. While the forced diversification of supplies may have added operational burdens to the Pakistani armed forces, the sheer numbers of weapons coming into the country may have been higher if Pakistan had complied with US demands.

The US inconsistency was met by a consistent, and increasingly entrenched, Pakistani pursuit of the nuclear weapons option, despite several dramatic changes in government. The resultant consequence of the inconsistencies in US policies and Pakistani intransigence has been that while Pakistan may have suffered economically, but it gained mileage with respect to pursuing its nuclear program. The ineffectiveness of sanctions and coercive measures in attaining the announced nuclear-non-proliferation policy goals is evident in all core areas of Pakistan's nuclear weapons programs: the quest for fighter aircraft, the procurement of ballistic missiles, the production of nuclear material and the nuclear tests.

As the polity has been dominated by the military leadership, the pursuit of strategic policies in Pakistan has shown enough aggressive components. The Pakistani case demonstrates the limits of sanctions in a case where economic costs of a policy were overwhelmed by what is perceived to be in the interest of national security by national decision-makers.

NOTES

1. For example, see news reports of an interview with A.Q. Khan by Kuldip Nayar, an Indian journalist, who quoted Khan as saying Pakistan possessed a nuclear bomb. A.Q. Khan said, "They told us that Pakistan could never produce the

bomb and they doubted my capabilities, but now they know, we have done it." *The Observer*, 1 March, 1987.

2. The US government revealed in late 2004 that there had indeed been a Pakistani-run clandestine supply network of nuclear material and technology. The head of this network, the "father" of the Pakistani nuclear program, A.Q. Khan, claimed that government officials had no knowledge of his activities. Still, the government punished A.Q Khan with not more than a few restrictions on his personal mobility, see for example, Monterey Institute Center for Nonproliferation Studies, Khan's Nuclear Network, December 2004, http://www.nti.org/f_wmd411/f2i6.html

3. For details about Pakistan's efforts to acquire nuclear technology, see Leonard S. Spector (1984).

4. The DIA report described the company as being under the direct control of the State Council, which was chaired by Prime Minister Li Peng and constitutes the nation's top policy-making group.

5. Beg stated that the former had a range of 80 km and the latter of 300 km.

6. Prime Minister Benazir Bhutto addressing a press conference at Karachi airport in November 1993 stated that the roll back of the nuclear program was not possible. See *Defence Journal*, Vol. XX, nos. 3–4, 1994.

7. SIPRI 1999, p. 523.

REFERENCES

Anthony, I. (2002). Sanctions applied by the European Union and the United Nations. In: *SIPRI yearbook 2002, armaments, disarmament and international security*. Oxford: Oxford University Press.

Asia Society Publications. (1998). Proceedings of a roundtable workshop on "South Asia after the nuclear tests: Where do we go from here?" July 1. Available at http://www.asiasociety.org/publications/south_asia_after.4.html

Asian Recorder. (1992). February 26–March 3, p. 22175. New Delhi: Ashish Printers and Publications.

Bureau of Economic and Agricultural Affairs. (1998). *Fact sheet: India and Pakistan sanctions* (June 18).

Bush, G. W. (2001). Presidential Determination No. 2001–28. "*President Waives sanctions on India, Pakistan*." September 22. Available at http://www.whitehouse.gov/news/releases/2001/09/20010922-4.html

Diamond, H. (1998). India, Pakistan commit to sign CTB treaty by September 1999. *Arms Control Today*, October.

Federal Register. (2001). Bureau of Nonproliferation: imposition of missile proliferation sanctions against a Chinese entity and a Pakistani entity. Vol. 66, no.176, September 11, 2001, in Stockholm International Peace Research Institute. 2002. *SIPRI Yearbook, 2002*. Oxford: Oxford University Press.

Financial Times. (1984). Cited in Spector, L. S., *Nuclear proliferation today* (p. 101). Cambridge: Ballinger.

Foreign Appropriations Act. (1999). Section 508 at http://www.mac.doc.gov/sanctions/sect508.htm

Government of Pakistan. (2002). *Economic survey of Pakistan, 2001–2002* (Available at http://www.finance.gov.pk/survey/fore.pdf).

Government of Pakistan. n.d. Government report on "Three Years of Reform", Available from: http://www.pak.gov.pk/Factsheets/three_years_of_reforms.htm

Harney, A., & Bokhari, F. (1998). Pakistan fired N. Korean missile. *Financial Times*, (Internet edition), September 25, Cited in SIPRI year book, 1999, p. 696.

Iqbal, A. (1998). Mass production of Ghauri missile begins: Qadeer, *The News* (Islamabad), June 1, in Stockholm International Peace Research Institute. 1999. *SIPRI Yearbook, 1999*. Oxford: Oxford University Press.

Jones, R. W., McDonough, M. G., with Dalton, T. F, & Gregory D. K. (1998). *Tracking Nuclear Proliferation: A Guide in Maps and Charts*. Washington, DC: Carnegie Endowment for International Peace.

Kak, K. (1999). Missile proliferation and international security, *Strategic analysis* (New Delhi), Vol. 23, No.3, in Stockholm International Peace Research Institute. 2000. *SIPRI Yearbook, 2000*. Oxford: Oxford University Press.

Lavoy, P. R. (1994). Civil-military relations, strategic conduct, and the stability of nuclear deterrence in South Asia. In: S. D. Sagan (Ed.), *Civil-military relations and nuclear weapons*. Stanford, CA: Center for International Security and Arms Control, Stanford University.

Leventhal, P. (1987). Testimony on Pakistan and U.S. nuclear non-proliferation policy before the house foreign affairs committee, October 22. Nuclear Control Institute. Available at http://www.nci.org/t/t102287.htm

Mistry, D. (1999). Diplomacy, sanctions, and the U.S. non-proliferation dialogue with India and Pakistan. *Asian Survey*, (Sept.–Oct.), 753–771.

Monterey Institute. (n.d.). Center for Nonproliferation Studies, US Non-proliferation Sanctions Against China And/or Chinese Entities at http://www.nti.org/db/China/sanclist.htm

Palit, D. K., & Namboodiri, P. K. S. (1979). *Pakistan's Islamic bomb*. New Delhi: Vikas.

Public Opinion Trends and Analyses (POT). (1993). *Pakistan Series*, December 15. New Delhi.

Rizvi, H-A. (1994). Pakistan's threat perception and weapons procurement. In: W. T. Wander, E. H. Arnett & P. Bracken (Eds), *The diffusion of advanced weaponry: Technologies, regional implications, and responses*. Washington, DC: American Association for the Advancement of Science.

Smith, R.J. (1998). A feared scenario around the corner, *Washington Post*, May 14, p. A29, in Stockholm International Peace Research Institute. 1999. *SIPRI Yearbook, 1999*. Oxford: Oxford University Press.

Spector, L. S. (1984). *Nuclear proliferation today*. Cambridge: Ballinger.

Spector, L. S., with Smith, J. R. (1990). *Nuclear ambitions: The spread of nuclear weapons 1989–1990*. Boulder, CO: Westview.

Spector, L. S., McDonough, M. G., with Medeiros, E. S. (1995). *Tracking nuclear proliferation: A guide in Maps and Charts*. Washington: Carnegie.

Stockholm International Peace Research Institute. (1998). *SIPRI yearbook, 1998*. Oxford: Oxford University Press.

Stockholm International Peace Research Institute. (1999). *SIPRI yearbook, 1999*. Oxford: Oxford University Press.

Stockholm International Peace Research Institute. (2000). *SIPRI yearbook, 2000*. Oxford: Oxford University Press.

Stockholm International Peace Research Institute. (2001). *SIPRI yearbook, 2001*. Oxford: Oxford University Press.

United States Information Agency. (1998). *Presidential determination on India and Pakistan*. PD no.99-7. December 1, White House, Office of the Press Secretary: Washington, DC, Available at http://www.usia.gov/regional/nea/sasia/docs/doc82.htm; in *SIPRI Yearbook 1999: Armaments, Disarmament and International Security*, New York, NY: Oxford University Press, 1999.

United States International Trade Commission. (1999). Overview and analysis of the economic impact of U.S. sanctions with respect to India and Pakistan, investigation no. 332–406, September.

Wagner, A. (2001a). Bush waives nuclear-related sanctions on India, Pakistan. *Arms Control Today*, October.

Wagner, A. (2001b). Bush authorized to lift sanctions on Pakistan. *Arms Control Today*, November.

CHAPTER 5

TIGHTENING THE SCREWS IN WEST AFRICAN ARMS EMBARGOES

Maraike Wenzel and Sami Faltas

United Nations Security Council (UNSC) sanctions prohibit countries to export arms into the sanctioned state. However, international arms trade is a large and lucrative business, and arms dealers do not give up easily. In Liberia and Sierra Leone, war itself became a profitable activity for various internal and external actors. Material gains derived from controlled territory proved a powerful disincentive to ending the war (Adebajo, 2002, p. 66). Taking this special dynamic into account, this chapter argues that "old-fashioned" sanctions such as in the case of Liberia and Sierra Leone had no major positive effects until they were combined with other measures. The following chapter will explore the cases of Liberia and Sierra Leone. In both conflicts the UNSC imposed – next to other sanctions - arms embargoes. These could not entirely stop the further influx of weapons into the sanctioned states. In addition to the loopholes that these sanctions offered, it is necessary to analyze what factors pushed the UNSC and UN member states to impose sanctions in the first place. In both cases, a network of profit-seeking actors was involved in breaching the arms embargoes.

The UNSC developed a set of so-called smart sanctions to increase the pressure on a sanctioned state. When these new instruments (travel sanctions, diamond sanctions, freezing of financial assets, etc.) were applied

Putting Teeth in the Tiger: Improving the Effectiveness of Arms Embargoes
Contributions to Conflict Management, Peace Economics and Development, Volume 10, 101–136
ISSN: 1572-8323/doi:10.1108/S1572-8323(2009)0000010009

in the case of Liberia and Sierra Leone, they changed the dynamics of the conflicts. The effects will be discussed and analyzed here. First, an arms embargo is a political decision taken by countries or the UNSC, which aims at restoring peace by directly influencing the policy of actors involved in a war (governments and rebels). The instrument of the arms embargo therefore functions as a signal both to the political parties and the international system. Second, the imposition of sanctions is a physical means to completely stop or hinder the import of weapons used in combat. But embargoes can also have negative effects on the conflict. In some cases, sanctions can have a criminalizing effect on states in the region, giving criminal elites extra opportunities to conduct illegal business (Kopp, 1999, p. 348; Peter, 2005). This severely affects neighboring countries by criminalizing the neighboring economy. The Sierra Leone conflict was exacerbated by the already ongoing conflict in Liberia. Sierra Leone's illegal sector became dependent on the Liberian criminal network.

This chapter will show how the UNSC reacted to the conflicts in Liberia and Sierra Leone. It analyzes UN policy and draws conclusions regarding the effectiveness of the sanctions regimes. Owing to the interconnection of the conflicts in Liberia and Sierra Leone, a joint analysis is performed.

BACKGROUND TO THE CONFLICTS

Liberia

On December 24, 1989, an armed insurrection began in Liberia. Charles Taylor, a former government official, led a rebel force, the *National Patriotic Front of Liberia* (NPFL), into the north-eastern Nimba County. A breakaway faction, the *Independent National Patriotic Front* (INPFL), led by Prince Yormie Johnson gained control of central Monrovia – the capital – and killed the President Samuel Doe. The *Economic Community of West African States* (ECOWAS) intervened in August 1990, sending monitoring troops (the ECOWAS Military Observer Group, ECOMOG), and convened a national conference which elected an *Interim Government of National Unity*. In October 1990, ECOMOG established a neutral zone in Monrovia where Dr. Amos Sawyer was installed as Interim President in November. Various different factions and opposition groups were formed and clashes between the rebel groups and the Liberian army continued.

In this violent situation, the arms embargo was imposed by UNSC resolution 788 (1992). In early March 1994, the UN deployed an observer mission (UNOMIL) while hostilities continued. Another year of violent incidents followed until a peace agreement was signed in Abuja in August 1996, and Taylor's NPFL was transformed into the civilian National Patriotic Party (NPP). Elections were held the following year and the former rebel leader Taylor became president of Liberia on August 2, 1997. Despite the peace treaty, violent conflict continued in much of the country such as in the northern Lofa County in 1998/1999. In July 2000, a new rebel insurgency, a Guinea-based group of dissidents under the name of *Liberians United for Reconciliation and Democracy* (LURD), began mounting attacks against the Taylor government.

In 2003, an additional armed group, the *Movement for Democracy in Liberia* (MODEL), emerged in Liberia. Fighting between LURD, MODEL and government forces escalated causing many civilian casualties. On August 18, 2003, a peace agreement was signed in Accra between the Liberian Government, LURD, MODEL and a number of political parties. The UNSC established the *United Nations Mission in Liberia* (UNMIL) in September 2003 (resolution 1509), and Charles Taylor went into exile in Nigeria.

The virulent conflict in Liberia had an intense effect on the whole sub-region. There is evidence of a strong connection between the conflicts in Liberia, Sierra Leone, Côte d'Ivoire and Guinea (UN, S/2004/396). From the beginning of the insurgency in Sierra Leone in 1992, Charles Taylor had been actively supporting the Sierra Leone rebels, the RUF, on multiple levels, by providing training, weapons, related materiel, logistical support and sanctuary (UN, 2000, S/2000/1195, para. 182). By instigating a second conflict in the region, Taylor planned to draw the attention of the international community away from Liberia. In the RUF, Taylor saw a potential vehicle to help him in his rebellion in Liberia, thereby distracting ECOMOG. A second factor was the diamond wealth of Sierra Leone that facilitated the purchase of military equipment for both conflicts. By providing logistical and military support to the RUF, Taylor gained access to Sierra Leone's diamond wealth, while Sierra Leone rebels relied on Liberian arms imports.

Sierra Leone

Charles Taylor's support for the RUF dates back to 1991. Personal connections between Charles Taylor and Foday Sankoh, former leader of the RUF, go back to the late 1980s when both were trained in Libya and both supported Blaise Campaoré in his power seizure in Burkina Faso.

Sankoh was already involved in Taylor's struggle as leader of NPFL to take power in Liberia in 1989 (*ibid.*, para. 180).

Foday Sankoh and two other future leaders of the RUF were trained in Libya in 1987 (Musah, 2000, p. 84). The Libyan connection opened the way for the creation of the RUF as well as for an alliance with Charles Taylor's NPFL. This alliance was instrumental in launching the incursion of the RUF, 1991, in Sierra Leone (*ibid.*). Thirteen months after the armed insurrection staged by the RUF, the military took over power and installed the *National Provisional Ruling Council* (NPRC). Toward the end of 1992, a new force entered the picture, the "Kamajors." Joined by a number of retired military personnel, the Kamajors soon became a force to contend with, fighting back not only against the RUF but also against the excesses of the NPRC government (Pratt, 1999).

In May 1995, the NPRC approached the South African Private Military Company (PMC) Executive Outcomes (EO). The Director of Branch Energy and Heritage Gas and Oil, Anthony Buckingham had introduced EO to the NPRC and had negotiated the contract with the PMC. The first EO contingent, 200 men in total, arrived in Sierra Leone in May 1995, and within ten days, they had managed to drive the RUF out of the capital Freetown. Their success was mostly due to their combat skills, excellent air support, first-rate communications equipment, skilled trainers, and to the assistance of a small group of Sierra Leone soldiers and Kamajors, by then a force of 2,000–3,000 men (Pratt, 1999). By early 1996, EO had pushed the RUF out of the strategically important diamond areas.

By 1996, foreign and domestic pressure forced the NPRC to hold general elections despite the ongoing war, and Ahmed Tejan Kabbah became the first freely elected president in 34 years. President Kabbah agreed to the expulsion of EO within five weeks of signing the Abidjan Peace Agreement, although LifeGuard, an EO offshoot, remained behind to protect the diamond areas (Pratt, 1999). The government was left exposed with few reliable security forces beyond the Kamajors and Nigerian troops, both acting under the umbrella of ECOMOG forces (Musah, 2000, p. 104). Within a year a group of renegade officers forced the new government to flee the country (May 1997) to Guinea.

The RUF welcomed the coup and formed an alliance with the new military government, the Armed Forces Revolutionary Council (AFRC). Exiled President Kabbah thereafter signed a contract with the British PMC *Sandline International*, a company traded on the Vancouver Stock Market, which had connections with EO and Branch Energy and Diamond Works (Pratt, 1999). EO and Sandline worked closely, partly reshuffling their personnel and using the same network to carry out the business part of their mercenary activities (Musah, 2000, p. 100). Their aim was to oust the AFRC and liberate the diamond areas. Financing was reportedly provided by Vancouver-based Indian national Rakesh Saxena who had business interests in Sierra Leone (Pratt, 1999). In February 1998, 28 tons of small arms arrived in Sierra Leone as a part of this deal but were officially impounded by ECOMOG as a contravention of a UN arms embargo (*ibid.*). After ECOMOG had forced the military junta (AFRC) out of office, the legitimate government (Kabbah) returned.

The military junta retreated and became a second rebel faction. In cooperation with the RUF, the rebel armies financed their participation in the war by mining diamonds and selling them through Liberia. Freetown was put under the authority of ECOMOG; however, large parts of the countryside remained in rebel hands. In January 1999, the AFRC and the RUF laid siege to the capital, but ECOMOG was able to repel the rebels. After it proved impossible to defeat the RUF militarily, all parties agreed to a regionally brokered cease-fire signed in Lomé in July 1999. The UNSC passed a resolution (1270) in October 1999 to mandate a peacekeeping force, the UN Mission in Sierra Leone (UNAMSIL). It replaced the largely Nigerian ECOMOG forces who left Sierra Leone in 2000 and who had been seen by the rebels as being a party to the conflict (Adebajo, 2002).

Disarmament began in 1999, although the RUF did not cooperate significantly in this program. In 2000, the Sierra Leone conflict gained attention in the western media when the RUF abducted and murdered UN peacekeepers. In an attempt to increase its efforts, the UNSC expanded the mission's troop contingent to 13,000 troops (resolution 1299) in 2000, and banned the sale of unauthorized Sierra Leone diamonds. On January 17, 2002, the RUF and the Government of Sierra Leone agreed to end the conflict.

SANCTION EPISODES

In both conflicts, the UN had used arms embargoes to counter and contain the virulent conflicts and regional insecurity. However, the embargo must be seen in a broader context than just being a national issue. The West African region has been and still is awash with small arms. Civil wars in Senegal, Guinea-Bissau, Niger, Côte d'Ivoire, Liberia and Sierra Leone had increased the demand for weapons, with stockpiles being transferred from one crisis to another (Pugh & Cooper with Goodhand, 2004). Interconnection of private traders and criminals established a complex network dedicated to satisfy the demands of the conflict markets. Corruption and criminalization of certain states created additional opportunities for arms trafficking.

Liberia

In the violent situation of the year 1992, the first arms embargo was imposed on Liberia by UNSC resolution 788. The embargo was imposed as a response to the serious deterioration of the internal situation in the country. The UNSC opined that the instability was not conducive to the holding of free and fair elections, which offered the best possible framework for a peaceful resolution of the Liberian conflict (United Nations Sanctions Secretariat, 2000, p. 11).

Considering the fact that the deployment of UNOMIL had no major effect and hostilities continued, the UNSC decided to establish a committee to monitor the implementation of the sanctions with resolution 985 in 1995. The sanctions had no major effect on the availability of arms to fighting groups. Weapons continued to enter the country causing many casualties. After the UN Panel of Experts (appointed pursuant to Security Council resolution 1306 (2000), para. 19, in relation to Sierra Leone) had pointed out Liberia's involvement in financing the war in Sierra Leone and facilitating illicit diamond trade through Liberia, a complete embargo on diamond exports from Liberia was recommended (UN, S/2000/1195, para. 9). Between 1995 and 1999, 33.6 million carats originating from Liberia were exported to Belgium. This volume exceeded official Liberian exports and, more importantly, production capacity by far (*ibid.*, para. 112). The Panel of Experts provided conclusive evidence that Taylor fueled the war in Sierra Leone while earning revenue from the diamond trade. The international community realized that additional sanctions were required to cut Taylor's financing of military material. On March 7, 2001, the UNSC adopted resolution 1343, imposing a set of sanctions on Liberia for its support of the RUF and its involvement in illicit arms-for-diamonds-trade.

The arms embargo imposed by UN resolution 788 was replaced by UN resolution 1343 (2001) and a new embargo imposed for different reasons. Now UNSC imposed the sanctions because of Liberia's involvement in the conflict of Sierra Leone. In 1992, UNSC had placed an arms embargo on Liberia and had established a committee to monitor its implementation arguing that Liberia was a threat to international security. In 2001, the UNSC dissolved that committee and tightened the already existing arms embargo by prohibiting the sale or supply of arms and related material to Liberia (Adebajo, 2002, p. 72). A new committee was established that considered imposing additional embargoes on diamonds and travel if Taylor would not cease his support for Sierra Leone's rebel group RUF (UN, S/2002/83, para. 4). These additional embargoes on travel and diamonds came into force later that year. At the urging of most ECOWAS states, the UNSC delayed theses sanctions for three months. Taylor accused the UN and the major architects of the sanctions of attempting to overthrow his government and started a nation-wide public relations campaign making the UN responsible for the country's situation (*ibid.*, p. 73).

Taylor became aware of his precarious situation and started to make huge efforts to comply with UNSC's requests (Adebajo, 2002, p. 72). He invited international monitoring of Liberia's diamond sector, called for the deployment of UN monitors along Liberia's land and sea borders and announced the expulsion of RUF staff and the closure of the RUF office in Monrovia (*ibid.*). A debate evolved between the UNSC and the ECOWAS whether the policy of sticks without carrots was appropriate (*ibid.*). ECOWAS members claimed UNSC policy to be contradictory, on the one hand, urging Taylor to assist in obtaining the RUF's compliance to implement the Lomé peace plan in Sierra Leone and on the other hand punishing Taylor for supporting the RUF (*ibid.*).

Taylor was then accused of using timber revenues to purchase arms in violation of resolution 1343 (2001) while timber companies were alleged to be linked to illegal arms trade (UN, 2002, S/2002/83, para. 34).[1] The Panel of Experts, established pursuant to resolution 1343, provided evidence of arms purchases valued at US$1.5 million, generated by timber taxes and other logging industry fees (UN, S/2003/498, paras 152–153). Additionally there was strong evidence of tax misappropriation – in 2001 at least US$17 million per year remained unaccounted for in official balances. The UN reacted with resolution 1478 (May 6, 2003), which prohibited the import of Liberian timber.

In the Liberian conflict, international actors did not enforce the arms embargo properly. Systematic information and implementation were not given due to a lack of resources and infrastructure to tackle smuggling activities as well as due to the collusion of high-level national officials. The international community and especially the UN had no real means of enforcement. This rendered the arms embargo merely symbolic. First, in Liberia, the UNSC activity relied solely on the support of ECOMOG forces who were trying to end the civil war that had already erupted in 1989. Furthermore, the UN waited three years until the UNSC imposed a stand-alone arms embargo on Liberia with resolution 788, in 1992. There was no further action until UNSC established a committee to monitor the implementation of the Liberian embargo, three years after the embargo was imposed in 1992. The new committee did not have special monitoring mechanisms to ensure effective implementation and relied solely upon the cooperation of states and organizations in providing information. As pointed out before, many state officials in the region were not willing to help, often being involved themselves in the arms trade in the region. From 1995 to 2000, no real initiative was launched by the UNSC to enforce the sanctions.

On August 2, 2000, the UN Secretary General appointed a Panel of Experts to collect information on possible violations of measures imposed by resolution 1171 concerning Sierra Leone and to explore the link between the trade in diamonds and the trade in arms-related materiel in Sierra Leone. As a consequence of the findings of the Panel of Experts concerning Sierra Leone, the arms embargo imposed on Liberia was modified in resolution 1343 (2001). Hereafter, the UNSC established a five-member Panel of Experts to monitor the implementation of the sanctions and to investigate any violations. In effect, nine years after the imposition of the sanctions, a profound investigative procedure was started in the Liberian case.

Clearly defined goals and the adherence to a consistent and all-embracing implementation of the goals are the core requirements for the initiator (UNSC) to commence an effective sanction process. In the Liberian case, it becomes obvious that international action was inconsistent. The ambiguity of stressing the importance of sanctions against Liberia, but failing to introduce any practical measures during a long period of the Liberian war, has resulted in criticism of the international action.

First, the UNSC waited more than two years after the crisis erupted before imposing its stand-alone arms embargo, which was little more than a token gesture until UNSC started an investigation by the Panel of Experts in 2001. In the course of the investigation conducted by the Panel of Experts, it became clear that a large variety of state and non-state actors were involved in the arms trafficking. Additionally, the regional and economic aspect of the conflict became obvious, and the UNSC started to elaborate targeted sanctions to counter the special dynamics of the conflict. The following chapter will focus on national and international actors who were involved in the breach of the Liberian arms embargo (see Table 1).

Sierra Leone

Stabilization seemed close in Sierra Leone when Ahmed Tejan Kabbah became the first freely elected president in Sierra Leone in 1996. But already in May 1997 the military took power and formed a new government, the

Table 1. Timeline for Sanctions on Liberia.

1989	Start of Liberian civil war
1992	Arms embargo (resolution 788)
1995	Establishment of SC Sanctions Committee (SCSC)
2001	New SCSC and Panel of Experts established, arms embargo accompanied by diamond sanctions, travel ban (resolution 1343)
2003	Timber sanctions added

AFRC. The international community intervened with the imposition of various sanctions. In contrast to the Liberian case, the UNSC imposed the arms embargo as part of a broader package of sanction measures. The arms embargo, oil embargo and travel sanctions were initially imposed in 1997 (resolution 1132, October 8, 1997) with the justification that the military coup of May 25, 1997, constituted a threat to international peace and security in the region.

When the legitimate government under President Kabbah had been reinstalled with the military help of ECOMOG, the UNSC lifted the oil embargo in resolution 1171 (March 15, 1998). The UNSC confirmed the removal of sanctions on the government and re-imposed the arms embargo and the travel ban on leading members of the RUF and of the former military junta. Additionally, the UNSC established the UN Observer Force in Sierra Leone (UNOMSIL). ECOWAS strongly encouraged the sanctions against the RUF (Cortright, Lopez, & with Gerber, 2002; p. 6).

After the arms embargo on the RUF and AFRC military junta was re-imposed in 1998 (resolution 1171), no further concrete steps were taken by the UNSC in the following two years. The arms embargo was strengthened by an additional diamond embargo in July 2000 (resolution 1306) and a Panel of Experts was established. Resolution 1306 banned the direct and indirect import of rough diamonds from Sierra Leone not certified by the Government of Sierra Leone through a *Certificate of Origin* (Adebajo, 2002).[2] Additionally a Panel of Experts was mandated to collect information on possible violations of the arms embargo and the link between the diamond sector and arms trade. The Panel's mandate was to examine opportunities and possibilities for launching air traffic control systems in the region as well recommend further steps to the UNSC (United Nations Sanctions Secretariat, 2000, p. 11).

Until 2001 UNSC resolutions did not take account of the regional dynamic of diamond and arms trade. The great majority of Sierra Leone diamonds were exported through Liberia and declared as Liberian diamonds. The Panel of Experts pointed to Liberia's involvement in smuggling activities and the UNSC reacted with the imposition of a diamond embargo on Liberia in resolution 1343 (2001).

Direct steps toward implementing the arms embargo were entrusted to ECOWAS. Resolution 1196 (1998) authorized ECOWAS, in cooperation with the democratically elected government of Sierra Leone (at that time still exiled in Guinea), to ensure strict implementation of the provisions of the resolution. ECOWAS was required to report to the Committee every 30 days on all activities undertaken in that regard. The Military Observer Group (ECOMOG) of ECOWAS maintained observations of the implementation of the arms embargo and related measures (United Nations Sanctions Secretariat, 2000, p. 12). There was no embargo enforcement taken up by the UNSC until the Lomé peace agreement formally ended the country's eight-year civil war in July 1999.

In December 1999 – after showing that the regional force (ECOMOG) had no real capacity to halt illegal weapon inflows – UN peacekeeping forces took over the responsibility of the Sierra Leone mission. The UNSC authorized the establishment of the United Nations Mission in Sierra Leone (UNAMSIL) with a maximum authorized strength of 6,000 military personnel, including 260 military observers. On February 7, 2000, the UNSC unanimously decided to strengthen UNAMSIL and raised the maximum troop strength to 11,000 and in 2001 up to 17,500 (Malan, 2003b, p. 53). The UN peacekeeping mission had no special mandate to enforce the international arms embargo against the rebels.

Several states unilaterally supported peace efforts (UK sent warships and a battalion, the US expanded logistical assistance to UNAMSIL, Canada provided military cargo specialists), and the ECOWAS member states and other countries put significant pressure on Taylor to negotiate with the RUF about the abducted peace keepers (Berman, 2002, p. 2). The international community invested an enormous amount of time and over US$2 billion in the peacekeeping mission in Sierra Leone. This investment made the parliamentary and presidential elections in May 2002 possible (Malan, 2003a, p. 13). However, after the disarmament program was officially completed in January 2002 suspicions of hidden arms caches remained (*ibid.*, p. 15) (see Table 2).

ARMS TRAFFICKING TO LIBERIA

The Liberian arms-trafficking network involved several states as well as non-state actors. State actors can be put in two groups: first, arms exporting

Table 2. Timeline of Sierra Leone Sanctions.

1991	RUF insurrection
1992	Military coup, National Provisional Ruling Party (NPRC)
1996	Freely elected president Kabbah
1997	Military coup, RUF forms an alliance with the new military government, the Armed Forces Revolutionary Council (AFRC)
	UNSC imposes arms embargo, oil embargo and travel sanctions, initially to all parties in resolution 1132
1998	Reinstallation of the Kabbah government
	UNSC lifts arms embargo on government, imposes arms embargo and travel ban on AFRC and RUF, resolution 1171, establishment of the UN Observer Force in Sierra Leone (UNOMSIL)
1999	Lomé peace agreement
2000	Imposition of diamond embargo, resolution 1306
2002	Presidential election

countries (in this case Eastern Europe: Ukraine, Serbia, Belarus, Slovakia, Kyrgyzstan, Moldavia) and second, countries facilitating illegal arms shipments through false end-user certificates (EUCs) or as transit points (predominantly Libya, Burkina Faso, Guinea, Sierra Leone, Democratic Republic of Congo, DRC). Taylor's sanction violating apparatus involved many key individuals around his person, predominantly a network of businessmen linked with the timber, diamond, cargo and arms industries. Taylor and both major rebel groups had developed close connections with neighboring countries to get access to war materiel in breach of the arms embargo. The rebel groups LURD and MODEL acquired arms mainly through connections in the region. Neighboring countries such as Sierra Leone, Côte d'Ivoire and Guinea were involved in arms trafficking with the rebels (UN, S/2002/1115, para. 6), while Taylor's arms-trafficking networks involved a range of international actors besides neighboring allies.

Arms-Exporting Countries

The UN Panel of Expert for Liberia named Ukraine, Moldova, Slovakia as well as Kyrgyzstan in its reports as states of origin for the actual or attempted arms shipments to Liberia. These shipments were arranged by individuals or companies based in these countries as well as companies from other states. The core problem in the arms sector is the accountability of EUCs. EUCs are documents that are provided by the purchasing governments that guarantee that it is the ultimate end user of the military equipment they purchase. In many cases, they are false or the shipments do not end in the country that claims to be the end user.

Charles Taylor's Allies

The Guinean *Pecos* Company supplied various false EUCs to the smuggling network of Victor Bout, an internationally known arms dealer (HRW, 2001, p. 3). These shipments originated from Kyrgyzstan, the Republic of Moldova and Slovakia in 2000 and 2001. Several false Guinean EUCs had also circulated in Eastern Europe (Belarus, Slovakia) in late 2002 (UN, S/2003/498, p. 31, box).

Via Cairo spare parts and rotor blades for military helicopters were exported from Kyrgyzstan to Liberia (HRW, 2001, p. 3). An Egyptian arms broker imported several tons of small arms in 2000 into Liberia although they were officially destined for Uganda (*ibid.*). In August 2000, a Kyrgyz helicopter was repaired in Slovakia and sent back to Kyrgyzstan. Flight records show that from there it was transported to Liberia. One year later, another Kyrgyz helicopter was brought to Slovakia. After repairing it the Slovak authorities halted the shipment of the helicopter to Guinea, were *Pecos* had provided an EUC (*ibid.*). Moldova also blocked a shipment of two helicopters to Guinea where they were to have been repaired before being exported to Namibia. The deal was not completed, because Moldavian authorities stressed that Guinea had no helicopter repair facilities and there was no export authorization (*ibid.*).

Other EUCs were provided by Côte d'Ivoire. An EUC from Côte d'Ivoire authorized a Russian company to transship arms to Côte d'Ivoire that were reported to have been diverted to Liberia. In July 2000, Ukraine approved the export of 113 tons of ammunition to Côte d'Ivoire based on an EUC signed by the Ivorian head of state Gen. Robert Guey (*ibid.*, p. 4). The majority of this shipment was transferred from Côte d'Ivoire to Liberia.

A similar incident had taken place in Burkina Faso in March 1999. Sixty-eight tons of weapons were exported from Ukraine to Burkina Faso, finally ending up in Liberia (HRW, 2000). An EUC issued in Burkina Faso authorized a brokering company registered in Gibraltar to obtain arms. These arms were designated for and shipped to Liberia. Charles Taylor relied mainly on Burkina Faso to cover up his illegal arms imports. Regular night flights from Burkina Faso to Monrovia Robertsfield International Airport continued through early August 2003 (HRW, 2003a).

False EUCs from Nigeria were used by companies from Belgrade, Nigeria and Liechtenstein to ship weapons to Liberia between June and August 2002 (UN, S/2002/1115, para. 24, Box). In one case a false Nigerian EUC was used for the delivery of 200 tons of arms originating in Belgrade in violation of the embargo in June–August 2002 (*ibid.*, para. 6). Taylor relied heavily on the Serbian connection. A major part of the illegally imported weapons to Liberia originated from Serbia. Taylor even admitted having violated the arms embargo in March 2003, referring to Article 51 of UN Charter for self-defense purposes.

The Belgrade-based company *Temex* obtained false Nigerian EUCs for arms shipments (UN, S/2003/498, para. 69). *Temex* brokered these shipments, while the Moldavian company *Aerocom* and a Belgian affiliate of *Ducor World Airlines* transported the weapons to Liberia (*ibid.*, para. 70). The Panel found evidence that Slobodan Tešic, a *Temex shareholder*, functioned as the chief sanction buster. Taylor's economic adviser, Mr. Emmanuel Shaw was managing director of *LoneStar Airways*. *LoneStar* aircraft flew from Burkina Faso to Liberia in November/December 2002 and February 2003. These flights are suspected to have carried military supplies. In February Shaw signed a lease agreement with a Belgrade-based company on the Serbian register. The range and capacity of these aircrafts are ideal for arms transport according to the Expert Panel (*ibid.*, para. 90).

DRC EUCs from February 2003 requesting Serbian weapons have found to be identical with Liberian weapons already acquired in violation of the arms embargo (see earlier) and might have been designated for Liberian use as the actual end-user (*ibid.*, para. 92). The Panel has identified a number of cargo flights originating from the DRC that landed in Liberia.

How Rebel Groups Acquired Arms: LURD, MODEL

The rebel groups were mainly supported by neighboring allies. Although LURD was primarily sponsored by Guinea, MODEL was supported by Côte d'Ivoire (UN, 2003). Côte d'Ivoire was actively involved in arming the MODEL, but detailed information is lacking (UN, 2003, para. 113).

Guinea is known to have supported LURD rebels. It provided regular logistical support and LURD fighters were being hosted in Guinean military barracks in Macenta and provided with ammunition and weapons. These weapons were trucked to LURD headquarter at Voinjama, Liberia (HRW, 2002). In July 2000, there was an indication of a possible arms violation incident in Guinea. A Liberian registered plane named *West Africa Air Services* landed in Conakry, Guinea. The plane carried a Moldavian crew and had started its journey in Kyrgyzstan heading for Burkina Faso, then to Guinea and finally Liberia. Cargo and client documents were false, and the plane was not registered at the Liberian register (UN, S/2000/1195, para. 219). Guinea also provided cross-border long-range artillery for LURD operations in late 2002 and early 2003 (UN, S/2003/498, para. 68). The Guinean mining company *Katex Mine* has been cited in helping to arm LURD, executing several flights in late December 2002 (*ibid.*, para. 110). Through legitimate EUCs, Guinea provided arms and ammunition. However, false Guinean EUCs had also been used to obtain arms. In late 2002 several forged Guinean EUCs had circulated in Eastern Europe (Belarus, Slovakia) (*ibid.*, p. 31, Box). In one specific case, LURD was found to have weapons that had been supplied by the United Arab Emirates to Guinea as military assistance (UN, S/2002/1115). In June/July 2003 LURD supposedly received 81- and 82-millimeter mortars from Guinea (HRW, 2003a).

In addition, it has to be stressed that Guinea is a recipient of US military aid (*ibid.*). It is proven that military material supplied by the US to Guinea has been used in the Liberian conflict.

Arms Suppliers in Perspective

Ukrainian, Moldavian, Slovakian as well as Serbian and Kyrgyz arms were used in the Liberian conflict. The shipments in breach of the UN arms embargo were facilitated by false and original EUCs from allied neighboring states as well through a network of companies. According to UN expert panel reports, false and original EUCs from following states were used to obtain military equipment: Guinea, Nigeria, DRC, Côte d'Ivoire, Burkina Faso and Libya.

Taylor relied heavily on Burkina Faso and Libya as his backers. Côte d'Ivoire actively supported MODEL, whereas Guinea policy backed LURD rebels. It is striking that the US and the United Arab Emirates were providing military assistance to Guinea although Guinea was a close ally to a rebel group under an arms embargo. Another important fact is the US and Guinean membership of the UNSC while mentioned violations were conducted.

As we have seen, UN policy toward Liberia was on a low burner in the first years of the conflict. Sanctions were imposed, but not effectively implemented. Liberia failed to implement thirteen major peace agreements for six years (Adebajo, 2002, p. 66). This can be explained by assessing the complex interactions at the domestic, regional and international level. International action failed to take domestic and regional interests into account in the first years of the conflict. Although national actors profited from the war and illegal trade, ECOWAS lacked political unity and military tools to intervene effectively in the war (*ibid.*). The international community failed to actively support regional efforts to resolve the conflict and did not understand the regional and economic dimension of the conflict for a time. As we have seen almost all neighboring countries were to some extent militarily, logistically or politically involved in the conflict, supporting one or the other of the warring parties. The Sanction Committees and the Reports of the Expert Panels brought to light the complex interactions of subnational and national actors facilitating the breaches of the embargo. The results of the Expert Panels helped raise awareness of false EUCs in the international community. This had a positive effect on the conflicts. The fact that arms sales and trade routes (Kyrgyzstan, Serbia etc.) were revealed led to a greater scrutiny of shipments and final destinations, especially in the case of Guinean EUCs.

In the following section, we will focus on the trade channels that facilitated the circumvention of the arms embargo.

Transport Routes

Weapons transports were conducted through airplanes or ships. In both cases lax aviation and maritime controls favored an easy breach of UN sanctions.

Air transportation is traditionally the preference of sanction busters. Owing to the uncontrolled air surveillance in the region, illegal commodities are flown in or out of sanctioned states. In 2002 only Ghana had up to date radar systems in the region that allowed a limited control of airspace (UN, S/2002/1115). In addition to the lax air surveillance, the so-called *flags of convenience* are helpful for sanctions busters to cover their activities. The fraudulent use of registration of aircraft in different country registers was a much used instrument in the case of Liberia and Sierra Leone. It was apparent that planes registered in the Liberian registry (EL) operating in Africa and from airports in the United Arab Emirates were involved in arms trafficking (UN, S/2000/1195, para. 223). Through different brokering companies, sanction busters cover their business and hire planes with flags of convenience which usually declare false air routes and refuse to contact aviation authorities of the countries they fly over. The respective Panel of

Experts undertook detailed investigations that brought to light the trade channels that facilitated the circumvention of the arms embargo. In the following section, we will focus on these trading channels and instruments used by the sanction busters. UN policy as well as the policies by the member states tends to include the knowledge about sanction busting mechanisms more and more in their policies. Owing to the importance of this fact, we will focus in a detailed manner on the findings of the Panel of Experts to highlight the necessity to counter the busting mechanisms to make sanctions more effective.

A company incorporated in the Liberia registry does not necessarily have its head office located in Liberia. In most cases business is conducted in another country. Neither names nor corporate officers or shareholders need to be filed or listed, nor is a minimum capital required. It is possible to obtain a legal existence within one day. The same phenomenon happens with lax maritime laws that provide owners of ships with discretion. Even the most superficial regulatory oversight is lacking (UN, S/2000/1195, para. 221).

Because of its lax license and tax laws, Liberia has been a flag of convenience for the air cargo industry, especially firms operating on the fringes of legality. Companies incorporated in Liberia can execute their business from all over the world and are provided with maximum discretion (UN, S/2000/1195, para. 221). Because of the fraudulent activities and registrations of Liberia, several countries (e.g. Belgium, South Africa, UK, and Spain) have banned Liberian aircraft from their airspace. There is evidence that Liberian aircraft loaded with weapons have touched down for fuel in Cairo, Nairobi, Entebbe and all over West Africa (UN, S/2000/1195, para. 29). As noted before many planes with illegal cargo either do not contact air authorities or use false documents to cover up their criminal activity.

One well-known supplier to embargoed states is the Russian national Victor Bout. He oversees a complex network of airline companies throughout the world, operating in the United Arab Emirates and using Liberian and other registrations (Swaziland, Brazzaville, Central African Republic) extensively (UN, S/2000/1195, para. 230).

One of Bout's planes registered in several different countries simultaneously was used in July and August 2000 for arms deliveries to Liberia. The cargo included attack helicopters, spare rotors, anti-tank and anti-aircraft systems, missiles, armored vehicles, machine guns and almost a million rounds of ammunition (UN, S/2000/1195, para. 27, 223). The shipments were delivered with the help of Gus Kouwenhoven of the *Royal Timber Company*, which operated in Liberia (*ibid.*).

Several unscheduled suspect cargo flights were identified between October 2002 and February 2003. The Panel of Experts detected a total of 104 flights that did not appear in the Robertsfield International Airport logs. Victor Bout had used the Liberian aviation register extensively and made use of Sharjah Airport, United Arab Emirates, as an "airport of convenience" for planes registered in many other countries (*ibid.*, para. 27). False flight plans and EUCs indicate that customs officials were paid off by sanctions busters (*ibid.*, para. 28). Insufficient controls in the cargo and transport sector make violations of arms embargoes possible. According to the Panel of Experts (UN, 2002), the following deception tactics were used (UN, S/2002/1115, para. 62):

- multiple requests filed to civil aviation authorities in various countries for flights at the same time, all using the same aircraft
- use of various brokering companies to issue these flight requests for the same aircraft
- use of insurance for several operators, all using the same plane at the same time
- use of false flight plans and routings
- refusal of the pilots involved to contact the control towers or aviation authorities of the countries they fly over
- complex corporate structures showing the registration of the aircraft, the insurance for the plane, the insurance for the cargo, the operating agent of the aircraft and the owner of the aircraft all registered in different countries and sometimes represented by third parties
- Flexible and sometimes fraudulent use of call-signs and flight numbers
- Use of forged documents regarding the registration, operating licenses or airworthiness certificates of aircraft used in the trafficking
- Constant search for new flags of convenience for the registration of the aircraft concerned
- Sequences of flights, usually three or four different flights, to deliver the total amount of the ordered weapons
- Use of false declarations on the cargo manifests to misrepresent the cargo

Maritime and Corporate Registry

Similar tactics are used in the maritime transport sector. Lax maritime laws in Liberia provide owners of ships with similar benefits enjoyed by aircraft operations. Liberia has the second largest maritime fleet in the world – having 11,715 ships registered under its open registry (flag of convenience) in

October 2002 (UN, S/2002/1115, para. 174). Funds from the registry provided US$18 million a year for the government. Irregularities in figures suggest off-budget diversion of funds at the source (*ibid.*, para. 176).

Liberia has four ports (Buchanan, Monrovia, Greenville and Harper), whereas Monrovia is the main port. Because of the containerization of cargo, it has become hard to identify the real cargo.

The allegation that logging ships were used to import weapons is difficult to prove (UN, S/2003/498, para. 105). It is assumed that logging companies took part in illegal arms trafficking stating their official cargo was timber although weapons were transported. The government used an elaborate network of foreign bank accounts to hide extra budgetary income and expenditure (*ibid.*, para. 153). Between May 1999 and April 2001 US$7,500,000 were transferred to seven different bank accounts (*ibid.*, para. 153.). Through off-budget spending and payments from revenue that bypassed the central bank, weapon purchases were made. In at least one case, money was transferred to an affiliate of the *Oriental Timber Corporation* (OTC). Through the OTC and other timber companies, the Taylor government violated the arms embargo. In several reports, the Panel examined the timber industry and documented in one case that it had provided funds for weapons (UN, S/2002/1115, para. 189). This knowledge led to the timber embargo resolution 1478 in 2003.

Now that we have seen how the warring parties in Liberia arranged illegal business, we can conclude that the existence of valuable natural resources helped financing the breaches of the embargo. In the Liberian case, natural resources were evidently linked to the finance of sanction busting. After having used the Sierra Leone diamond sector as the financial basis and as a cover for illicit imports of weapons (UN, S/2002/1115) – in many cases mining companies were cover companies to hide illegal arms trafficking – Taylor misused the timber industry to finance and cover illegal arms trade (*ibid.*).

In the Liberian case, it has been shown that the embargo was tightened through further specification of the embargo (including war-related materiel). The investigations held by the Panel of Experts led to a broader understanding of the economic dynamics of the war and smart sanctions were imposed. The further specification of the arms embargo can be seen as a contribution to the end of the war. The detailed investigations by the Expert Panels showed the great amount of revenues that generated the trade with natural resources. First, the diamond embargo aggravated the Liberian war economy. Taylor then depended on the national timber industry for his financial revenues. After these were cut off by the targeted sanctions in 2003, Taylor's financial and military situation worsened and regional and international actors took their chance to pressure Taylor into peace negotiations.

ARMS TRAFFICKING TO SIERRA LEONE

Arms-Exporting Countries

During the 1970s and 1980s, the government of Sierra Leone received military assistance from Nigeria and the UK. In 1991 the government concluded negotiations with China (Berman, 2002, p. 10), who supplied Sierra Leone with 1,000 AK-47-type rifles, machine guns, grenades and other war material (*ibid.*, p. 11). After the RUF rebellion started, Guinea donated several consignments of ammunition and Nigeria donated rifles and ammunition to the government of Sierra Leone (*ibid.*).

When it proved impossible to defeat the RUF militarily between 1992 and 1996, the government first turned to Guinean and Nigerian troops and later engaged a PMC to fight against the rebels. The first contracted PMC were *Gurkha Security Guards Limited* and EO. During the NPRC's rule, weapons were mainly obtained from Romania, Russia and Ukraine through a third party (Berman, 2002, p. 12). Under the Kabbah government arms procurement remained with the same sources, using the same brokers – like the diamond merchant Serge Mueller (*ibid.*). EO as well provided weapons to the government of Sierra Leone. When EO departed in January 1997 (Kabbah had to end the relationship because of the November 1996 peace agreement), it provided about ten tons of arms (*ibid.*).

The accumulated information from UN expert panel reports indicates that the RUF received its weapon shipments mainly from Ukrainian, Bulgarian and Slovakian stocks. The shipments were arranged with the assistance of private companies engaged in the cargo and diamond business as well as states such as Burkina Faso and Liberia. Especially Liberia played a very important role in the RUF's military strategy: Taylor was the connecting person in almost all the arms transfers already having close business contacts with arms producers, brokers and cargo companies.

The set of sanctions was initially imposed on Sierra Leone in 1997 (resolution 1132, October 8, 1997) due to the military coup. In contrast to Liberia, the UNSC decided to amend the sanctions in June 1998 when Kabbah was reinstalled and the set of sanctions targeted only the former NPRC and the RUF (Musah, 2000). Here, it is especially interesting to look at the involvement of the UK, the former colonial power. The British government had made no secret of its determination to restore Kabbah to power and had supported the exiled government from the outset (*ibid.*, p. 101).

China is another UNSC member that reportedly provided weapons to the government of Sierra Leone right after the embargo was amended. In 1999 China provided various small and light weapons. Chinas main motivation was to limit Taylor's influence in the region because of Monrovia's close relationships with Taiwan in the timber sector (Berman, 2002, p. 13).

As in the Liberian case, this chapter will first focus on the arms procurement of the government of Sierra Leone. Second, it will outline how the rebel faction, the RUF, acquired arms.

The Sandline International Affair

The UNSC adopted the British-sponsored resolution including oil, arms and travel sanctions in October 1997. At that time, Britain, the former colonial power, started to make unusually strong gestures in support of the Kabbah government (Cornwell, 1998, p. 77). UK's High Commissioner to Sierra Leone, Peter Penfold, who had followed Kabbah into exile, supported and consulted with the exiled government. Some sources claim that he had introduced *Sandline International,* a PMC, to Kabbah as an option for reinstalling his government in Sierra Leone (*BBCNews*, 1999b: Arms to Africa row re-surfaces). According to *Sandline International* lawyers, the first contact was initiated by Peter Penfold (Cornwell, 1998, p. 76).

When Kabbah, who had previously been working in the UN for some twenty years (*ibid.*, p. 74), was forced into Guinean exile in May 1997, he contracted *Sandline International*, which had close ties to EO and *DiamondWorks,* PMCs already involved in Sierra Leone between 1995 and 1997, to restore his rule. *Sandline International* ignored the sanctions and attempted to ship weapons to Sierra Leone. Through the shipment, *Sandline International* violated the UN arms embargo – with the knowledge of officials in the British government (*ibid.*, p. 73). *Sandline International* arranged a 35-ton shipment of arms to assist ECOMOG in restoring Kabbah's government (Berman, 2002, p. 12). *Sandline International* bought the weapons in Bulgaria and flew them via Lagos to Lungi airport, near Freetown (O'Loughlin, 2000). The British air cargo company, *Sky Air,* flew from Bulgaria to Nigeria.[3] The consignment consisted of about 1,000 Soviet assault rifles, mortars, light-machine guns and ammunition (*ibid.*). With the significant contribution of *Sandline International*, ECOMOG was thought to be able to repel the rebels and the AFRC. The funding was arranged through Rakesh Saxena who had his own diamond operations in Sierra Leone (Cornwell, 1998, p. 76).[4]

The weapons were intended for militias allied to Kabbah, but soon controversy ensued due to the legality of the shipment (O'Loughlin, 2000). Nigerian peacekeepers impounded the weapons and stopped their distribution. On January 27, 1998, first clashes began between ECOMOG and junta troops. By February ECOMOG held the majority of Sierra Leone.

With the publication of the involvement of a British PMC in the violation of an arms embargo, major investigations started in the UK. The Intelligence and Security Committee (ISC) of the Members of Parliament of the UK stated that Penfold had close contact with Kabbah and was well informed about the *Sandline International* contract. Penfold claimed that this information had not been transmitted to the British government due to logistical problems (Evans, 1999). In contrast *Sandline International* insisted that it acted in a legal frame and with full knowledge of the British government (*ibid.*). Then Penfold claimed that he himself had told the Foreign Office about what *Sandline International* was up to (Lockwood, 1999). A scandal broke out about whether the *Trade Office* or the *Foreign Office* had been informed about the breach of the arms embargo.

The involvement of Robin Cook, then UK Foreign Secretary, who had loudly and repeatedly committed the Blair administration to the pursuit of an ethical policy, is especially interesting (Cornwell, 1998, p. 73). When it became official that papers had circulated within the ministries mentioning the shipment, Cook accused his officials of failing to inform him about the shipment of arms by *Sandline International* in February 1998. In the end no responsible party was found. In 2004 Penfold said that he was unaware of the fact that the sanction applied to all parties in Sierra Leone and not just the rebels and that the Foreign Office was aware of the deal (*BBCNews*, 2002).

In conclusion, we can state that a very unsatisfactory investigation was conducted. In November 1997 already a report had been published in the *Globe and Mail*, Toronto, alleging that members of EO, *Sandline International* and mining companies (such as *DiamondWorks*) were engaged in planning a counter-coup in Sierra Leone to restore the Kabbah regime (Cornwell, 1998, p. 78). Three more articles were published in March 1998 before the scandal became public. The investigation started two months later (in May 1998) – at a time when Kabbah already had been successfully reinstalled. Instead of investigating the British breach of the embargo, the UN sanctions on the government of Sierra Leone were amended in 1998, and the UK became Sierra Leone's biggest arms supplier. In 1999 the UK announced its intention to spend £4.5 million to help train and equip the armed forces in Sierra Leone. Another £5 million were pledged to fund the African ECOMOG peacekeeping force (BBCNews, 1999a, UK Politics, UK funds for Sierra Leone military). After the *Sandline International* scandal, the UK government stressed that supplying equipment (boots, uniforms, rifles and ammunition) would not violate the arms embargo because sales to the Sierra Leone government were legal (*ibid.*). According to Robin Cook, £30 million were spent on the former British colony Sierra Leone since the restoration of President Kabbah in 1998 (Lockwood, 1999). The UK provided the following arms supplies in 1999: 132 light machine guns with two millions rounds of ammunition, 7,500 rifles, 800,000 rounds of training ammunition, 24 81-mm mortars with 2,000 rounds of ammunition and various gear including uniform, and 2000 10,000 self-loading rifles, 5 million rounds of ammunition and 4,000 mortars (Berman, 2002, p. 13).

The British involvement has to be seen in a broader context than just the involvement of arms exporting or allied countries. In this case, a UNSC permanent member was involved in launching a resolution on sanctions in Sierra Leone, while being involved in supporting other instruments of reinstalling the legitimate government. In addition, the involvement of the British PMC *Sandline International* in a breach of UNSC sanctions with the knowledge of (parts of) the British government raises questions on the consistency of UN sanctions. British policy toward Sierra Leone aimed at the reinstallation of the Kabbah government. But the applied strategies differed in the bilateral and multilateral dimension.

Allies of RUF and AFRC

Having no access to the sea, the RUF was dependent on arms imports by land or by air. Therefore, regional neighbors were vital for the RUF's supply chain. During the civil war in Sierra Leone, the RUF had established external supply lines for the provision of military equipment, taking advantage of neighboring countries and existing infrastructure. The weapons shipped into the RUF territory were transshipped to at least two other countries between the point of origin and the RUF (UN, S/2000/1195, para. 202). Especially Burkina Faso and Liberia were involved in arms shipments to Sierra Leone. Liberia was therefore responsible for the breach of its own arms embargo as well as for the arms embargo against Sierra Leone. This fact led to the imposition of a set of new sanctions on Liberia in 2001. In almost all cases, weapons first arrived in Liberia before getting transshipped to the RUF. In other cases arms deliveries to Sierra Leone are reported to have been directly flown in from Burkina Faso. Additionally, Libya and Côte d'Ivoire functioned as weapons intermediaries.

The Liberian Connection

Typically, arms smuggling from a supplying country to the RUF includes several stopover and cross-border shipments to obscure the illegal activity. In many cases private arms dealers participated. In the early years of the Liberian insurgency, Taylor's military assistance to the RUF was limited (Berman, 2002, p. 4). Liberia had a limited number of aircraft (two small Mi-2 light helicopters acquired from Libya), so Taylor mostly used private aircraft companies in the region to transship weapons to the RUF (*ibid.*). In exchange for weapons, Taylor was paid with diamonds and became dependent on Sierra Leone diamond revenues. Taylor and private businessmen had developed a well-organized sanction-busting apparatus that included international crime networks. For Taylor, the Sierra Leone conflict became a lucrative business. There are various incidents that prove Liberia's involvement in arms trafficking with Sierra Leone. Different sources claim that in October 1999 sixty 122-mm rockets for the BM-21 were transported from Liberia to Sierra Leone under the guise of relief materiel (HRW, 2000). In addition to war related materiel, Taylor also provided training to the RUF. In July 2000, the RUF troops under the command of Sam Bockarie were trained and heavily armed with surface-to-surface missiles, assault rifles and anti-tank weapons from Liberia (Farah, 2000). Taylor is believed to have provided large quantities of arms, fuel, ammunition, food and medicines throughout the years of civil war. In almost all cases, the last transit point before reaching Sierra Leone had been Liberia. The weapons reached Liberia either by air or by sea using *flags of convenience*.

The Taylor arms-trafficking network was also applied in Sierra Leone. A key individual was a Lebanese businessman named Talal El-Ndine. He connected Monrovia with businessmen and possible investors, negotiating payments for brokers, shippers and aircraft staff, mostly Russian or Ukrainian nationals (UN, S/2000/1195, para. 214). Gus Kouwenhoven, a Dutch national well known in the arms-trafficking scene, arranged the logistical aspects of many arms deals and transfers from Monrovia to Sierra Leone (UN, S/2000/1195, para. 215). Simon Rosenblum, an Israeli businessman with interests in the timber industry in Liberia, provided trucks for arms shipments to Sierra Leone (UN, S/2000/1195, para. 216).

The RUF is reported to also have obtained weapons from Bulgaria and Slovakia (Berman, 2002, p. 7). Via Gambia and Liberia, Bulgarian and Slovakian arms shipments got transported to Sierra Leone in January 1999 (*ibid.*). UK-based and Belgian-owned airlines carried out the deal, while in July 1999 a Dakar-based Aviation Company delivered 68 tons of weapons deals originating Bulgaria (*ibid.*).

Transshipments via Burkina Faso

Most of the weapons ending up in Sierra Leone and Liberia originated from Eastern Europe and in many cases were transshipped via Burkina Faso (*ibid.*, p. 6). In many cases arms were flown in via Ouagadougou to Robertsfield (Liberia) from where arms were transported to the RUF. Even after the Lomé agreement, it was fairly easy to transport arms across the Liberia-Sierra Leone border without detection (HRW, 2000). The Burkinabé General Ibrahim Bah handled much of the financial, diamond and weapons transactions between Liberia, the RUF and Burkina Faso (*ibid.*).

Burkina Faso officially bought Ukrainian weapons and was accused by one ECOMOG commander in Sierra Leone of shipping arms to the RUF (HRW, 2000). This accusation referred to a shipment dated March 14, 1999. A Ukrainian-registered cargo plane had delivered 68 tons of weapons and ammunition to the Burkinabé capital Ouagadougou. From Ouagadougou, the cargo was transported to Liberia by a smaller aircraft and then onward by land to the RUF (*ibid.*). In June 1999 the Ukrainian government stated that it had sold the weapons to the government of Burkina Faso referring to an EUC stating Burkina Faso as "the final consumer" (*ibid.*). The Gibraltar-based Chartered Engineering and Technical Company, Ltd. had bought the weapons in Ukraine on behalf of the Burkinabé government. The same company had then contracted the British company *Air Foyle*, a trade agent of Ukrainian air carrier *Antonov Design Bureau,* a division of the Ukrainian aircraft giant *Antonov*, to fly the cargo to Burkina Faso (Walsh, 2001). The further shipment was then observed to have been carried by smaller planes to Liberia and Sierra Leone (*ibid.*).

Other External Sources to RUF and AFRC

Libya was an important ally and donor of military assistance, providing arms, logistical support and training (Berman, 2002, p. 6). The transit country for shipments from Libya to Sierra Leone was either Liberia or Burkina Faso.

Côte d'Ivoire under President Félix Houphouöt-Boigny provided safe passage through its territory for the transportation of war materiel. His successors are believed to have followed his example. Côte d'Ivoire was sympathetic to Taylor's government and therefore indirectly to the RUF. In the early 1990s, Côte d'Ivoire provided training to Liberian rebels and to the RUF (UN, S/2000/1195, para. 195).

Guinea is said to have delivered arms to Sierra Leone in a small-scale trade (Berman, 2002, p. 7). Officially policy plays down allegations of supporting the RUF with weapons. The AFRC received arms from the traditional backers of the RUF, Liberia and Burkina Faso. (*ibid.*, pp. 12–13).

Disarming – Seizure from ECOMOG/UNAMSIL

Arms were not only obtained by illegal trade. The RUF was able to get large quantities of weaponry from the government forces (*ibid.*, p. 8). Sources claim that within the Sierra Leone Army soldiers sold weapons and ammunition to rebels (UN, S/2000/1195, para. 1779). Another source of war-related materiel was seizures from ECOMOG and UNAMSIL troops. Instead of disarming after the Lomé agreement, the RUF rebels obtained further weapons through these seizures. Seizures of weapons in combat cannot be put under the label of a *breach of the arms embargo*. But in many cases, there is a strong indication of bribery.

In December 1998, the RUF captured all ECOMOG weapons stationed at Kono where the West African force had stationed most of its materiel (Musah, 2000, p. 109). On other occasions, the RUF rebels disarmed troops after ambushes and in some cases even bought weapons from ECOMOG troops (Berman, 2002, p. 8). In another case the RUF stole 500 automatic rifles, six heavy artillery pieces, anti-aircraft guns, three armored vehicles and five trucks from Kenyan and Guinean "Blue Helmets" (HRW, 2000). In an incident in May 2000, a Zambian peace-keeping battalion was detained by the RUF, and it is widely believed that the battalion lost some 500 AK-47 rifles, a few dozen machine guns, assorted mortars, and several tons of small arms ammunition (Berman, 2002, p. 9). Some sources also claim that it is very likely that Guinean troops had sold the materiel to the rebels (*ibid.*). This would signify that UN peacekeepers were actively involved in the breach of the sanctions, while their mandate was to assure the contrary. The UN was therefore involved in activities that weakened the sanction regime and the peace process.

Private Brokers

One key individual is the aforementioned Lebanese businessman Talal El-Ndine (UN, S/2000/1195, para. 23). El-Ndine paid Liberian fighters active in Sierra Leone to bring him diamonds out of Sierra Leone. El-Ndine also hired aircraft staff to conduct the smuggling. Another businessman, Victor Bout, a well-known supplier of war materiel, was involved in several countries and violation if international embargoes (Angola, DRC, Liberia, Sierra Leone). He oversees a complex network of over 50 planes and cargo charter companies involved in smuggling and shipping illicit cargo. He was later assisting the US army logistically in Iraq (Rémy, 2004). As in Liberia, private actors were able to ship large quantities of weapons to the region through false or fraudulently used EUC and the so-called *flags of convenience*. In many cases their assistance in breaching the embargoes is well known, however, international opposition was lacking. In the eyes of the authors, the case of Victor Bout raises many questions on the consistency of UN embargoes. As we have seen, he was never held responsible for his actions although being an important person of international arms-brokering network.

EFFECTIVENESS OF THE ARMS EMBARGOES

As we have seen, the arms embargoes in Liberia and Sierra Leone were undermined by several actors. Two structural problems limited the effectiveness of the embargoes. First, in both cases a lack of monitoring and implementation of the embargo in the region reduced the embargo to a symbol. Only when the ineffectiveness became obvious as a result of a regionalization of the conflict, the UNSC responded with additional sanctions. The additional sanctions were also a result of the Panel of Expert's investigations installed by the UNSC.

Second, the UNSC did not integrate the special regional and economic dynamics into its strategy. In Liberia and Sierra Leone, a special conflict dynamic (called war economy) had emerged. The control and trade of valuable resources enabled individuals and rebel groups to circumvent the embargoes – either through arms-for-resources deals or through plowing back profits of natural resources into the arms trade.

The international community only slowly understood this dynamic and for a long time failed to take into account the regional aspect of both conflicts: The interconnections between rebel leaders, their common connections, goals, trade and smuggling efforts were not taken into consideration until the imposition of secondary sanctions. With the imposition of secondary sanctions, the main loopholes of the sanctions were targeted and diminished the possibilities and opportunities to conduct arms deals and profit from these.

How did it remain possible for the actors to acquire weaponry? The analysis will focus on three questions:

- What enforcement capabilities did the respective actors have to execute/carry out/strengthen the sanction regime?
- Were the respective actors willing to enforce the sanctions properly?
- What loopholes existed that facilitated breaches?

Sanction Enforcement Capabilities and the Willingness of Actors

Sanctions are complex. They involve a wide range of stakeholders including the UN, international and regional organizations, states, companies, and entrepreneurs, non-governmental organizations as well as individual persons (Dhanapala, 2000, p. 41). The Expert Panels on Liberia and Sierra Leone have given much attention to individual arms traffickers and to the transport networks they used to illegally deliver weapons to abusive end-users (HRW, 2001, p. 2). These illegal activities intersect with arms-trading policies and practices of governments. Arms dealers are able to camouflage their operations because of lax controls by governments that facilitate arms exports as well as smuggling through their territory. It therefore does not suffice to analyze sanction busting apparatus and violation instruments (EUC, flags of convenience) that primarily involve private entrepreneurs. These private actors are the responsible parties for the illegal transactions yet are dependent on state actors. In many cases, the state offers opportunities through weak controls, not enforcing regulations on their territory or through state officials being themselves involved in illegal activities (like in Liberia, Burkina Faso). Non-state actors take advantage of existing loopholes in national and international regulations or weak state institutions. So if a state is not capable of enforcing justice and law within its territory, it will not be able to hinder actors who violate sanctions. The enforcement capability is one very important variable and must be analyzed on a regional and an international level. As we have seen, especially neighboring countries play a major role in securing, jeopardize or destabilize a sanction regime.

In the West African cases, it must be considered that the geographical conditions along the border of Sierra Leone and Liberia are such that full governmental control is virtually impossible given the available resources in the region (UN, S/1998/1236, para. 23). When the UNSC imposed sanctions on Liberia, the conflict was acute and there was no possibility to secure the border area to stop incoming arms-even less so when the Sierra Leone conflict started. So one predominant prerequisite, local enforcement capabilities, was not given. In both cases, the UNSC did not take immediate action to enforce the sanction regime on the international level. Instead it was left up to regional forces to resolve the conflict. However, ECOWAS did not possess the physical and financial assets necessary for securing the border area. The UN would have been capable to invest more energy to ensure a strict implementation of the sanctions regime, but showed little willingness to do so in both conflicts.

The willingness of actors to implement sanctions is a second very important variable when analyzing the effectiveness of sanctions. In the cases of Liberia and Sierra Leone, a wide range of national and international actors were involved in the sanction process, and it is necessary to focus on their respective interests in the conflicts. In the Liberian case, the international community and especially the US was interested in a quick end of the conflict. The Liberian conflict caused severe instability and insecurity in the region, and a large range of states were interested in ending Taylor's influence in the region. In the Sierra Leone case, the UK, as the former colonial power, took the initiative and played a predominant part in the sanction process. ECOWAS in both cases was mandated to execute the sanction regime. ECOWAS (with Nigeria as the political leader) was willing to carry out the international mandate because it coincided with regional and national (Nigerian) interests. However, in both cases ECOWAS was not fully capable to enforce the arms embargo properly.

What Went Wrong?

The UN as an international actor intervened late in both conflicts and did not follow through with an effective sanction process until the late 1990s. A clear definition of the common goal, the enforcement instruments and financial resources to enforce them are vital requisites for an effective imposition of sanctions. In both cases the arms embargo initially lacked a clearly defined strategy and remained primarily symbolic. The UN condemned the violent situation in both cases and imposed sanctions on

Liberia (1992) and Sierra Leone (1997) arguing that the conflicts were a threat to international peace and security in the region. Further UN action was inconsistent. The primary aim of the embargoes was to stop the influx of arms and halt a deterioration of the violent conflicts. The overall aim was to stabilize the region. However, in both cases the UNSC failed to take into account the regional and the economic dimension of the conflicts. An initial comprehensive strategy was lacking.

The UN imposed the sanctions without much consideration toward their enforcement, making them a regional responsibility overseen by ECOWAS. ECOMOG troops initially mandated in 1990 to establish peace in Liberia were subsequently given the additional task of intervening in the Sierra Leone conflict (Berman, 2002, p. 1). Regarding ECOWAS willingness, it must be stressed that ECOWAS member states had different individual interests in the conflict, often violating the sanctions themselves. Especially Nigeria played an important role in both conflicts as Nigerian troops represented the largest contingent within ECOMOG. In the case of Nigeria, national interests concerning an establishment of Nigeria's undisputed hegemony in West Africa have to be taken into account (Musah, 2000, p. 103). So the willingness to deal with the conflict by regional actors was not primarily influenced by an urge to ensure stability but also by the satisfaction of personal interests.[5] In the Liberian conflict, ECOMOG troops (mainly Nigerian contingents) had already garnered a rather bad reputation being accused of robbery and smuggling of cars, electronic goods and other material goods: Liberians referred to ECOMOG as Every Car or Moving Object Gone (Ellis, 1999). ECOWAS troops were therefore not seen as neutral peacekeepers but as a party to the conflict. ECOMOG soldiers and officials themselves took part in the sanction violating apparatus by selling arms to the warring parties (*ibid.*). The lack of financial means and international observers to verify a proper implementation of the sanctions regime led to a steady violation of the regime by the respective actors.

In March 1997 Nigeria had signed a defense pact with Kabbah's government and consequently intervened in Sierra Leone with 900 Nigerian troops when the military took power in the May 1997 coup. Nigeria acted unilaterally at first, though claiming an ECOWAS sanction, which was eventually forthcoming. Regional actors were not willed or capable to enforce the UN embargo, although they played a part in bringing about the ECOWAS moratorium. Member states such as Guinea, Côte d'Ivoire and Nigeria took an active part in the violation of the regional initiative of the PCASED. In 2002 the Panel of Experts (Liberia) suggested that the ECOWAS moratorium should be more effectively used to monitor and combat illicit trafficking and sanction busting, hinting that the moratorium had little success (UN, S/2002/1115, para. 8).

This shows the UN's awareness of the fact that regional actors did not enforce the regional initiative properly to combat illegal arms trade. At the same time the UN stressed the necessity that ECOWAS enforce an international arms embargo. Here it needs to be considered that the UN failed to effectively enforce its own sanction in Liberia and Sierra Leone while expecting such enforcement by the regional actors. The UN formally delegated the responsibility to monitor the arms embargo to ECOWAS. After noting the limited capacity of the regional forces to halt the illegal influx of arms, UN peacekeeping forces began taking over responsibility for the Sierra Leone mission in December 1999 (HRW, 2000). However, here too a mandate to actually enforce the international arms embargo against the rebels was missing. The UN peacekeepers' mandate did not include border monitoring or other related measures (*ibid.*). In the case of Liberia, monitoring responsibility was left to ECOWAS, although its capabilities in this respect were limited and it urged the UN to improve enforcing measures for the embargo it had imposed (*ibid.*).

Secondary Sanctions - Smart Sanctions?

The imposition of secondary sanctions on the governments that have breached embargoes was pursued in the case of Liberia. It was subjected to a tighter arms embargo as well as a travel ban, diamond sanctions and later timber sanctions, in response to its support for rebels in Sierra Leone, a fact that violated the UN embargo. In Sierra Leone, various smart sanctions and a traditional arms embargo were imposed from the beginning. Here the UN began to understand the special economic dimensions of the conflict, realizing that the Sierra Leone diamond revenue helped Sierra Leone and Liberian actors to finance their illegal arms trade. Special regional and economic aspects of the conflict and the arms trade were incorporated in the UN strategy to recreate peace and stability.

A certification regime for diamonds that covered the entire region was developed with the help of ECOWAS and succeeded in curbing the flow of illicit diamonds out of Sierra Leone. This measure limited the financial revenues available for further illegal arms shipments. Nevertheless, the RUF was still able to mine diamonds illegally (UN, S/2002/1115, para. 50), however, on a smaller scale.

Once the UN took the specific regional and economic factors into account and incorporated them into its secondary sanctions, an important step was made to understand the special dynamics of the civil wars in Liberia and Sierra Leone. However, the implementation and monitoring of the newly elaborated instruments still had shortcomings.

Allies of Sanction Busters

The Liberian embargo applied to the Liberian government as well as to the rebel forces in the country. Still, many private actors as well as states made breaches possible. The Burkinabé president was accused by the Panel of Experts of directly facilitating Taylor's arms-for-diamonds trade. In contrast, Guinea was involved in assisting the Liberian rebels. The government of Guinea violated the UN arms embargo on Liberia while serving as a member of the UNSC. It is proven, that Guinea supplied weapons that Liberian rebels (LURD) used to commit atrocities (HRW, 2003b). When LURD forces ran out of ammunition – possibly because of the sanctions - and retreated in June 2003, the rebels only renewed the offensive in July after having received fresh supplies via Guinea (*ibid.*). The Guinean government had imported the munitions from Iran. Although being member of the ECOWAS, Guinea did not adhere to the moratorium from 1998 on the import or transfer of small and light weapons. Furthermore, the US publicly backed Guinea with military assistance even though Guinea had been involved in the neighboring conflict and had breached an international mandatory arms embargo. Officially it has been known for a long time (since 1999) that Guinea facilitated the illicit supply of arms to the LURD (HRW, 2003b, p. 15). HRW even alleged that in April 2003, LURD received weapons deliveries from Guinean peacekeepers involved in the UNAMSIL peacekeeping operation in Sierra Leone (*ibid.*). Taylor also accused the US of being part of a conspiracy (Mbakwe, 2003, p. 21) that caused the war through support for the LURD rebels (HRW, 2003b, p. 27).

Allies of sanction busters were private and state actors. But official investigations through the Expert Panels focused mainly on private actors. The involvement of states, as has been described, needs to be considered as well.

Great Britain had a strong influence on the conflict in Sierra Leone. The British Government had initiated the sanction process as resolution 1132 was mainly British sponsored. Sir Franklin Berman, chief legal advisor to the ministry of Foreign Affairs, drafted large parts of resolution 1132 that, among other things, prohibited the supply of arms to Sierra Leone (Cornwell, 1998, p. 79). Berman's staff also drafted the order in the Council, giving it effect in British law. The original interpretation was that the arms embargo applied equally to all Sierra Leone parties that would mean that *Sandline International* had acted in breach of the embargo (*ibid.*). UN lawyers changed their minds by the end of May 1998 arguing that the resolution aimed at restoring the elected government and that *Sandline International* and ECOMOG (who's intervention was strongly encouraged by UN members) must therefore enjoy an implied partial exemption from the embargo (*ibid.*). This interpretation supported internal British government efforts to excuse its knowledge of the breach by the British PMC and took pressure off of the British government. This new definition of the embargo's general aim makes a final evaluation difficult. Great Britain, as the initiator, encouraged and drafted a main part of the resolution, incorporating it into national law, but then did not take action when a national company acted in breach of the sanction. With *Sandline International*'s help, the restoration of a legally elected government was achieved, however, in breach of international and national law. Arms embargoes are international law and have to be applied universally by every state. Breaches and violations of such embargoes must then equally be confronted and punished universally. For the consistency of a UN arms embargo, it is of great importance that exemptions are well considered and explicitly included in the resolution.

SUMMARY

This chapter has shown that political will and enforcement capabilities of those imposing the sanctions in the two conflicts were initially very weak. In both cases the UNSC acted late. As described, the Sierra Leone crisis might have been prevented or at least contained by earlier action (such as greater border controls enforcement). The international community for a long time failed to take action against suppliers and private or state sanction busters. The cases show that it does not suffice to impose sanctions if there are no implementation and enforcement mechanisms. When enforcement became stronger, and particularly when additional sanctions began to limit the financial means of conflict parties, arms logistics became a problem for at least some of them. In the end, the arms embargoes, as part of larger sanction packages, helped to bring the conflicts to an end.

The cases show that enforcement has to work on a sub-national, national and supranational level. Internationally standardized EUCs need to be developed that are more transparent (UN, S/2002/1115, para. 102). The main problem with EUCs is that the brokers who are mainly registered in tax havens or badly regulated countries can remain anonymous (UN, S/2002/1115, p. 24, Box). The acceptance of EUCs by arms-exporting countries without prior questioning is a severe problem. There is an urgent need to check the authenticity of these certificates. Furthermore, better communication with countries that import arms is required (*ibid.*). The Panel of Experts (UN, 2002, p. 24) stated in 2002 that

> The ease with which end-user-certificates can be forged or obtained proved to be a vital weakness in the observance of United Nation arms embargoes. The lack of standardized, universally recognizable end-user certificates makes it easy for illicit arms brokers to forge them and apply for arms export licenses in producer countries.

Another major problem with the arms embargoes against the two countries that only slowly tackled was the bad air surveillance and lax controls in the cargo business. It has been described how private arms dealers use flags of convenience to circumvent controls and embargoes. Here, the international community has to take action and develop controls in the international transport sector as well as in international law.

Sufficient manpower or the general willingness to commit troops is another prerequisite for an effective sanction regime. Only a small UN Observer Mission in Sierra Leone (UNOMSIL) received a mandate in July 1998 to serve alongside the ECOMOG troops. Finally, in October 1999, UNSC decided to replace the observer mission with a peacekeeping force (UN Mission in Sierra Leone). In Liberia the UN reacted in early March 1994, five years after the civil war erupted, and deployed a UN observer mission (UNOMIL) while hostilities continued. Arms embargo enforcement would likely increase if it became a key task for UN peacekeeping operations.

The strategy of the UN to combine "traditional" arms embargoes with additional sanctions has had major impacts on the war economies in Liberia and Sierra Leone. Taylor, the RUF and other profiteers from the smuggling activities were cut off from their revenues that financed their war activities. The major incentives for war were therefore eliminated by the UNSC. This highlights the predominant importance of the combination of arms embargoes with secondary sanctions as a peace-rendering instrument for the UN. In general, it can be stated that the UN failed to influence the wars in Liberia and Sierra Leone in the early 1990s. However, the peace agreements in Liberia (2003) and Sierra Leone (1999) need to be seen as a consequence of the stronger influence of the UNSC through an extensive sanction process. The lack of revenues pressured the warring parties into peace negotiations. The fact remains that strong implementation and monitoring mechanisms are the core requirements for an effective handling/execution of a sanctions regime.

NOTES

1. Liberia has a substantial forest cover: about 40 percent of land area is forest (UN, S/2003/779, para. 31).

2. In resolution 1446, December 4, 2002 the SC lifted the embargo on official Sierra Leone diamond exports after a Certificate of Origin regime had been developed.

3. The UK private companies were allowed to arrange arms deals where both the supplier and purchaser remained outside the UK (http://www.amnesty.org.uk/news/mag/jul98/killing.html). No UK controls apply if the equipment remains outside the UK (*ibid.*).

4. His motivation was to restore peace through his funding of Sandline and being able to protect and extend his diamond interests (Cornwell, 1998, p. 76).

5. For further information and details about Nigeria's interests and strategies in West Africa, see Musah: 103–104.

REFERENCES

Adebajo, A. (2002). *Building peace in West Africa. Liberia, Sierra Leone and Guinea Bissau.* International Peace Academy Occasional Paper Series, Boulder: Lynne Rienner.

BBCNews. (1999a). *UK politics, UK funds for Sierra Leone military,* March 31, 1999.

BBCNews. (1999b). *Arms to Africa row re-surfaces,* May 13, 1999.

BBCNews. (2002). *Hero's welcome for ex-ambassador,* February 8, 2002.

Berman, E. G. (2002). Re-armament in Sierra Leone: One year after the Lomé Peace Agreement, Small Arms Survey, Occasional Paper No. 1.

Cornwell, R. (1998). Sierra Leone: RUF diamonds? *African Security Review,* 7(4) Available at http://www.iss.co.za/pubs/asr/7No4/Contents.html

Cortright, D., Lopez, G.A. with Gerber, L. (2002). *Sanctions sans commitment: An assessment of UN arms embargoes,* Project Ploughshares, Working Paper 02/2.

Dhanapala, J. (2000). Final expert seminar on smart sanctions. The next step: Arms embargoes and travel sanctions. "Keynote Address." In: Brzoska, M. (ed.), *Smart sanctions: The next steps. The debate on arms embargoes and travel sanctions within the 'Bonn-Berlin Process'.* Baden-Baden: Nomos.

Ellis, S. (1999). *The mask of anarchy. The destruction of Liberia and the religious dimension of an African Civil War,* London: Hurst.

Evans, M. (1999). Foreign office 'farce' over Sierra Leone. *The Times,* May 14.

Farah, D. (2000). Liberia reportedly arming guerillas. *The Washington Post,* June 18.

HRW. (2000a). *Neglected arms embargo on Sierra Leone rebels*, Briefing Paper, New York, May 15. Available at www.hrw.org

HRW. (2000). *Burkina Faso arms inquiry urged. Weapons transferred illegally to rebels in Sierra Leone, Angola*, March 30. Available at www.hrw.org

HRW. (2001). *No questions asked: The Eastern Europe arms pipeline to Liberia*, Human Rights Watch Briefing Paper, November 15. Available at www.hrw.org

HRW. (2002). *Liberian refugees in Guinea: Refoulement, militarization of camps, and other protection concerns*, November. Available at www.hrw.org

HRW. (2003a). *Liberia: Where the arms come from*, by Peter Takirambudde, published in the International Herald Tribune. Available at www.hrw.org

HRW. (2003b): *The regional crisis and Human Rights abuses in West Africa*. A briefing paper to the U.N. Security Council, June 20. Available at www.hrw.org

Kopp, P. (1999). Embargo und wirtschaftliche Kriminalisierung. In: Jean, F. & Rufin, J.-C. (Eds), *Ökonomie der Bürgerkriege*. Hamburg: Hamburger Edition.

Lockwood, C. (1999). Britain discovers the high price of its role in a country at war. *The Telegraph*, August 7. Available at http://www.telegraph.co.uk/htmlContent.jhtml?html = /archive/1999/08/08/wsie208.html

Malan, M. (2003a). Introduction. In: M. Malan, S. Meek, T. Thusi, J. Ginifer & P. Coker (Eds), *Sierra Leone: Building the road to recovery*. Pretoria, South Africa: Institute for Strategic Studies.

Malan, M. (2003b). UNAMSIL after elections. In: M. Malan, S. Meek, T. Thusi, J. Ginifer & P. Coker (Eds), *Sierra Leone. Building the road to recovery*. Pretoria, South Africa: Institute for Strategic Studies.

Mbakwe, T. (2003). Liberia. The untold story. *New African*, August/September.

Musah, A. F. (2000). A country under siege: State decay and corporate military intervention in Sierra Leone. In: A. F. Musah & K. Fayemi (Eds), *Mercenaries: An African security dilemma* (pp. 76–116). London: Pluto Press.

O'Loughlin, E. (2000). Sandline international scandal arms shipment reaches forces. *Independent*, May 22.

Peter, A. (2005). Criminalizing consequences of sanctions. *International Studies Quarterly*, 49(2), 335–360.

Pratt, D. (1999). *Sierra Leone: The forgotten crisis*, Report to the Minister of Foreign Affairs, the Honourable Lloyd Axworthy, P.C., M.P. from David Pratt, M.P., Nepean-Carleton, Special Envoy to Sierra Leone, April 23, 1999. Available at http://www.sierra-leone.org/pratt042399.html

Pugh, M., & Cooper, N. with Goodhand, J. (2004). *War economies in a regional context. Challenges and transformation*. A Project of the International Peace Academy, IPA. Boulder: Lynne Rienner.

Rémy, J.-P. (2004). The trafficker viktor bout lands US aid for services rendered in Iraq. *Le Monde*, May 18.

UN. (1998). (S/1998/1236). *Report of the Security Council Committee Established Pursuant to Resolution 1132 (1997) Concerning Sierra Leone*, United Nations, New York.

UN. (2000). (S/2000/1195). Report of the Panel of Experts appointed pursuant to paragraph 19 of SC resolution 1306 (2000) in relation to Sierra Leone; United Nations, New York.

UN. (2002). (S/2002/1115). Report of the Panel of Experts appointed pursuant to Security Council resolution 1408 (2002), paragraph 16, concerning Liberia, United Nations, New York.

UN. (2003). (S/2003/498). Report of the Panel of Experts appointed pursuant to paragraph 4 of
    SC resolution 1458 (2003) concerning Liberia, United Nations, New York.
UN. (2003). (S/2003/779). Report of the Panel of Experts appointed pursuant to paragraph 25
    of SC resolution 1478 (2003) concerning Liberia, United Nations, New York.
UN. (2004). (S/2004/396). UN Report of the Panel of Experts appointed pursuant to paragraph
    22 of SC resolution 1521 (2004) concerning Liberia, United Nations, New York.
United Nations Sanctions Secretariat, Department of Political Affairs. (2000). *The experience of
    the UN in administering arms embargoes and travel sanctions*, Informal background
    paper. Available to http://www.un.org/sc/committees/sanctions/background.pdf
Walsh, D. (2001). Ex-Citijet link to weapons. *Sunday Business Post*, January 14.

CHAPTER 6

FROM FAILURE TO SUCCESS: THE IMPACT OF SANCTIONS ON ANGOLA'S CIVIL WAR

Wolf-Christian Paes

Angola's civil war presents a fascinating case study of the effectiveness of a sanctions regime against a non-state actor. The target of the sanctions, the *União Nacional para a Independência Total de Angola* (Union for the Total Independence of Angola – UNITA), was locked in armed conflict with the government in Luanda (and its colonial predecessor) for the better part of four decades. This war came to a sudden end in March 2002, following the death of UNITA leader Jonas Savimbi in battle and the decision of the UNITA leadership to return to the negotiating table. Since then, UNITA's armed forces have been demobilized, and the former insurgent movement is searching for a new political role. Meanwhile, the Angolan government has prided itself on succeeding where a string of United Nations (UN) peacekeeping missions in the 1990s failed – bringing to an end one of Africa's longest and most bloody conflicts.

On previous occasions – in 1992 and 1994–1998 – international intervention led to intervals of relative peace followed by a return to the battlefield. But by the end of 2002, the movement's military muscle had been thoroughly destroyed, in large part due to the post-war disarmament, demobilization, and re-integration (DD&R) process (Porto & Parsons, 2003; Porto, Alden, & Parsons, 2007). While some UNITA weapons remain

Putting Teeth in the Tiger: Improving the Effectiveness of Arms Embargoes
Contributions to Conflict Management, Peace Economics and Development, Volume 10, 137–162
ISSN: 1572-8323/doi:10.1108/S1572-8323(2009)0000010010

at large, most likely hidden in caches in the countryside, the organization's remaining leadership has been incorporated into the country's political oligarchy, while the common soldiers have either returned to civilian life or been integrated into the national army. This development caught most international observers by surprise. Many of them had argued, even in late 2000, that UNITA would keep on fighting, buoyed by receipts from the sale of conflict diamonds, and motivated by the implicit complicity of government forces and rebels in using the war as a pretext for the continued looting of Angola's vast mineral resources (Cortright & Lopez, 2000; de Jonge Oudraat, 2000; Global Witness, 1998).

As this chapter illustrates, UNITA's real military strength was exaggerated by most international observers, who conceded that the movement was losing ground to government troops, while at the same time claiming that it would be able to destabilize Angola's periphery for years to come (Hodges, 2001; Human Rights Watch, 1999; Cornwell & Potgieter, 1999). The end of Angola's civil war has also forced the international community to re-evaluate the impact of the comprehensive sanctions adopted by the United Nations Security Council (UNSC) from 1993 onward. They were rated a "failure" by international analysts as late as 2000 (Cortright & Lopez, 2000; Human Rights Watch, 1999), more recent accounts (Cortright & Lopez, 2002; Kevlihan, 2003; Mills & Sidiropoulos, 2004) are more cautious in their judgment. New information on UNITA's arsenal, which has become available during the course of the disarmament process, has allowed us to revisit the question of these embargoes effectiveness.

UNITA's return to the negotiating table and subsequent demobilization seem at first glance to be the result of Savimbi's death and the successes of the *Forças Armadas Angolanas* (Angolan Armed Forces – FAA) on the battlefield. Upon closer examination, it becomes clear that the sanctions regime put in place by the UNSC has played an important role in contributing to UNITA's loss of the arms race against the government. To procure weapons abroad, the FAA could tap into the revenue from Angola's significant oil exports, estimated at more than US $3 billion per year at the end of the last decade. UNITA, conversely, found it increasingly difficult to procure sufficient amounts of food, ammunition, and fuel to keep its forces operational. This chapter will argue that this was the result of a number of interrelated developments in Southern African politics, including the increasing isolation of the movement from former international backers such as South Africa and the United States of America; the loss of control over important diamond fields in 1998; the pressure applied by Angola's government on regional governments suspected of assisting UNITA; and, last but not least, the impact of the UNSC sanctions regime, which led to the end of the civil war. While international sanctions alone would have been unlikely to force UNITA back to the negotiations, they did play an important role in tipping the scales of the military stalemate between UNITA and the FAA in favor of the government.

THE ORIGINS OF THE CONFLICT

The drama of Angola's recent history must be seen against the backdrop of political developments in Southern Africa, which had a direct impact on the turn of events in the civil war. During the 1960s and 1970s, the conflict was widely regarded as a prominent example of a liberation struggle against the Portuguese colonial regime. In contrast, the bitter battle in the 1980s and early 1990s between UNITA and the *Movimento Popular de Libertação de Angola* (Popular Movement for the Liberation of Angola – MPLA), the party which has dominated the government in Luanda since independence, was seen as a proxy war between the superpowers over the control of a key African state. During the final phase of the conflict, from the mid-1990s to early 2002, Angola was viewed as a quintessential resource conflict, a power play over access to valuable commodities such as diamonds and crude oil (Global Witness, 1998; Global Witness, 1999). All these categorizations – which reflect the dominant themes in conflict analyses of their time – fall somewhat short of grasping the complex reality of the Angolan conflict. Nevertheless, the shifting position of much of the industrialized world – particularly of the United States at the end of the Cold War – goes a long way toward explaining how the FAA managed, during the mid-1990s, to turn a decade-long military stalemate on the battlefield into a decisive victory. Looking at the geo-strategic picture also helps to explain why it took the comprehensive sanctions regime against UNITA so long to become effective in cutting the supply lines for arms, ammunition, and fuel.

Both UNITA and MPLA can trace back their origins to the final decades of Portuguese colonial rule. During this period, three distinct streams of Black Nationalism emerged in Angola (Cornwell, 1999). First, among the small mestiço elite in the urban centers on the coast in the early 1950s, the communist stream emerged and ultimately led to the establishment of the MPLA in 1956. In 1959, following repression by the Portuguese secret police, the MPLA went underground. The armed struggle started with an uprising – which was quickly crushed – in Luanda in February 1961. In the wake of this military defeat, the MPLA moved its military operations to the Dembos region, hoping to find support among the rural Mbundu population.

The second center of nationalist agitation developed among the Kigongo-speaking people of northern Angola in the 1950s. Operating from bases in Belgian Congo (today's Democratic Republic of Congo (DRC)), and under the leadership of Holden Roberto, the *Frente Nacional de Libertação de Angola* (Angolan National Liberation Front – FNLA) began an armed uprising against the Portuguese in March 1961. Following some territorial gains during the early weeks of the fighting, Roberto was defeated, in September of 1961, and had to cross the Congolese border, where he found support among his ethnic kinsmen. While MPLA and FNLA initially discussed military and political cooperation, these talks failed and fighters from both insurgent groups began to target each other in addition to the Portuguese colonial army. While some elements of the FNLA ultimately joined the MPLA, one prominent FNLA politician, Jonas Savimbi, decided to form his own group, UNITA, in 1966. Savimbi cultivated support among his Ovimbundu community and thereby creating the third major "liberation movement."[1] Whereas the MPLA received support from the USSR, Holden Roberto's comparatively moderate position made the FNLA popular with pro-Western African states (such as Mobuto's Congo) and their European and North American backers. Savimbi, for his part, initially courted Beijing, which was interested in establishing a foothold in Angola to balance Moscow's influence (Schicho, 1999).

The division of the nationalist forces into three distinct camps – hostile to one another and each claiming a separate ethnic and social constituency – had a devastating effect on the anti-colonial struggle. While talks between the groups about closer coordination did take place during the 1960s, they did not lead to the establishment of a united front against the Portuguese. UNITA operated from rear bases in Zambia, whereas FNLA used Congolese territory for their supply lines. The MPLA, which by now had emerged as the favorite of the Afro-Asian block, received support and training from the Soviet Union and Cuba through Congo-Brazzaville. Accounts vary about the role of UNITA vis-à-vis the two other armed groups. Among others, Cornwell (1999, p. 54) states that Savimbi initially sought an alliance with the MPLA but was rebuffed. Others (Schicho, 1999, p. 197) claim that UNITA formed a coalition with the Portuguese forces (and their South African allies), in effect becoming a proxy for the Lisbon government.

Portugal reacted to the insurgency by pouring additional military forces into the country. At the end of the 1960s, more than 70,000 Portuguese soldiers served in Angola. The colonial army had become more effective in their anti-guerilla warfare during the late 1960s and early 1970s – using the unrivalled air superiority to deal devastating blows, particularly to the MPLA. At the same time, the Portuguese conscript army was overstretched, fighting simultaneously against liberation movements in Angola, Guinea-Bissau, and Mozambique. More than 12,000 were dead and 40,000 soldiers of the African wars were wounded, which contributed to a climate of political anger in Portugal that culminated in the April 1974 coup. The new government declared its intention to hold elections in Angola in October 1975, to be followed by the colony's independence in November 1975.

That year marks the end of the anti-colonial struggle in Angola and the beginning of the civil war that was to last another 27 years. Rather than prepare for the elections, all three movements sought a military victory. FNLA received substantial support from France, Belgium, the United States, and China. Supported by regular Congolese forces, Holden Roberto marched on Luanda from his northern strongholds. Meanwhile, MPLA had conquered the oil-rich Cabinda enclave and forged an unlikely alliance with some 3,000 Katanga Gendarmes – former secessionists from neighboring Zaire, which had sought refuge in north-eastern Angola following the end of Tshombe's experiment. Their only bond was shared animosity toward the Mobuto government.

Meanwhile, UNITA had discarded its Maoist rhetoric and turned for assistance to the United States, playing off Washington's fear a communist take-over in Luanda and its wider implications for the region (Wright, 1995). The group also received support from conservative Portuguese settlers as well as from South Africa, whose troops had crossed the Angolan border in August 1975 under the pretext of defending South Africans strategic interests in the Ruanca dam project (Thomashausen, 2002, p. 22). The government in Pretoria was afraid that a MPLA victory in Angola would boost anti-South African resistance in Namibia, then under South African administration, and destroy the *cordon sanitaire* formed by other settler states around its borders. While the Portuguese withdrawal became a rout, MPLA emerged as the dominant military force in Luanda and quickly declared the "People's Republic of Angola."

Being simultaneously threatened by FNLA and its Congolese allies from the North, and UNITA and its South African allies from the South, the newly formed government sought (and received) support from Cuba and the Soviet Union to defend its self-proclaimed sovereignty. The first months of independent Angola were marked by heavy fighting on both fronts. Supported by substantial numbers of Cuban "military advisors," the MPLA dealt a decisive blow to the FNLA and the latter disintegrated as a military force in January 1976. Meanwhile, fearing another Vietnam, the US congress passed the Clark Amendment (to the Security Assistance Bill), forcing the administration to withhold military support from FNLA and UNITA, and tipping the scales in favor of the MPLA (Cornwell, 1999). Following a series of military setbacks in March 1976, the South African troops also withdrew from Angola. The MPLA emerged as the victorious party and the government by default, owing its position as much to its military prowess as to the association of its enemies with Apartheid – South Africa, a reality that tarnished the reputation of UNITA in the eyes of many African observers.

ANGOLA'S CIVIL WAR IN A REGIONAL CONTEXT

The second phase of Angola's armed conflict saw MPLA and UNITA emerging as the main actors on the battlefield and in the political arena. After the initial defeat of FNLA and UNITA, Savimbi managed to re-group his forces and to establish himself in the Angolan hinterland, whereas MPLA controlled much of the coast as well as some urban centers further inland. Luanda received massive military support from the Soviet Union and other Warsaw Pact countries, which aimed to defend this socialist enclave in Southern Africa against UNITA and its Western backers. Angola's armed forces were trained according to the Warsaw Pact military doctrine and received modern Soviet weaponry, including T-54/55 battle tanks, BTR-60 armored personnel carriers, and long-range artillery systems. By the 1980s, the Angolan government had bought weapons worth more than 1.5 billion US dollars from the Warsaw Pact states, mortgaging future oil production to pay for them (De Beer & Gamba, 1999, p. 77). The Angolan Air Force received MiG-23 and Su-22 fighter jets, as well as helicopter gun ships of various makes. With the air force suffering from a lack of indigenous pilots, the planes were mostly manned by nationals from socialist "brother countries." Combat pilots and Soviet military advisors (numbering several hundred during the 1980s) were not the only foreign nationals fighting alongside the MPLA; the largest contribution came from Cuba, which increased the number of its troops from 4,000 in 1978 to 23,000 in 1981 (Wright, 1997, p. 91).

While the Angolan government was busy building a conventional army, Jonas Savimbi pursued a guerilla strategy, focusing his activities on the central highland and on Cuando Cubango. UNITA attacked targets of economic importance, such as the strategic Benguela Railroad, which provided an important lifeline for copper exports from landlocked Zambia. Though the lightly armed UNITA infantry units were frequently outgunned by government troops, Luanda's mechanized units were limited to the road and railway network for deployment, a situation that gave UNITA the military edge in rural areas. According to James (1992), UNITA had managed to raise some 18 million US dollars abroad, mostly from Arab, Iranian, and French interests. The bulk of this assistance was channeled through South Africa (Potgieter, 1999, p. 260).

Following the election of Ronald Reagan to the White House, the United States repealed the Clark Amendment in 1986 and resumed limited assistance to UNITA. Dubbed a policy of "constructive engagement," the Reagan administration lobbied for a Cuban withdrawal from Angola, linking this issue to independence for South West Africa (present-day Namibia). At the same time that Jonas Savimbi and his movement were courted by Western governments, Savimbi himself made repeated visits to Washington DC (De Beer & Gamba, 1999, p. 77). In 1986, he was received by President Reagan, who used the opportunity to speak of UNITA "winning a victory that electrifies the world." From 1986 to 1991, UNITA received about 250 million US dollars in covert aid from the United States (Wright, 1997, pp. 125–162; Stiff, 1999, p. 150). Additional military assistance was provided by a number of American allies in Europe and Africa, most notably by South Africa. The Apartheid state had become Savimbi's key ally and provided for most of UNITA's military needs. Concerned about his reputation as an African freedom fighter, Savimbi sought to downplay his association with the regime in Pretoria by stressing that his organization paid for these services with the revenue from diamond mining (Potgieter, 1999, p. 260).

However, while UNITA certainly received some revenue from the sale of diamonds, hardwood and ivory during the 1980s, the movement was also bankrolled by the South African state to the tune of some 400 million Rand (about 200 million US dollars) per year (Breytenbach, 1997, p. 247). As a guerilla army without any arms manufacturing capacities of its own, UNITA was totally dependent on arms and equipment either seized from the enemy or imported from abroad. Originally, most of these shipments came from South Africa through the territory of present-day Namibia. With Namibian independence looming in the late 1980s, UNITA moved its main logistics base to Cazombo because of its proximity to the borders of Zambia and Zaire. After the resumption of US military assistance in 1986, the air base at Kamina in Zaire became the main transit point for arms, ammunition, and other equipment to UNITA (Potgieter, 1999). These land-based supply lines were augmented by frequent flights to UNITA airstrips, which imported military equipment, exported valuable commodities such as diamonds or ivory, and facilitated travel for high-ranking UNITA cadres. While many of these flights were operated by South African Air Force planes, UNITA also used the services of private freight airlines such as Santa Lucia Airways, then a Zairean subsidiary of SABENA (Peleman, 1999, p. 299). The network of private contractors, warehouses, and foreign offices established during this period allowed UNITA to survive in later years, even after UNITA lost official support from South Africa and the United States.

TOO LITTLE, TOO LATE: THE UNITED NATIONS IN ANGOLA

The UN' role in Angola was hampered during the Cold War because the major powers blocked each other on the Security Council, effectively paralyzing the institution's most important executive organ. This situation of deadlock changed profoundly during the early 1990s. As the decade-long confrontation between both blocks faded away, the role of the UNSC as an instrument of collaborative peace-enforcement was strengthened. At the same time, the withdrawal of Soviet military assistance meant that numerous proxy wars came to an end, often assisted through the mediation of the UN. Assisted further in South Africa by the crumbling of the Apartheid state and Namibian independence, this global development encouraged hope for a peaceful solution for the Angolan civil war.

Early Intervention and Failure

In May 1991, during negotiations in Bicesse (Portugal), the MPLA and UNITA agreed on the terms of a peace agreement. The main elements of the accord included the demobilization of UNITA, the creation of a unified national army, as well as democratic elections by September 1992. This process was to be monitored by the United Nations Verification Mission in

Angola (UNAVEM II^2), which was to deploy throughout the country with the consent of both parties. While UNAVEM suffered from a lack of resources and a limited mandate, both conflict parties were obstructing elements of the peace plan (Anstee, 1997).

Voting took place in September 1992 as planned and was considered by international observers to be "free and fair." MPLA won an absolute majority of 54 percent of the votes in the parliamentary elections, UNITA gained a share of 34 percent, and the balance was carried by minor parties. During the presidential elections, MPLA candidate Eduardo dos Santos won 49.6 percent of the vote, compared to 40.1 percent for UNITA's Jonas Savimbi (Hodges, 2001). This defeat came as a surprise to UNITA and its Western backers, and Savimbi was quick to denounce the MPLA for stealing the elections. Within days, UNITA was back at war.

Initially, UNITA made some impressive territorial gains. For the first time since the mid-1970s, UNITA was able to conquer and hold large cities, including Caxito, Huambo, M'banza Kongo, Ndalatando, and Uige, and to engage the enemy in pitched battles (Hodges, 2001). One of the reasons for these early successes was the fact that UNITA had demobilized its own troops on a much smaller scale than the MPLA, giving Savimbi the military edge –a fact largely overlooked by UNAVEM II. By the end of 1993, UNITA controlled more than 70 percent of Angola's territory (Human Rights Watch, 1999, p. 15), while the government's presence in the hinterland was reduced to besieged garrison towns. During this period, Angola's civil war was at its deadliest. According to the UN, between May and October 1993, as many as 1,000 people were dying every day (Human Rights Watch, 1994). While UNITA could no longer draw on military assistance from the United States and South Africa, Savimbi continued to capitalize on the close relationship with President Mobuto in neighboring Zaire. During this period, UNITA intensified exploitation of the diamond areas under its control and, benefiting from the glut on the international arms market following the end of the Cold War (Hodges, 2001, p. 15), used the sales revenue to buy surplus weapons from Eastern Europe.

Early Sanctions

In light of this situation, and with Savimbi in blatant violation of the Bicesse peace accords, the UNSC for the first time decided to impose sanctions against UNITA.^{3} This move was motivated by a policy shift among the Western members of the Security Council, many of whom had supported

UNITA during the Cold War. With the end of the Soviet threat in Southern Africa, Savimbi had lost his strategic importance. Meanwhile, the MPLA began to court Western investors, dropping the socialist rhetoric and increasing oil production. In this situation, the international community decided to ignore the blatant corruption and widespread human rights abuses of the Luanda government and to bet their political chips on a MPLA victory (Mills & Sidiropoulos, 2004). The sanctions also provided a welcome opportunity for the US government to publicly dissociate itself from Savimbi. Adopted on 15 September 1993, resolution 864 imposed an arms embargo against UNITA and stipulated that the sale of petroleum products to Angola would be restricted to ports designated by the Angolan government. The resolution created a sanctions committee and established 1 November 1993 as the deadline for more comprehensive sanctions should the Secretary-General continue to find UNITA in violation of the peace accords (Cortright & Lopez, 2000). The combination of the threat of further sanctions and a reversal of UNITA's military fortunes forced Savimbi back to the negotiation table. While the parties discussed in Lusaka, the fighting in Angola continued. Nevertheless, after the November deadline expired, UN Secretary-General (UNSG) Boutros-Ghali claimed that the ceasefire was holding and that the talks were making progress (UNSC, 1993). In response to his report, the UNSC decided to place more comprehensive sanctions against UNITA on hold and passed resolution 890 instead, threatening stronger sanctions but without giving a timetable for their imposition. (Cortright & Lopez, 2000).

A New Peace Effort and Failure

By the second half of 1994, UNITA had suffered a series of military setbacks and had lost most its urban strongholds. The withdrawal of US (and later South African) covert military assistance certainly was partially responsible for this change in military fortunes. Savimbi returned to the negotiation table and on 20 November 2004 accepted a comprehensive peace agreement, the Lusaka Protocol. The signing of the agreement heralded the beginning of a four-year period during which the country oscillated between war and peace. As localized fighting between UNITA and FAA continued, UNAVEM publicly pursued a strategy of appeasing Savimbi. Alioune Blondin Beye, the special representative of the UN in Angola, reported that the peace process was on track and that a return to war was unlikely (Angola Peace Monitor, 30 November 1996). While the gap between diplomatic perception and Angolan reality was widening in the mid-1990s, in December 1996, the UNSC passed resolution 1087, authorizing the withdrawal of UNAVEM III in 1997. This decision was based on the optimistic reports of Beye regarding the prospects of the Lusaka peace process and was probably also the result of a certain donor fatigue, as international attention was captured by the conflicts in the Balkans. UNAVEM III was replaced by a smaller observer mission (MONUA) with some 1,500 military observers.

Both sides used the lull in the fighting to regroup their armed forces and to procure new weapons abroad. In this, the Angolan government had the edge, given its access to oil revenue and the fact that it was excluded from sanctions. In 1995–1996, the government bought MiG-23 and Su-22 fighter planes, as well as Mi-17 and Mi-24 attack helicopters worth more than 300 million US dollars. T-55 tanks and BMP-2 infantry fighting vehicles were purchased to strengthen the army, along with small arms, ammunitions, and other military equipment. Most of the weapons were bought from Angola's traditional suppliers in Russia, but Brazil, France, and Switzerland were also suppliers (De Beer & Gamba, 1999, p. 84). This shopping spree was financed by proceeds from the oil sector, which experienced a bonanza during the 1990s as investor confidence in the Angolan government grew and production was expanded significantly. As the Angolan state fell more deeply in debt to international donors, the government devised a clever scheme by which oil revenue was channeled into off-shore accounts and then used to pay directly for arms purchases. Allegedly, these funds also supported the luxurious lifestyle enjoyed by Luanda's small, but enormously wealthy elite, without ever being accounted for in Angola's state budget (Global Witness, 1999). Due to the opaque nature of the Angolan oil sector and the fluctuating price of its product, it is very difficult to give a reliable number for oil revenues during the period. For 2000, the International Monetary Fund (2000, p. 47) put the figure at 3.3 billion US dollars.

In clear breach of UN sanctions but buoyed by the receipts from diamond sales from the mining areas under its control, UNITA was also rearming in 1996–1997. The diamond market is believed to have provided Savimbi's movement with up to 700 million US dollars in cash during the mid-1990s (Global Witness, 1998). According to De Beer and Gamba (1999, p. 84), UNITA bought a BM-27 multiple rocket launcher from the Ukraine, in addition to SA-6 surface-to-air missile systems and BM-2 infantry fighting vehicles. This build-up of a conventional arsenal improved UNITA's capability to face the FAA in a pitched battle, but also increased its dependency on reliable fuel supplies to operate the mechanized units. Other vital supplies such as small arms, ammunition, uniforms, fuel, and other equipment were flown in by privately owned air cargo companies from Central Africa. Until the end of the Mobuto regime in May 1997, the hub for these "sanction-busting" flights was Kinshasa's N'Djili international airport. UNITA then moved its supply operation to the Maya international airport in neighboring Brazzaville (in the Republic of Congo), until this base was also lost due to fighting between militia groups in September 1997. UNITA subsequently moved its supply center to Pointe Noire on Congo's Atlantic coast, where it remained until an insurgency backed by the Angolan government replaced the UNITA-friendly Congolese government (Human Rights Watch, 1999, pp. 112–114).

Despite the fact that both UNAVEM officials and independent observers were aware of some of these developments, the UN continued to pursue a strategy of quiet diplomacy. Some members of the Security Council, most notably the United States and the United Kingdom, were lobbying for a total ban on arms exports to Angola (which would have included the government), but found that this was opposed by the Russian and Brazilian government, both of which were important suppliers of weaponry to the government in Luanda (Human Rights Watch, 1999). While the UNSC would frequently threaten stronger sanctions, UNITA always managed to deflect these by making conciliatory gestures. According to Cortright and Lopez (2000, p. 156), the rationale behind this strategy was that senior UN diplomats believed that the supposedly moderate Savimbi should be strengthened vis-à-vis more radical voices in his own camp. This view was apparently also shared for some time by the Clinton administration, which, having made the Angolan peace process a foreign policy priority, stopped the dialog with Savimbi only in late 1998 (Human Rights Watch). In Angola, the reluctance of the UNSC to impose tougher measures on Savimbi discredited the UN and led to a situation in which many observers believed that the Security Council tolerated UNITA's violations of the peace agreement. By the time the UNSC finally acted, it was too late. In August 1997, the council adopted resolution 1127, imposing travel sanctions against senior UNITA cadres, closing its offices abroad, and banning f lights to and from UNITA-held territory. The implementation of these measures was suspended for another two months while the UNSC waited in vain for UNITA to make credible steps toward disarmament, and they finally became effective in October 1997. In June 1998, after these steps failed to have an impact on UNITA, the UNSC voted for resolution 1173, which took aim at the economic base of the movement, freezing all UNITA assets and banning all financial transactions with it. Most importantly, the resolution targeted the resource base of Savimbi's organization by imposing an embargo on diamond exports not certified by the Angolan government.

A Limited Role in the End Game

By this time, the government in Luanda had given up all hopes for a diplomatic solution to the conflict. President Dos Santos used the fourth congress of the MPLA in December 1998 to declare that "the only path to peace is war" and called for the withdrawal of the UN from Angola and for the end of the Lusaka Peace Process (Human Rights Watch, 1999, p. 16). FAA immediately initiated large-scale attacks against UNITA positions, while the UN decided to withdraw the last remaining peacekeepers[4] because, as Human Rights Watch (1999, p. 17) pointedly put it, "there was no longer any peace to keep." MONUA's withdrawal in February 1999 marked the end of the UN's direct engagement on Angolan soil. The mission left demoralized from the death of special representative Beye in an air crash as well as from the shooting down of two UN-chartered planes, probably by UNITA. Meanwhile, during the course of 1999, FAA dealt major blows to UNITA, driving the movement from its strongholds in Bailundo and Andulo back into the Angolan bush. Savimbi's gamble – using his newly acquired arsenal and conventional tactics to fight the enemy – failed. This was partially the result of insufficient fuel supplies, which had to be trucked in from across the Zambian border, and which meant that UNITA's mechanized units were occasionally running out of fuel during battles with FAA (United Nations Security Council, 2000). There is some evidence from post-war interviews with UNITA leaders that from 1999 onward, the impact of the sanctions was acutely felt by the movement (Kevlihan, 2003, pp. 100–101). The lack of spare parts, ammunition, and in particular fuel rendered most of the heavier weapons obsolete. The travel sanctions also began to take effect at about this time and international isolation of Savimbi increased as a result.[5] UNITA, which had control over two-thirds of the country's territory when the Lusaka Protocal was signed, had to abandon conventional warfare and returned to fighting a guerilla war by the end of 1999, targeting government towns in quick "hit-and-run" operations and denying FAA a target for its superior air power. These attacks were often motivated by the necessity to loot weapons, food, and other supplies, as individual UNITA had increasingly to fend for themself.

DIAMONDS ARE A GUERILLERO'S BEST FRIEND

To understand the survival of UNITA as a military organization following the end of external assistance and the imposition of targeted sanctions, one needs to take a closer look at the nature of Savimbi's international supply network. Some countries, most notably Zaire until the end of the Mobuto regime and a few other West African states, were willing to tolerate the use of their territories for the shipping of supplies to UNITA. This lenience depended to a large extent, however, on the ability of Savimbi to secure their support through frequent payments. Among the African rulers receiving such payments were the President of Burkina Faso, Blaise Compaoré, the President of Togo, Gnassingbe Eyadema, and the President of Zaire, Mobuto Sese Seko (Hodges, 2001, p. 156). UNITA also had to procure weapons, ammunition, fuel, and food on the international market – a difficult undertaking given the movement's increasing political isolation. The UN sanctions regime also played a role in weakening Savimbi's position in the arms market. While the international body had few possibilities to make sure that "sanction-busting" did not take place, the international publicity generated by the UNSC, as well as by international non-governmental organizations such as Global Witness and Human Rights Watch, drove the trade further underground. UNITA was forced to rely on a complex network of intermediaries for its transactions. From the mid-1990s onward, arms shipments to UNITA-controlled territories extracted a premium, as the government began to reassert its authority vis-à-vis neighboring states and by making air-borne sanction-busting more difficult through the use of mobile radar units and more frequent patrol flights.

The key resource allowing UNITA to continue its struggle for another decade was rough diamonds from areas under the movement's control. Diamond mining has a long tradition in Angola, dating back to 1912 when the first stones were discovered in a river in the Lunda region of the northeast (Hodges, 2001, p. 148). Five years later, industrial exploitation began under the auspices of the *Companiha de Diamantes de Angola* (DIAMANG), at one time the largest corporation in the Portuguese colonies. DIAMANG had a workforce of some 70,000 laborers and a network of company farms, hospitals, and schools to provide food and services in the underdeveloped Angolan hinterland. The country's diamond production peaked in 1971 at 2.4 million carats, making it the fourth largest producer in the world (Dietrich, 1999a, p. 144).

The end of colonial rule and the deteriorating security situation had a devastating effect on diamond production. UNITA's involvement in diamond mining dates back to this period. According to one source, during the 1980s, the movement was generating between 50,000 and four million US dollars per month from diamonds in 1986–1987 (Bridgland, 1988). This was done through the exploitation of sites abandoned by commercial mining companies as well as through the taxation of independent artisanal miners, known locally as *garimpeiros*. It is important to note that UNITA's forays into diamond mining predate the end of South African and US military assistance by several years, even though the changing geopolitical situation certainly sped up the process (Le Billion, 1999). After the Bicesse peace accords, the number of garimpeiros increased dramatically, and by August 1992, more than 50,000 illegal diggers were working in Angola (Dietrich, 1999b, p. 174). After fighting resumed later that year, UNITA quickly occupied the country's most lucrative alluvial diamond areas. Under an agreement with Zaire's President Mobuto, 100,000 contract miners were imported from Zaire to assist UNITA in the exploitation of the mines (ACTSA, 2000, p. 18).

While UNITA soldiers initially worked some of the mines themselves, the movement quickly turned from direct exploitation to taxation. This worked through a "production-sharing" agreement by which the garimpeiro was allowed to keep a part of his production, while UNITA provided some degree of security for the mining operation. Foreign entrepreneurs were also invited by Savimbi to establish mining operations on UNITA territory in exchange for license fees. Under this setup, UNITA took care of the recruitment of the garimpeiro labor and provided security at the mines (Dietrich, 1999c, pp. 277–278). The foreign investor would be responsible for the necessary capital investments. While UNITA's share of the production was channeled back to Savimbi's headquarters and exported from there, the garimpeiros were free to sell their share (usually 20 percent) to independent diamond buyers both in Angola and across the borders in Zambia and Zaire.

It is extremely difficult to come up with reliable data on UNITA's profit from diamond production. Global Witness (1998, p. 4) gave the figure of an "estimated minimum revenue of 3.72 billion US dollars" for the period from 1992 until 1998, when UNITA was dislodged from most of its diamond-producing areas. In hindsight, this number, repeated subsequently in many publications, seems to be inflated. Hodges (2001, pp. 152–153) argues that the number seems to be based on the market value of all Angolan rough diamonds sold through the "outside market," that is, not through the official channels licensed by the Angolan government. The total revenue for UNITA would be lower because of the share taken by the various middlemen before reaching the global market, as well as by the fact that substantial numbers of diamonds were smuggled out of government-controlled mines as well. Alternative industry sources quoted by Hodges (2001, p. 153) put the cumulative value of UNITA diamond exports for the 1992–1998 period at a more conservative two billion US dollars, but still making Savimbi's movement probably the richest insurgent group of the time.

It seems that UNITA preferred to keep much of its funds in diamonds, rather than selling them for cash, because diamonds could be moved easily in case of enemy attack and because foreign bank accounts were under the risk of closure following UN sanctions (Hodges, 2001, p. 156). Cash was only needed for some purchases (the majority seemed to have been barter trades) and also to raise funds for UNITA representatives and recipients (including some family members of the UNITA leadership) of UNITA scholarships abroad.

UNITA's diamond bonanza, which prospered during the uncertainty of the "no peace, no war" situation between 1994 and 1998, came to a sudden end with the resumption of all-out fighting and the loss of UNITA's main supply base in Andulo in the Central Highlands at the end of 1999. As the location of the movement's principal airport, the loss of Andulo meant that flights in and out of UNITA territory became much more difficult. For the remainder of its existence as a military force, the movement never again established a fixed headquarters of this magnitude – its existence reduced to comparatively small groups of soldiers operating from temporary bases. According to Hodges (2001, p. 156), however, UNITA's diamond-producing capacity was probably already past its peak before the Lusaka peace process faltered. He gives two reasons for this development. First, during the 1990s, the movement had gradually exhausted the alluvial sites to which it had access, basically picking from sites identified and prepared for exploitation by commercial mining companies. Hodges argues that without prospecting or investments such as river diversions, it would have been difficult for UNITA to sustain the record level of production enjoyed during the mid-1990s. Secondly, UNITA had surrendered its main mining areas to government control toward the end of 1997, a step foreseen under the Lusaka Protocol and which went largely unnoticed abroad. While UNITA had stalled the handover, the eventual transfer is a clear indication that the movement's leadership was aware that the mines were almost exhausted. It seems likely that UNITA retained some secondary mines after the defeats of 1999 (UNSC, 2002a, paragraphs 113–114), but industry sources reported a steep decline in the number of rough stones from unofficial Angolan sources from 1998 onward. This drop was a strong signal that the movement's main source of revenue was drying up.

MEASURING THE IMPACT OF SANCTIONS

Looking back at more than a decade of UN sanctions against UNITA, it is not easy to judge the extent to which the resolutions passed by the UNSC had a direct impact on the cessation of hostilities in Angola. International sanctions were certainly not the only or even the most important factor in ending Angola's agony. Nevertheless, in retrospect, it seems clear that there were two distinct phases of UN sanctions during the 1990s.

A First Phase of Negligence

From 1993 to 1997, sanctions against UNITA were largely declaratory, their scope limited to an arms and petroleum embargo, leaving out such crucial elements as sanctions against the trade in diamonds or a freezing on UNITA's overseas assets. While SCR 864 had also established a sanctions committee to oversee the implementation of the arms and petroleum embargo against UNITA, this committee remained passive for much of the 1990s. Canada's outspoken ambassador to the UN, Robert Fowler, once likened the sanctions regime against UNITA to "traffic rules" and was quoted (in Hodges, 2001, p. 154) as saying that since "nobody enforced them, people drove where they wanted and parked all over the place. It was a complete disaster." In short, the problem of the UN sanction regime against UNITA was the lack of enforcement.

This seems to be all the more surprising given the fact that the UNSG actually had the necessary manpower at his disposal during this period to supervise the implementation of the sanctions regime. When resolution 864 was passed by the UNSC in 1993, Angola already hosted a sizeable UN peacekeeping mission (UNAVEM II), which was even expanded with the deployment of UNAVEM III in 1995. The mandate of the observer mission specifically included verifying whether the two conflict parties were disarming their military wings as agreed during the Lusaka negotiations. While the UN mission in Angola suffered from many logistical problems, marring the deployment of its observers, there can be no doubt that it misjudged the extent to which Savimbi was not only not disarming but rather building a new arsenal. The UN followed an extremely cautious line in dealing with Savimbi, alternating between strong public statements about UNITA's lack of compliance with the terms of the Lusaka protocol on the one hand and attempts at quiet diplomacy to secure such compliance on the other.

MacQueen (1998, p. 415) argues that "the gamble for the UN was that the pace of the process, although still extremely slow, was fundamentally irreversible and that UNITA's continued obstructiveness had become a mere habit rather than a purposeful political strategy."

When the Lusaka peace process finally failed, it became apparent that the UNSC had misjudged both the political aims and the military capabilities of UNITA. Following the military successes of FAA at Andulo, Bailundo, and Jamba, the Angolan government claims to have seized more than 15,000 tons of material from UNITA arms dumps, including 27 tanks and 40 armored personnel carriers, 16 million rounds of small arms ammunition, 120 artillery pieces, and 30 anti-aircraft missiles (ACTSA, 2000, p. 8). With most of these weapons having been recently acquired, it seems quite clear that the arms embargo had no substantial impact on the movement's ability to procure weapons abroad. Resolution 864 also included a ban on the sale of petroleum products to Angola with the exception of ports of entry designated by the government in Luanda. UNITA's newly acquired conventional arsenal relied on the continuous supply of fuel to ensure combat readiness. Fuel was transported by air from Zambia, South Africa, Togo, Cote d'Ivoire, and Burkina Faso, as well as by road from Zambia and Namibia. During the late 1990s, the supply of fuel had become a major strategic problem for UNITA, as it was dislodged from its positions on the Namibian border and had to rely increasingly on the very costly practice of securing fuel flown in by chartered planes. Zambia, another important source of fuel supplies during the 1990s, became less reliable when a fire destroyed the country's single oil refinery at Ndola in 1999. According to a prominent UNITA defector, the movement had only about half a million liters of fuel when the fighting erupted (ACTSA, 2000, p. 15). Fuel scarcity was a significant military disadvantage as UNITA's mechanized units were running out of fuel during set battles with FAA and had to abandon large amounts of military equipment. However, while the lack of fuel played an important role in UNITA's defeat during the FAA's 1999 campaign, there is no indication that this was predominantly the result of the UN embargo.

Improvement in the Second Phase

The second phase was almost concurrent with the withdrawal of the UN peacekeepers from 1997 onward. Sensing that its engagement on the ground had failed to bring about an end to the conflict, the UNSC chose a more comprehensive approach. With resolutions 1127 (August 1997) and 1173 (June 1998), the scope of the sanctions regime was extended to include a freeze on all UNITA-held accounts. They forced the closure of UNITA offices abroad and, most importantly, imposed an embargo on diamond imports not authorized by the Angolan government. While these measures again intended to bring Savimbi back to the negotiation table, unlike the preceding phase, this time they were meant to hit the movement where it hurt most, in its financial resources. Enforcement remained a problem though, and with the UN presence in Angola gradually being reduced, the UNSC sought a new instrument to monitor the implementation of the sanctions regime. This instrument was found in the sanctions committee, which previously had played a fairly minor role, but gained a new importance with the appointment of Canadian Ambassador Robert Fowler to its chair. Not content with viewing developments from New York, the committee adopted "a more assertive monitoring and enforcement role" under his leadership (Cortright & Lopez, 2002, p. 65). He set out on an extended trip to Central and Southern Africa in May 1999, followed by another trip to the diamond center of Antwerp in July of the same year. Fowler talked with both governments and private sector representatives with the aim of finding ways to enhance the effectiveness of sanctions against UNITA. The reports of his missions, collectively also known as the "Fowler report," were issued in the summer of 1999 and detailed a number of recommendations on how to improve the effectiveness of the embargo (UNSC, 1999a, 1999b).

One key recommendation from the Fowler report was the creation of a panel of experts, which was to track developments with regard to the sanctions regime and report back to the UNSC. Originally, the UNSC had passed resolution 1237 (7 May 1999) with the aim of creating two independent panels: one investigating UNITA's finances and the other scrutinizing arms transfers to the movement. But at their first meeting, the panel members decided to amalgamate their tasks and thereafter they functioned as a single unit under the Chairmanship of Swedish Ambassador Anders Möllander (Cortright & Lopez, 2002, p. 66). The panel of experts continued the investigative work started by the Fowler report. Presented in March 2000 (UNSC, 2000), its report created an enormous stir in diplomatic circles. In plain language, the report implicated Togo and Burkina Faso as countries assisting UNITA in sanction-busting, pointing toward the respective presidents Eyadema and Compaorè as receiving direct payments from Savimbi for their services. It was equally hard-hitting on the providers of military equipment in breach of sanctions and mentioned several Eastern

European countries, including Bulgaria, Belarus, and Russia as sources of UNITA's newly acquired arsenal. Finally, the report criticized Belgium, as the host of the world's most important diamond bourse, for its "lax regulatory environment" regarding diamond imports (UNSC, 2000, paragraphs 89 and 90).

While much of the information collected by the panel had been available among experts working on Angola, the fact that this information was publicly discussed in the UNSC raised the profile of the allegations and triggered a cascade of media reports. This practice of "naming and shaming" provoked angry reactions by the representatives of the states mentioned in the report, with the Togolese representative calling the report "rumor, hearsay and scraps" (*New York Times*, 16 March, 2000). The direct impact of the panel report is difficult to measure, but a number of states mentioned in the report either started inquiries of their own following its publication or changed their respective national legislation in the fields concerned. As Cortright and Lopez (2002, p. 67) note, "despite the controversy generated by the report – perhaps even because of it – the work of the panel of experts produced results." The use of expert panels has since then become a favorite tool for the UNSC, monitoring sanctions against Somalia, Liberia, Sierra Leone, and Cote d'Ivoire, as well as investigating the illegal exploitation of natural resources in the DRC.

The work of the panel of experts was continued by a monitoring mechanism created through resolution 1295, passed by the UNSC on 18 April 2000. The mechanism had a similar structure and *modus operandi* as the panel of experts, however as Cortright and Lopez (2002, p. 69) put it, "unlike the panel, however, it did not single out heads of state" to avoid stirring resentment among regional governments. In the pursuit of its mandate to collect information on "sanction-busting," the mechanism sought the cooperation of both governments and private companies, as well as that of international law enforcement agencies such as INTERPOL. However, as the mechanism notes in its final report (UNSC, 2002b, paragraph 15), "it was neither empowered with subpoena authority nor did it possess a search warrant"; that is, it had to rely on information volunteered by national governments, non-governmental organizations, or individuals. While the mechanism's reports contributed greatly to our understanding of UNITA's supply network, the most important contribution to ending the conflict arguably lay in its use of "quiet diplomacy"[6] – in convincing governments that they needed to do more to stop violations of the UN sanctions regime.

Sanctions and the End Game

On 22 February 2002, three years after the appointment of Robert Fowler signaled a more hard-nosed approach toward UNITA, Jonas Savimbi died on the battlefield.[7] His death removed the main obstacle to the resumption of negotiations between the government and the remaining political leadership of UNITA and eventually to the demobilization of UNITA during the course of 2003 (Porto & Parsons, 2003). During the final two years of Angola's civil war, after UNITA had been dislodged from its permanent bases in the Central Highlands, the movement essentially had been fighting a rearguard action. Its supply situation had deteriorated to such an extent that many UNITA fighters, including members of Savimbi's personal protection force, were on the brink of starvation and required immediate medical attention when reporting to the quartering areas (Author's interviews in Luanda, 2003; UNSC, 2002b, paragraph 42; Kevlihan, 2003, p. 101). The movement was also rapidly running out of ammunition – the remaining arsenal handed over to the FAA after the ceasefire included some 26,000 small arms, 861 mortars and artillery pieces, as well as 8 anti-aircraft guns. While this might seem impressive for a defeated army, only about 290,000 rounds of ammunitions, missiles, and artillery shells were handed over. Therefore, even without accounting for the differences in caliber, a ration of 10.7 units of ammunition per gun shows that the fighting capacity of UNITA was much diminished. As a matter of fact, the ratio for heavier weapons systems was even worse. In one instance, the number of mortars actually outnumbered the number of available shells. While bands of UNITA combatants surrendered 15 of Angola's 18 provinces, UNITA's heavier weapons were concentrated in one province, indicating that the movement's lack of fuel supply had prevented their wider deployment (UNSC, 2002b, paragraphs 39–42).

It is very difficult to measure the extent to which this deteriorating supply situation was the result of the UN sanctions regime. It seems likely that the sanctions were but one element that led to the ultimate defeat of UNITA. By isolating Savimbi from his former allies in West Africa and by making a determined effort to track the arms flows to UNITA, the monitoring mechanism certainly had made it more difficult for the movement to acquire weapons on the international market. While the sanctions probably did not manage to stop the flow of guns from reaching Savimbi, they increased the premium his organization had to pay to obtain them. Equally important is the fact that UNITA lost its main airport at Andulo to government forces during the 1999 offensive, making it much more difficult to receive shipments by air, as the other airstrips still under the movement's control were too small to receive larger transport planes. Transporting supplies overland from Zambia became more difficult as well during the final years of the conflict, as government troops made an effort to push UNITA away from the border, while stepping up diplomatic pressure on Zambia to improve border controls on their side. The fact that the government in Luanda intervened militarily in both Zaire and the Republic of Congo to topple governments, which in the past had provided Savimbi with rear bases, certainly left an impression with other governments, including the one in Lusaka.

It is also very difficult to measure the extent to which the UN embargo against diamonds had a significant impact on the ability of UNITA to finance its operation. As mentioned earlier, by the time the UNSC passed resolution 1173 in June 1998, UNITA had already lost control over important mining areas to government forces. The monitoring mechanism states that diamonds worth one million US dollars continued to be smuggled daily from Angola right until 2002 (UNSC, 2002b, paragraph 5), but it seems questionable that this trade was linked to UNITA mining and trading operations. Up to the present day, no trace of the UNITA diamond treasure has been found. Given the highly centralized nature of UNITA's diamond operations, it seems likely that Savimbi would have had the movement's "war chest" with him during the final months of the conflict. The mechanism notes that "four suitcases containing respectively diamonds, dollars and bank transfer papers, documents and personal possessions" were found with Savimbi's corpse (UNSC, 2002a, paragraph 98) and that the remaining UNITA leadership attempted to sell some parcels of diamonds through Zambia in the weeks after Savimbi's death (UNSC, 2002a, paragraph 99). If these possessions represent the remainder of UNITA's fortunes, the movement seems to have burned up most of its financial reserves during the final two years of fighting. It would seem to be result of attrition rather than an effect of the sanction regime. Nevertheless, the publicity generated by the reports of the monitoring mechanism, as well as by various non-governmental organizations working on the issue of "conflict diamonds," certainly made it more difficult for UNITA to market its stockpile of diamonds after 1998. It also played an important role in jump-starting the so-called Kimberley Process, which led to the establishment of a mandatory global certification scheme for diamonds.

CONCLUSIONS

After nearly a decade of uncoordinated and on-again, off-again attention to the civil war in Angola, by 1999, the establishment of an institutionalized organ to monitor the enforcement of its sanction regime indicated the UN had become more focused and committed to help end this costly struggle. The combination of "quiet" and "public" diplomacy of the international body, in addition to the successes of the Luanda government, both on the battlefield and in the diplomatic arena, combined with the deterioration of options and resources available to UNITA because of the sanctions, finally created the necessary preconditions for UNITA's surrender. Evidence indicates that only the personal charisma of Jonas Savimbi kept many in UNITA holding to the fight, even as the supply situation deteriorated to such an extent that the looting of food became the most important military objective and confrontations with government forces were avoided (UNSC, 2002a, paragraphs 5–8). After almost four decades of civil war and almost 15 years of UN intervention, the fighting has finally come to an end in most parts of Angola (the exception being the Cabinda enclave). The international community had an opportunity to learn many lessons from its engagement in Angola – lessons, one hopes, that will ultimately benefit the population of other war-torn countries. As far as the Angolan people are concerned, one wishes that the UNSC had shown more determination during the early 1990s, when the international community's handling of Savimbi with kid gloves allowed him to continue the conflict by another decade, extending the suffering of hundreds of thousands of ordinary people.

NOTES

1. The fourth movement fighting the Portuguese was the *Frente de Libertação do Enclave de Cabinda* (Front for the Liberation of the Cabinda Enclave – FLEC). Unlike the other three insurgent groups – which claimed to represent all Angolans – FLEC fought for the independence of the oil-rich enclave rather than for an independent Angola. FLEC has continued its low-intensity military campaign against the government until the present time (Porto, 2003).

2. An earlier and much smaller UN verification mission (UNAVEM I) had been deployed in Angola from 1989 to 1991 to monitor the withdrawal of the Cuban military forces under the terms of the New York Accords, which led to the independence of Namibia (Hodges, 2001).

3. While this was the first time that the UNSC imposed sanctions against UNITA, it was by no means the first time the organ dealt with Angola. As early as 31 March

1976, the UNSC had adopted resolution 387, condemning "South Africa's aggression against the People's Republic of Angola." In November 1977, this was followed by UNSC resolution 418, which imposed an arms embargo against South Africa, inter alia because of South Africa's "persistent acts of aggression against neighboring states" (Thomashausen, 2002, p. 25).

4. While the UN withdrew MONUA, it retained a small mission in Luanda tasked with observing the political developments and the human rights situation. However, with the end of MONUA, the UN ceased to be a relevant actor within Angola.

5. Kevlihan (2003, p. 100) notes that UNITA's "foreign minister" Alcides Sakala did not travel overseas since 1997 and that UNITA personnel abroad apparently faced significant financial difficulties from 1998 onward.

6. On occasion, this could also take the form of heated debates, for example, when "government officials who, even when presented with conclusive proof of violations, had to be emphatically reminded of the legal and moral obligations of their Governments under the Charter of the United Nations. In those instances, the Mechanism's reports to the Security Council became powerful instruments for exposing non-compliance" (UNSC, 2002b, paragraph 13).

7. The precise circumstances of his death remain shrouded in mystery. Both UNITA and the government claim that he died during combat in Moxico province, when he and his bodyguards were trapped against a riverbank by government forces. His bullet-riddled body was later shown to the news media. However, some international observers in Angola claim that he in essence committed suicide (by seeking the firefight with government troops) because he was aware that his movement could not fight for much longer (Author's interviews in Luanda, 2003).

ACKNOWLEDGMENT

The author gratefully acknowledges the editorial assistance of Christopher Fitzpatrick.

REFERENCES

ACTSA. (2000). *Waiting on empty promises – The human cost of international inaction on Angolan sanctions.* London: Action for Southern Africa.

Anstee, M. (1997). *Orphan of the cold war.* London: Macmillan.

Breytenbach, J. (1997). *Edens exile: One soldier's fight for paradise.* Cape Town: Queillerie Publishers.

Bridgland, F. (1988). *Jonas Savimbi: A key to Africa.* London: Hodder and Stoughton.

Cornwell, R. (1999). The war for independence. In: J. Cilliers & C. Dietrich (Eds), *Angola's war economy: The role of oil and diamonds.* Pretoria: Institute for Security Studies.

Cornwell, R., & Potgieter, J. (1999). *Angola: Endgame or stalemate?* Occassional Paper No. 30. Pretoria: Institute for Security Studies.

Cortright, D., & Lopez, G. (2000). *The sanctions decade: Assessing UN strategies in the 1990s.* Boulder: Lynne Rienner Publishers.

Cortright, D., & Lopez, G. (2002). *Sanctions and the search for security: Challenges to UN action.* Boulder: Lynne Rienner Publishers.

De Beer, H., & Gamba, V. (1999). The arms dilemma: Resources for arms or arms for resources. In: J. Cilliers & C. Dietrich (Eds), *Angola's war economy: The role of oil and diamonds.* Pretoria: Institute for Security Studies.

Dietrich, C. (1999a). Inventory of formal diamond mining in Angola. In: J. Cilliers & C. Dietrich (Eds), *Angola's war economy: The role of oil and diamonds.* Pretoria: Institute for Security Studies.

Dietrich, C. (1999b). Power struggles in the diamond fields. In: J. Cilliers & C. Dietrich (Eds), *Angola's war economy: The role of oil and diamonds.* Pretoria: Institute for Security Studies.

Dietrich, C. (1999c). UNITA's diamond mining and exporting capacity. In: J. Cilliers & C. Dietrich (Eds), *Angola's war economy: The role of oil and diamonds.* Pretoria: Institute for Security Studies.

Global Witness. (1998). *A rough trade: The role of companies and governments in the Angolan conflict.* London: Global Witness.

Global Witness. (1999). *A crude awakening – The role of the oil and banking industry in Angola's civil war and the plunder of state assets.* London: Global Witness.

Hodges, T. (2001). *Angola from Afro-Stalinism to Petro-Diamond capitalism.* Oxford: James Curry.

Human Rights Watch. (1994). *Angola: Arms trade and violations of the law of wars since the 1992 elections.* New York City: Human Rights Watch.

Human Rights Watch. (1999). *Angola unravels – The rise and fall of the Lusaka peace process.* New York City: Human Rights Watch.

International Monetary Fund. (2000). *Angola statistical annex.* Washington DC: IMF.

James, M. (1992). *A political history of the civil war in Angola 1974–1990.* New Brunswick: Transaction Publishers.

de Jonge Oudraat, C. (2000). Making economic sanctions work. *Survival, 42*(3), 105–127.

Kevlihan, R. (2003). Sanctions and humanitarian concerns: Ireland and Angola 2001–2. *Irish Studies in International Affairs, 14*, 95–106.

Le Billion, P. (1999). *A land cursed by its wealth? Angola's war economy (1975–1999).* Helsinki: United Nations University/WIDER.

MacQueen, N. (1998). Peacekeeping by attrition: The United Nations in Angola. *The Journal of Modern African Studies, 36*(3), 399–422.

Mills, G., & Sidiropoulos, E. (Eds). (2004). *New tools for reform and stability. Sanctions, conditionalities and conflict resolution.* Johannesburg: South African Institute of International Affairs.

Peleman, J. (1999). The logistics of sanctions busting: The airborne component. In: J. Cilliers & C. Dietrich (Eds), *Angola's war economy: The role of oil and diamonds.* Pretoria: Institute for Security Studies.

Porto, J. G. (2003). *Cabinda – Notes on a soon-to-be-forgotten war.* ISS Paper No. 77. Pretoria: Institute for Security Studies.

Porto, J. G., Alden, C., & Parsons, I. (2007). *From soldiers to citizens: Demilitarization of conflict and society.* Aldershop: Ashgate Publishers.

Porto, J. G., & Parsons, I. (2003). *Sustaining the peace in Angola: An overview of current demobilisation, disarmament and reintegration.* BICC Paper No. 27. Bonn: Bonn International Center for Conversion.

Potgieter, J. (1999). Taking aid from the devil himself – UNITA's support structures. In: J. Cilliers & C. Dietrich (Eds), *Angola's war economy: The role of oil and diamonds*. Pretoria: Institute for Security Studies.

Schicho, W. (1999). Angola. In: S. Walter (Ed.), *Handbuch Afrika* (Vol. 1). Frankfurt/M: Brandes & Apsel.

Stiff, P. (1999). *The silent war – South African recce operations 1969–1994*. Alberton: Galago Publishing.

Thomashausen, A. (2002). Angola: The role of the international community. *South African Journal of International Affairs, 9*(2), 17–42.

United Nations Security Council. (1993). *Report of the Secretary-General on the situation in Angola*. S/26872, 13 December. New York City: United Nations.

United Nations Security Council. (1999a). *Letter dated 4 June 1999 from the Chairman of the Security Council Committee established pursuant to resolution 864 (1993) concerning the situation in Angola addressed to the President of the Security Council*. S/1999/644, 4 June. New York City: United Nations.

United Nations Security Council. (1999b). *Letter dated 28 July 1999 from the Chairman of the Security Council Committee established pursuant to resolution 864 (1993) concerning the situation in Angola addressed to the President of the Security Council*. S/1999/829, 28 July. New York City: United Nations.

United Nations Security Council. (2000). *Report of the panel of experts on violations of Security Council sanctions against UNITA*. S/2000/203, 10 March. New York City: United Nations.

United Nations Security Council. (2002a). *Additional report of the monitoring mechanism on sanctions against UNITA*. S/2002/486, 26 April. New York City: United Nations.

United Nations Security Council. (2002b). *Additional report of the monitoring mechanism on sanctions against UNITA*. S/2002/1119, 7 October. New York City: United Nations.

Wright, G. (1995). United States foreign policy and Angola. In: K. Hart & J. Lewis (Eds), *Why Angola matters*. Cambridge: African Studies Centre.

Wright, G. (1997). *The destruction of a nation: United States Policy towards Angola since 1945*. Chicago: Pluto Press.

CHAPTER 7

UN ARMS EMBARGOES IN THE GREAT LAKES, 1994–2004

Marc von Boemcken

From the start of the Rwandan civil war in 1990, the genocide in 1994 and right up to the conflict in the Democratic Republic of Congo (DRC), international policy has failed to effectively curtail arms supplies to the Great Lakes region. Whilst the United Nations (UN) arms embargo against Rwanda, which was imposed on May 17, 1994, could have presented a useful opportunity for achieving this objective, it lacked any sort of framework to ensure its proper enforcement. The most striking characteristic of the embargo can be identified in the stark dissonance between Security Council Resolution 918, which installed the sanctions, and the actual policies of UN member states before, during, and after the genocide of 1994.

The first section of this chapter will briefly examine the role of the international community in the run-up to genocide between 1990 and 1993. Despite a multitude of indicators for the looming catastrophe, a number of external actors continued to fuel the spiral of violent escalation, not least through the direct supply of weaponry and military aid.

As the terrible consequences of these assistance measures became ever more apparent in the first months of 1994, the international community failed to take any decisive action that might have forestalled a foreseeable worsening of the already violent situation. Here, the second section will pay particular attention to the widespread dissemination of small arms

Putting Teeth in the Tiger: Improving the Effectiveness of Arms Embargoes
Contributions to Conflict Management, Peace Economics and Development, Volume 10, 163–188
Copyright © 2009 by Emerald Group Publishing Limited
ISSN: 1572-8323/doi:10.1108/S1572-8323(2009)0000010011

in early 1994 and their often-underestimated function in the ensuing massacres.

It took up to six weeks of genocide and hundreds of thousand of victims before an arms embargo was eventually imposed against Rwanda. Since a robust peacekeeping mission failed to deploy in time, the embargo ended up being the only concrete measure taken by the international community. However, as the third section will illustrate, its immediate impact was minimal at best. Up to July 1994, weapons deliveries to the genocidal Rwandan government continued, seemingly uninterrupted. Indeed, Resolution 918 contained no provision for effective implementation. Although a small group of experts, the so-called UN International Commission of Inquiry (UNICOI) was later tasked by the Security Council to investigate embargo violations, none of its final recommendations on how to improve effectiveness were eventually put into practice.

Fourth, the chapter will look into the second phase of the arms embargo, beginning in August 1995. Pursuant to Resolution 1011, sanctions were lifted against the new government in Kigali. They continued to stay in place, however, against the forces of the exiled *genocidaires*, who had retreated into neighboring countries, eastern Zaire in particular (now the DRC).

Despite the unsettling conclusions drawn by the UNICOI in 1998 on illegal arms deliveries to the ousted Rwandan Hutu regime, within the Security Council, the arms embargo seemed to have somewhat vanished into obscurity only two years later. Although it clearly overlapped with the mandate of a UN peacekeeping mission (Mission to the Democratic Republic of Congo (MONUC)) deployed to the DRC in 1999–2000, the embargo did not receive a single mentioning in the relevant UN resolutions and documents. Apparently, the arms embargo and the peacekeeping mission were treated as two completely separate undertakings. As a consequence, and repeating the very same mistake that United Nations Assistance Mission to Rwanda (UNAMIR) had made 10 years earlier, the problem of small arms – both in terms of their import and in terms of their ongoing internal circulation – was largely neglected.

The chapter will nevertheless conclude on a carefully optimistic outlook. In 2003, the Security Council imposed a new arms embargo against rebel groups in the eastern provinces of the DRC, including, incidentally, those groups already embargoed pursuant to Resolution 1011. In comparison to earlier sanction regimes, this embargo displayed some significant improvements with regard to implementation. This new approach may well become a role model for the implementation strategy of future UN arms embargoes.

THE BUILD-UP OF THE RWANDAN MILITARY, 1990–1993

In the early 1990s, the single-party regime of the *Mouvement Révolutionnaire Nationale pour le Développement* (MRND), headed by President Juvénal Habyarimana, came under growing pressure both internally and externally. Rwanda experienced widespread destitution and famine as state revenues from coffee exports fell from an annual US $144 million in 1985 to a mere US $30 million in 1993 (Debiel, 2003, p. 166). A Structural Adjustment Program (SAP), imposed upon Rwanda by the Bretton Woods institutions in September 1991, was largely irrelevant, if not conducive, to the rising impoverishment of the Rwandan people (Chossudovsky, 1994, p. 21). Between 1989 and 1993, the proportion of the population consuming less than 1,000 calories a day doubled from 15 percent to 31 percent (Maton, 1994).

In October 1990, the rebel army of the Rwandan Patriotic Front (RPF) seized the opportunity of an economically shaken Rwanda and lauched an invasion against Kigali from Ugandan territory. The RPF was founded in 1987 by members of the ethnic Tutsi minority, which had been disposed as the ruling elite of Rwanda by the Hutu majority in a series of bloody massacres in the early 1960s. Nourished by social desperation and a Rwandan President bent on using the rebel invasion as a pretext for crushing any kind of internal – mainly Tutsi – opposition to the MRND, these tensions progressively radicalized and polarized Rwandan society throughout the early 1990s. According to a 1992 report by Amnesty International, following the RPF invasion, Habyarimana detained more than 8,000 civilians "on account of their ethnic [. . .] origins, political views or family connections with government opponents rather than because there was any evidence of their participation in the rebellion" (Amnesty International, 1992).

Although human rights abuses perpetuated by state officials were regularly reported – a coalition of Belgian non-governmental organizations (NGOs) even proposed sanctions against Rwanda as early as 1991 (Adelman, 1998) – the Habyarimana regime continued to receive massive aid from Western countries. Accompanying the imposition of the SAP, the total development aid volume to Rwanda rose by one quarter in 1991 (Debiel, 2003, p. 166). As powerfully argued by Peter Uvin (1998, p. 82, 237), this continuation of "business as usual" sent a strong signal to the MRND that the donors did not care about "government sponsored racist attacks against Tutsi."

The substantial rise of development assistance to Rwanda in the early 1990s was paralleled by an intensive process of militarization within Rwanda itself (Uvin, 1998, p. 88). Although there is no conclusive proof, it would appear that a "sizeable portion of [development aid] had been diverted by the regime [...] toward the acquisition of military hardware" (Melvern, 2000, pp. 66–8).

At the time the civil war in Rwanda began in October 1990, the *Forces Armées Rwandaise* (FAR) numbered between 3,000 and 5,000 soldiers. However, the Habyarimana regime soon embarked upon a frenzied recruitment campaign. Since the number of urban unemployed and landless peasants had dramatically increased, enlisting new recruits did not pose a problem (Chossudovsky, 1999, p. 124). By mid-1991, the FAR had swollen to 15,000, by the end of that year to 30,000 and, by 1992, to approximately 50,000 soldiers (Prunier, 1995, p. 113).

The main challenge was to secure the procurement of weapons necessaitated by such a dramatic rise in manpower. Military expenditures climbed from 1.8 percent of the gross domestic product (GDP) in 1989 to 5.6 percent in 1991 (SIPRI, 2001). By 1992, a staggering 38 percent of the government budget was devoted to the military (World Bank, 1994, p. 24). It was only through external support that the regime could sustain such a massive military build-up. As Chossudovsky and Galand (1996, Secn., 2.5, 5.4) concluded in their thorough study, "through intervening with loans and donations, the donors covered the National Defense's budgetary deficit, and by doing so financed the war."

A large segment of the international community can hardly plead ignorance for this strengthening of what was effectively a brutal and proto-fascist dictatorship. For in addition to the diversion of development aid, much of the costs for arms purchases and the military build-up was softened with foreign revenues specifically allotted to military purposes. Kathi Austin concluded that "[b]etween 1992 and 1994, Rwanda was [sub-Saharan Africa's] third-largest importer of weapons (behind Angola and Nigeria), with cumulative military imports totaling US $100 million" (Austin, 1999, p. 31). Between 1990 and 1994, Rwanda received arms and military assistance from Belgium, the United States, China, South Africa, and Egypt (Braeckman, 1994, p. 152; Goose & Smyth, 1994; *Federation of American Scientists, U.S. Security Assistance Database*; *Federation of American Scientists, U.S. Arms Transfers Database*; Chossudovsky & Galand, 1996, pp. 3.6–7; McNulty, 2000, pp. 113–4). The largest supplier, however, was France, and the French assistance can be regarded as key to the Rwandan military build-up between 1990 and 1993 (Uvin, 1998, pp. 82–3, p. 97).

France increased its bilateral military assistance to Rwanda from FF 4 million (US $0.8) per year before 1990 to FF 55 million (ca. US $10 million) in 1993. According to various reports, this included the delivery of *Milan* and *Apila* missile systems, mortars, light artillery guns, armored vehicles, three Gazelle helicopters, and a *Mystère* Falcon jet for President Habyarimana's personal use (McNulty, 2000, pp. 110–3; Goose & Smyth, 1994).

France not only supported the Habyarimana regime with financial resources and arms but also deployed troops in and around Kigali. In October 1990, 370 French Foreign Legion paratroopers and Marines arrived in Rwanda. As RPF attacks gained renewed intensity in early 1993, this number was increased to 670 (Sellström & Wohlgemuth, 1996). The French soldiers were instrumental to the build-up of the FAR through facilitating arms transfers, providing combat training and securing strategically important installations and roads (Braeckman, 1994, p. 159). Eventually, President Habyarimana gave a French military officer overall command of counter-insurgency operations (Prunier, 1995, p. 149). As Africa Watch (1993, p. 26) rightly concluded: "[T]he importance of French soldiers and French military aid in terms of moral and political support for President Habyarimana is unquestionable."

France's open support for the Habyarimana regime prevented an early UN arms embargo that, in all likelihood, would have slowed the massive build-up of the FAR and constituted a strong international condemnation of the widely reported human rights violations.

THE UNITED NATIONS MISSION TO RWANDA, NOVEMBER 1993–MAY 1994

Despite foreign support to the Habyarimana regime, the RPF managed to launch a successful offensive against the FAR in February 1993. This sudden development gave renewed impetus to a series of peace negotiations culminating in the signing of the so-called Arusha Accords on August 4, 1993. The Accords provided for a power sharing agreement with the RPF, which be included in a Transitional Government and comprise 40 percent of the new armed forces, thereby ending 39 years of Hutu monopoly in Rwanda (Arusha Accords, 1993, Annex III and Annex V). Furthermore, they reinstalled the "suspension of supplies of ammunition and weaponry" to the warring sides (Annex I: Article II.2).

Both parties to the Arusha Accords asked the UN to assist in the implementation of the agreement, leading to the establishment of the UNAMIR, following Security Council Resolution 872 in October 1003. However, UNAMIR was fraught with severe shortcomings familiar to UN operations. The UN Security Council had constituted UNAMIR not as a peace enforcement operation under Chapter VII of the UN Charter but as a Chapter VI peacekeeping mission. In effect, this meant that it was assigned a monitoring role and not able to "guarantee overall security of the country" as envisioned in the Arusha Accord (Annex V: Article 54.1).

Violent demonstrations, roadblocks, assassinations of political leaders, and random killings of civilians continued within view of UNAMIR troops between November 1993 and February 1994. On the evening of April 6, 1994, the French-made *Mystère* Falcon jet carrying President Habyarimana was shot down by two ground-to-air missiles upon approaching Kigali. Within a couple of hours of the plane crash, the Presidential Guard and militias had erected roadblocks, conducted house-to-house searches, and began a campaign of organized murders. Most "priority targets" – such as political opposition leaders, civil rights activists, journalists, and influential Tutsi – were massacred within 36 hours (Prunier, 1995, p. 229, 243). Upon receiving this news, the RPF forces in the northern part of the country immediately broke the cease-fire and resumed their offensive campaign against Kigali. It took another 100 days until they finally reached the city and the massacres ended. By then, over three-quarters of the entire population registered as Tutsi had been systematically slaughtered.

Following the murder of 10 Belgian peacekeepers on the day following Habyarimana's death, the Belgian Defense Minister informed the UN Secretary-General of Belgium's intention to withdraw its contingent "forthwith and unilaterally" from UNAMIR. Thereafter, Belgium began lobbying for the entire UNAMIR mission to be withdrawn from Rwanda (Caplan, 2004, No. 8). Despite strong protest from the Organization for African Unity (OAU) and many African governments, Security Council Resolution 912, which was agreed on April 21, 1994, dramatically reduced UNAMIR to a strength of 270 people and restricted its mandate to mediation and humanitarian aid.

ARMS AND GENOCIDE

Small arms played a central part in the gradual increase of violent activity before and during the genocide (Klare, 1999, p. 20). Parallel to arming the growing number of FAR troops, the Habyarimana regime had launched a program of militarizing civilian life as early as 1991. Initially, the aim was to distribute a gun for "every unit of 10 households." This process was soon augmented by the arming and training of organized militia units, the so-called *Interahamwe* (Sellström & Wohlgemuth, 1996).

Following the RPF offensive of February 1993, the arming of civilians intensified and, by the end of 1993, the militia counted 50,000–60,000 combatants (Omaar & de Waal, 1994; Debiel, 2003, p. 175). Although the city of Kigali had been declared a "weapons-secure" area in UN Resolution 872, arms were still being openly handed out in the streets after the arrival of UNAMIR in December 1993 and January 1994 (Prunier, 1995, p. 206).

In fact, the Arusha Accords had specifically addressed this problem of weapon proliferation. A "Neutral International Force" was considered capable of providing a sufficient degree of security only when simultaneously mandated to "track arms caches and neutralize armed gangs" throughout the whole of Rwanda (Article 54 paragraphs 4, 6). UNAMIR, however, was merely to "contribute to the security of the city of Kigali *inter alia* within a weapons-secure area *established by* the parties in and around the city" according to Resolution 872. An authorization for the proactive recovery of weapons and single-handed disarmament of militias was notably absent from its mandate. UNAMIR's assignment to simply *assist* Rwandan authorities in the collection and recovery of weaponry, that is, not to take unilateral action, proved to be disastrously ineffective. By January 30, 1994, UNAMIR had conducted 924 mobile patrols and 320 foot patrols and established 306 checkpoints, yet collected no more than nine weapons (DesForges, 1999).

However, UNAMIR displayed some limited success in enforcing the ban on arms imports as contained in the Arusha Accords (Annex I: Article II.2). On January 22, 1994, a French plane loaded with 90 boxes of Belgian-made mortars arrived secretly at Kigali airport. Despite the French government later arguing that the delivery had been "technically legal" since it stemmed from a contract concluded before the conclusion of the Arusha Agreement, the entire shipment was confiscated by UNAMIR troops (Otunno, 1999, p. 38). Also, on at least three occasions in February and March 1994, UNAMIR refused requests from the Rwandan Minister of Defense to grant landing permits to planes carrying arms (Wood & Peleman, 1999).

However, the control of Kigali airport by UNAMIR was hardly enough to effectively terminate arms imports into Rwanda. On February 27, 1994, Belgian intelligence reported FAR arms purchases from UNITA rebels in Angola. The weapons were supposedly "delivered through the Zairean military base at Kamina. From there they were sent to Goma and then across the border into Gisenyi, in northwestern Rwanda" (DesForges, 1999). Following the outbreak of large-scale massacres and the reduction of UNAMIR in early April 1994, the arms flow into Rwanda seemed to intensify rapidly. Apparently, on April 10, 1994, a deal to obtain weapons from both Israel and Albania and deliver them to Rwanda through Goma in Zaire, was concluded with the British-based aviation company *Mil-Tec* for a reported US $1.6 million (Oxfam, 1998).

Officially, France imposed a unilateral arms embargo against Rwanda on April 8, 1994. However, the French military – which enjoyed immunity from UNAMIR controls –continued reportedly to fly weapons into Kigali for a couple of days. A report published by Human Rights Watch (1995, pp. 6–8) described several French weapons shipments to the FAR in May and June 1994. Indeed, in May, a FAR delegation paid a visit to the head of the *Mission militaire de Coopération* in Paris where it reiterated its "urgent need" for "munitions [. . .], clothing and transmission equipment" (McNulty, 2000, p. 116). Two days after this meeting, the FAR is reported to have submitted to the French state-controlled enterprise *Société Française d'Exploitation de Matériels et Systèmes d'Armement* an order for US $8 million worth of South African–made weapons and munitions (DesForges, 1999). As with all weapons deliveries to Rwanda at this time, Zaire apparently issued the required End User Certificates. The cargo was then transported overland across the border to Rwanda so as to circumvent UNAMIR controls at Kigali airport (DesForges, 1999). General Dallaire was aware of these deliveries through Zaire in violation of the Arusha Accords. On one occasion, he is quoted to have said "If they land their planes here to deliver their damn weapons to the government, I'll have their planes shot down" (Prunier, 1995, p. 287, n. 14).

No notable international pressure was put on France to terminate arms exports to Rwanda (Austin, 1998). Neither was an arms embargo considered seriously within the European Union. Indeed, despite the situation in Rwanda, *Mil-Tec* did not even require an arms export license from the UK to broker deliveries (Oxfam, 1998). All in all, the Rwandan government was able to purchase weapons on the European market with startling ease given the fact that it was, at the same time, widely disseminating arms for the deliberate purpose of preparing genocide. It was mainly due to the diplomatic pressure exerted by African states – Nigeria in particular – that the problem of small arms availability in Rwanda finally showed up on the agenda of the UN Security Council (Adelman & Suhrke, 1996). On April 30, 1994, the President of the Security Council issued a statement wherein the killings in Rwanda were referred to as taking place in a "systematic manner" and being facilitated by continuing arms imports (S/PRST/1994/21). After four years of civil war and almost four weeks of genocide, it was the first time that the international community openly pondered the possibility of cutting off arms supplies to Rwanda. However, the major powers in the Security Council remained largely disinterested and – for the time being – did "not express a sense of urgency" (Adelman & Suhrke, 1996).

It is often held that automatic rifles were largely irrelevant to executing the genocide. As Stephen Smith and Antoine Glaser, two well-known African experts, (Glaser & Stephen Smith, 1994, p. 35) contended in 1994, "[T]he hands which cut to pieces men, women and children were Rwandan. They were not puppets' hands. They weren't even hands equipped with our help. Because, horror upon horror for their victims, the killers used machetes and not firearms which we had delivered to them in abundance."

For obvious reasons, the impression excited by the images of naked bodies slaughtered by machetes stick in the mind as the most gruesome, most horrific iconography of the genocide. Moreover, they conveniently fit the Western stereotype of unleashed primitive savagery whilst at the same time relegating responsibility. However, small arms played an instrumental part in the particular way that the violence was organized and orchestrated. Small arms were essential on at least three different levels: a symbolic level, a military/strategic level, and a technical level.

First, continual arms shipments from the West instilled in Hutu extremists and the Rwandan government with the necessary support and confidence that they could get away with the genocide unpunished by the international community (Clapham, 1996, p. 156). Second, the *genocidaires* knew that if they were to go through with executing a "final solution," they were likely to provoke an attack by the RPF. Thus, they needed a strong and well-equipped military able to fend off the rebel attacks whilst the militias proceeded with the massacres well behind the battle lines. Third, given the dissemination of weaponry to militia units in early 1994, small arms were also commonly employed by the *Interahamwe*, thereby improving considerably their deadly efficiency. In this sense, Goose and Smyth (1994, p. 90) underline the usage of such weaponry as a key factor for enlarging the scope of violence: "The proliferation of weapons in Rwanda expanded the conflict. [...] Much of the killing was carried out with machetes, but automatic rifles and hand grenades were also commonly used. Their wide availability helped Hutu extremists carry out their slaughter on a horrendous scale."

Since the Rwandan government depended on arms deliveries to meet at least three different objectives, all related to executing the genocide successfully, it hardly comes as a surprise that great efforts were made to ensure their continued supply once the killings had started. Indeed, as DesForges (1999) note, at one point in late April, the *genocidaires* actually altered their deadly strategy to secure a steady influx of weaponry and ammunition. Wary of international condemnation, and at almost the same time that the possibility of an arms embargo emerged on the agenda of the Security Council on April 30, the Rwandan government declared a campaign of "pacification." The purpose was to curtail a certain randomness, which had by that time begun to take hold of the killings, often leading to large-scale massacres with a high degree of international visibility. "Pacification" aimed to give a more organized and less visible character to the genocide. Stronger coordination would enable a maximum of dispersal, thereby obscuring the true dimension of violence. This way, it was hoped, a strong international reaction, let alone an arms embargo, could be held at bay.

THE UN ARMS EMBARGO AGAINST RWANDA, MAY–JULY 1994

On May 17, 1994, the UN Security Council imposed an arms embargo on both the genocidal government of Rwanda and its enemy in the field, the RPF. The embargo was part of an ambitious resolution, which sought to enhance the effectiveness of UNAMIR, and it was preceded by a change of attitude toward Rwanda gaining momentum within the UN administrative structure during late April. Interestingly, the initiative to draft and introduce the resolution was not taken by the permanent members of the Security Council. Instead, it was very much a result of pressure exerted over several weeks by African states upon the Council and growing concern within the UN bureaucracy, which continually received alarming reports from General Dallaire as to the worsening situation on the ground in Kigali.

Supported by human rights groups, many African states had repeatedly expressed the need for a forceful intervention in Rwanda unless the international community was to appear as bystander to a genocidal tragedy (Adelman & Suhrke, 1996, p. 39). UN Secretary-General Boutros Boutros-Ghali reacted to this pressure on April 29. In a letter to the Security Council, he openly questioned the "viability of [. . .] resolution 912," which "does not give UNAMIR the power to take effective action to halt the continuing massacres." Acknowledging that "as many as 200,000 people may have died during the last three weeks," he then concluded that the situation demanded urgent, and if necessary "forceful" action on behalf of the international community (S/1994/518). Although some Council members – most notably the United States – remained hesitant, a draft resolution was put to the vote in the UN Security Council three days later. It entered into force on May 17, 1994.

Resolution 918 consists of two main parts. Part A spells out the mandate for a renewed UNAMIR mission, which would differ from the previous one in three significant ways. First, its area of operation was expanded. As the peacekeepers had thus far been confined to the city of Kigali, Resolution 918 authorized the establishment of "secure humanitarian areas" in the whole of Rwanda. Second, these safe havens could be protected by force if necessary. Third, and perhaps most importantly, the size of UNAMIR was boosted to a projected 5,500 troops for this purpose. The mandate of UNAMIR II was backed by a Chapter VII arms embargo contained in the second part (B) of the resolution. Whereas, in text at least, Part A appeared as a rather ambitious response, Part B already implied two major weaknesses. First, the sanctions were not specifically targeted, but vaguely directed against "Rwanda," which apparently included the government as well as the rebels, who were actively trying to stop the genocide. Second, the arms embargo was, in the words of Joost Hiltermann (1997), "not accompanied by concrete proposals to implement it or enforce its compliance by UN member states."

Security Council members adopted the establishment of UNAMIR II (Part A) unanimously. However, it took another two months and another UN resolution before UNAMIR II actually materialized on the ground, even though the measures mandated in the resolution would in all likelihood have immediately halted most of the violence. Given the failure of UNAMIR II to deploy in time, the arms embargo (Part B) remained as "the only concrete measure" taken by the Security Council in response to the genocide (Prunier, 1995, p. 276). It was adopted with 14 votes in favor and one against. Not surprisingly, only Rwanda, which had been a member of the Security Council since January 1994, voiced opposition to it. The embargo acknowledged the implication of the Rwandan government in large-scale massacres way behind the frontline.

The arms embargo sought to achieve a number of different objectives. Like many other embargoes of a similar composition, it was first and foremost designed as a symbolic gesture. Western states hoped that their support for a sanctions regime against Rwanda would carry a message catering to at least three distinct audiences. First, domestic TV viewers could be morally appeased by the ostensible termination of arms exports on behalf of their respective national governments. Second, African states had been increasingly criticizing the Western attitude of indifference toward violent conflict on their continent – an accusation not least supported by the flourishing business of arms trafficking by and large emanating from developed countries. To oppose an arms embargo against Rwanda would thus not only have been unwise in terms of domestic policy but also diplomatically vis-à-vis Western relations with Africa. Third, after six weeks of genocide, no stretch of the imagination could possibly justify continued Western support for the policy objectives of the Rwandan government, which had so far been symbolically transported through massive arms deliveries.

However, all three messages failed to achieve the desired effects. On the one hand, the embargo stopped short of conveying a putative ethical concern of Western powers for peripheral conflict areas to both domestic audiences and African governments. For any such impression was certainly undermined not only by the disastrous reduction of UNAMIR I and the failure of UNAMIR II to materialize in time. In the long term, it was also seriously compromised by the gradual disclosure of information signaling the degree to which the West had been both indirectly and directly complicit in preparing the material grounds for genocide over a period of at least four years. On the other hand, the decision to impose an arms embargo simply came too late to meaningfully alter policy choices of the Rwandan government. By May 17, the dynamic of genocide had reached an intensity that could no longer be halted through diplomatic intervention alone.

Apart from serving an initial symbolic purpose, it is unlikely that the embargo was ever thought to produce any concrete effects in the short-to-medium term. This is not to say, however, that there was no material impact at all. The next part of the study will, first, take a closer look at the embargo violations and examine the extent to which the quantity of arms imports to Rwanda was – if at all – limited (*Level II effectiveness*). Should this be the case, and given the already mentioned importance that the *Interahamwe* apparently attached to continued weapons deliveries, it shall second be asked whether the embargo might have had at least a minimal effect upon the target's policy (*Level I effectiveness*).

Almost one and a half years after the embargo imposition, the UN established an International Commission of Inquiry (UNICOI) (S/RES/ 1013). It was given the mandate to collect information and investigate reports on possible violations of the arms embargo. The Commission conducted its work from October 1995 to October 1996 and issued four reports. As Loretta Bondi (2001) pointed out, "this marked an extraordinary advance in efforts to investigate arms embargo violations." For the UNICOI reports were, in fact, the very first detailed and "aggressive investigation into embargo busting" ever commissioned by the UN (Lumpe, 2004).

In the course of its investigations, UNICOI documented one case of what it considered to be a "highly probable violation of the embargo" (S/1997/1010: 107). Accompanied by a leading figure of the Rwandan government, Willem Ehlers – a South African citizen and director of a company called *Delta Aero* – had traveled to the Seychelles in May 1994 to negotiate the purchase of US $330,000 worth of weapons. Although he used an end-user certificate to Zaire, some 80 tons of arms and ammunition from the Seychelles arrived shortly after at Goma airport in June 1994. They were apparently diverted across the border to embargoed FAR troops in Gisenyi. As the Commission notes, the "[g]overnment of Zaire, or elements within it, [...] aided and abetted that violation" (S/1997/1010: 107). For unknown reasons, Ehlers was never prosecuted for the reported violation. A second incident reported by UNICOI concerned a Nigerian registered aircraft, which apparently transported 39 tons of arms and ammunition, which may have been destined for Rwanda, from Madrid to Goma on May 24, 1994 (S/1997/1010: 57). However, UNICOI could not confirm whether a violation had in fact taken place.

UNICOI was reactivated on April 9, 1998, with substantially the same mandate. In a report published seven months later, it mentioned a second series of illegal arms deliveries, which took more or less the same route (S/1998/1096). Confirming earlier claims by NGOs and newspapers, the report refers to the British company *Mil-Tec*, which had been brokering arms sales to the Rwandan government from Albania and Israel since April 1994 and apparently continued to do so irrespective of the sanctions until mid-July. All together, the *Mil-Tec* shipments seem to have added up to a sum total of US $5.5 million worth of weaponry including rifles, ammunition, grenades, and mortar bombs (Elliott & Norton-Taylor, 1996). The reactivated commission approached the British government on this matter in 1998. Its reaction to the incident clearly illustrated the grave deficiencies evident in the failure to incorporate international embargoes into national legislation practices. The report summarized it as follows:

> The Government had concluded that there had been delays and omissions in implementing the United Nations arms embargo on Rwanda in the United Kingdom [...], which included the Isle of Man on which the Mil-Tec Corporation was registered. It had also concluded that "because the legislation imposing the embargo in the United Kingdom did not fully cover the supply of arms to neighbouring countries [of Rwanda], the Customs and Excise investigation was unable to take forward criminal proceedings against Mil-Tec for a breach of the United Kingdom law. (S/1998/1096: 74)

Although the bodies officially commissioned by the UN were only able to confirm two "highly probable" occasions of embargo busting for the period between May and July 1994, a Human Rights Watch report from 1995, whose validation criteria appears to have been somewhat less strict, drew attention to further illegal arms shipments. For example, it alluded to a shipment in mid-June 1994, which "arrived on an aircraft registered in Liberia, with a Belgian crew from Ostend, which picked up arms in Libya, including artillery, ammunition and rifles from old government stocks" (Human Rights Watch, 1995). Another case mentioned in the report concerned arms dealer Fred Zeller from the United States. In an interview conducted by Human Rights Watch, Zeller apparently admitted that he had been authorized by the Rwandan Central Bank "to act as a middleman for an arms transfer from private sources headquartered in Belgium to the FAR in Rwanda via Goma airport" (Human Rights Watch, 1995). Although the deal seems to have been eventually unsuccessful, the US government later refused to cooperate with UNICOI in investigating the precise involvement of Zeller in further weapons deliveries violating the embargo. As Kathi Austin (2002) later noted, "[a]s it turned out, the United States did not want to expose this broker's arms trafficking violations because his networks also catered to U.S. allies such as the Sudanese People's Liberation Army."

The Human Rights Watch report (1995) also accused the French government of having continued its arms deliveries to the FAR even after the imposition of the UN embargo on May 17. As it would appear, the embargo merely provoked the French to redirect cargo flights away from Kigali airport, where shipments had thus far been unloaded under the eyes of UNAMIR, and instead take the route through Goma-Gisenyi. According to Prunier (1995, p. 287), the French military attaché at the French embassy in Kinshasa "virtually admitted in mid-June that weapons were still being delivered to the FAR." When later confronted by UNICOI with these charges, the French government categorically denied any arms deliveries to Rwanda subsequent to May 17 (S/1996/67: 43).

Given these findings, the embargo appears to have simply effected a diversion of the supply route. Nevertheless, DesForges (1999) do mention some cases where the embargo seems to have, not simply slowed down but in fact, prevented at least some deliveries. Egypt, Libya, and South Africa reportedly called off arms deals with the Rwandan government as a consequence of the UN sanctions. Following publication of the embargo violation conducted from their territory, the Seychelles acted swiftly to cancel a third shipment of arms brokered by Ehlers to Rwanda. And finally, the supply of US $8 million worth of arms that the Rwandan government had negotiated with the French firm SOFREMAS in early May 1994 was eventually put on hold due to the embargo (DesForges, 1999). Yet, whereas total supplies did in all likelihood decline over June and July 1994, there is no evidence to suggest that the intensity of the killings actually decreased over the same period. However, the embargo might well have played a minor role in facilitating the military defeat and subsequent retreat of the FAR, and, thus, albeit indirectly, contributed to an end of the massacres. After all, the Rwandan government apparently relied on massive arms and ammunitions imports and had made great efforts to secure further deliveries before the embargo in April and May 1994.

PRELIMINARY CONCLUSION: EFFECTIVENESS OF UNSC RESOLUTION 918

The arms embargo had displayed a number of major shortcomings up to July 1994. Most importantly, it was not embedded in an effective international response to the Rwandan genocide. Quite simply, Rwanda was of no political, economic, or strategic interest to the international community. Although all weapons imports had already been explicitly forbidden in the Arusha peace agreement of August 1993, large amounts of arms and ammunition were allowed to pour into the country up to six weeks into the genocide. This is all the more tragic, since small arms were instrumental for the effective execution of the genocide on a number of different levels. It may well be speculated whether an early arms embargo would have had a decisive impact, particularly if it had been backed by a genuine interest for the plight of Rwanda on behalf of the Western powers. For example, a UN monitoring mission similar to the one positioned on the Ugandan border (UNOMUR) might have been deployed on the Zairian border, which in turn could have been threatened with sanctions itself in case of supporting attempts at embargo busting.

The Sanctions Committee, which consisted of all members of the Security Council, remained, by any standard, "completely inert for the embargo's duration" (Hiltermann, 1997). In addition, the embargo was not exclusively targeted against the FAR and *Interahamwe*, but also against the RPF – at the time the only serious force in the region that was actively trying to stop the genocide. Quite clearly, support for the embargo among permanent Security Council members was lukewarm at best. No country exerted any pressure on Zaire to prevent arms destined for Rwanda from passing through its territory. The United States refused to cooperate with UNICOI in investigating the possible involvement of one of its citizens in embargo violations. Britain failed to properly incorporate the embargo into its domestic legislation, thus effectively allowing a British company to continue brokering activities unprosecuted. Finally, the French government itself reportedly deliberately violated the embargo. All in all, the arms embargo seemed to be more of a tragic farce than part of an effective policy response to genocide during the first couple of months following Resolution 918.

THE UN ARMS EMBARGO AGAINST THE HUTU REBELS 1995–1998

On August 16, 1995, the UN Security Council lifted the arms embargo against the RPF, now the *Rwandan Patriotic Army* (RPA), which had taken control of the country in July 1994 (S/RES/1011). Now that the security situation within Rwanda itself had improved, the Security Council members not only acknowledged the need for establishing an effective security sector in the war-torn country but also recognized its legitimate right to self-defense with appropriate weaponry (S/PV.3566). The latter was all the more important, since the majority of ex-FAR and *Interahamwe* fighters had retreated into a number of camps located just across the border to Zaire from where they continually threatened to violently topple the RPA government. For this reason, the embargo remained active with regard to the supply of arms to all "non-governmental forces," which were both situated either within or "in states neighboring Rwanda" and intended to use weapons on Rwandan territory (S/RES/1011). In effect, this amounted to an embargo against the ex-FAR and *Interahamwe*, who in the meantime had merged to form the so-called *Armée pour la libération du Rwanda* (ALIR).

By pursuing a double strategy of lifting the sanctions against the new government in Kigali while at the same time extending it to include hostile forces across the border to neighboring countries, the Security Council hoped to attain two objectives. First, it sought to deter the Hutu extremists from re-igniting the war by launching a large-scale attack against the RPA government (S/PV.3566). Second, it wanted to deprive the exiled government from any sense of international legitimacy, thus conveying its approval of the status quo. However, as the next part of this chapter will attempt to demonstrate, it failed on both accounts. Indeed, the omission of properly enforcing the UN sanctions in the years following Resolution 1011 would prove disastrous to stability in the Great Lakes region in the following years.

During its investigations between October 1995 and October 1996, UNICOI produced ample evidence that ALIR was engaging in frequent military training, which was logistically supported by Zairian authorities and conducted with a view to attacking Rwanda. UNICOI also documented extensive recruitment, drug-peddling, and fund-raising activities of the ousted genocidal regime throughout the African continent (S/1997/1010: 80–9). The profit was apparently used to finance a range of arms procurements in violation of the UN embargo. Since ALIR forces tended to exert effective control over Hutu refugee camps in the border region, they were also able to divert international emergency aid for their own purposes. For example, food was hoarded and sold cheaply on local markets to purchase arms with the profits (Pottier, 1996). In late 1996, according to UNICOI, ALIR had been successfully re-equipped with "brand-new weapons, including Kalashnikovs and anti-personnel mines that were not available to them before the embargo was imposed" (S/1997/1010: 92).

In early 1996, ALIR was reported to comprise up to 70,000 soldiers and militia (UNDP, 2001, p. 10). Throughout 1995 and 1996, cross-border incursions into Rwanda occurred on a regular basis. Just as during the 1994 genocide, the international community reacted with silence and inaction.

Human Rights Watch published the first detailed analysis on continuing arms flows to the ex-FAR and *Interahamwe* (later ALIR) as early as May 1995. Eyewitnesses stated that planeloads of weapons destined for the ex-FAR continued to regularly arrive at Goma airport throughout the latter half of 1994 and early 1995 (Human Rights Watch, 1995). In most cases, the origin of these shipments could not be clearly established, though Human Rights Watch did allude to several arms deliveries flown directly from South Africa to Zaire in February and March 1995. In a matter of only a couple of months, the ex-FAR had fully recovered from its defeat and was duly waiting for the appropriate moment to stage its violent return to Rwanda.

According to the third UNICOI report, from December 1997, substantial rearmament and mobilization of ALIR forces continued unabated after Human Rights Watch and other NGOs had first drawn attention to this development (S/1997/1010). The report pointed to strong ties between the ex-FAR and the Forces Armées Zaïroises (FAZ), which assisted with military training and supplied heavy weaponry. It also drew attention to the ways in which the embargoed forces were formidably linked to a complex web of both regional and international arms traders (S/1997/1010: 93).

UNICOI made a number of recommendations to the international community. Besides calling upon UN member states to effectively incorporate sanction regulations into domestic law and prosecute citizens found guilty of embargo busting (S/1997/1010: 110), it suggested expanding the embargo to include "a freeze on assets [...] of individuals and organizations involved in raising funds to finance the insurgency" (S/1997/1010: 114). The report also raised the important issue of deploying UN military observers at selected sites in the Rwandan-Zairian border region, particularly at suspected arms transit points (S/1997/1010: 113). As Eric Berman (2001, p. 167) later noted, none of these recommendations was eventually implemented.

After waiting for more than two years, the RPA eventually decided to take matters in its own hands. It played an instrumental role in assembling various Zairian anti-Mobutu movements to form an organized rebel army, led by Laurent Kabila, which came to be known as the *Alliance des Forces Démocratiques pour Libération du Congo-Zaire* (AFDL). Together with RPA elements, the AFDL crossed the western Rwandan border into Zaire in October 1996. By mid-November, the offensive had succeeded in driving ALIR out of their major strongholds in the border region of Kivu. Kinshasa fell in May 1997, and Kabila became head of state of what was now renamed the Democratic Republic of Congo.

However, the victory of the AFDL did not lead to peace. Fighting between the RPA and ALIR continued. A dramatic shift of alliances occurred in mid-1998 when the Rwandan government, which had allegedly also begun to exploit Congolese diamond mines, refused to concede to Kabila's demand to withdraw its forces. The situation soon escalated into full war between Rwanda and the DRC, involving a plethora of different state as well as non-state actors from the region, and in the course of which Kabila eventually forged an alliance with ALIR. Rwanda, for its part, again reverted to the strategy of creating and supporting its own proxy rebel group, the *Rassemblement Congolais pour la Démocratie* (RCD).

At about the same time that the Congo war was rapidly approaching a new stage of intensity and violence, on April 9, 1998, the UN Security Council reactivated UNICOI (S/RES/1161). A final report was produced six months later and published on November 18 (S/1998/1096). In comparison to the first Commission, the reactivated UNICOI had only "relatively little success in documenting arms sales in contravention of the embargo" (Berman, 2001, p. 165). There were a number of reasons for this. On the one hand, Eric Berman points out that "standard of proof was much higher [...] for the Commission as a UN body than for an advocacy group [...] or journalists." On the other hand, the verification of information obtained was extremely complicated by four main factors. First, there was an ongoing war in the DRC which Commission members were unable to visit. Second, a lack of human resources in the investigation team hindered their efficacy. Third, the short time frame of only six months allotted to the Commission cut short efforts. Fourth, a bureaucratic delay in financing from the UN created another hurdle (Berman, 2001, pp. 168–9). Despite all these difficulties, the reactivated Commission produced some interesting findings with regard to the movements and whereabouts of ALIR since their expulsion by the RPA/AFDL from the border region of eastern Zaire in late 1996 (S/1998/1096: 13). According to the final Commission report, by August 1998, some 50,000 ex-FAR and *Interahamwe* fighters were located in "sizeable organized groups in nine countries" of the Great Lakes region (S/1998/1096: 12/13). They had often "intermingled with other rebel groups" (S/1998/1096: 15) from whom they received weapons (S/1998/1096: 87) not subject to UN sanctions, in turn making the identification of actual embargo violations extremely difficult, if not impossible.

In regard to the precise origin of weapons supplies, the Commission was not able to identify anything more but general trends. Outside the African continent, Eastern and Southeastern European surplus stocks as well as South East Asia were referred to as important sources (S/1998/1096: 72, 51). As far as African suppliers were concerned, the Commission named a number of important producers in the region, notably the "Kenyan arms factory in Eldoret, the Ugandan arms factory in Nakasongola, Zimbabwe Defense Industries, and various South African arms manufacturers" (Berman, 2001, p. 166). In August 1998, ALIR found a new friend in Laurent Kabila. The reactivated Commission encountered a "unanimity of views that the Government of the Democratic Republic of the Congo was now supporting the ex-FAR and *Interahamwe*," which it both trained and armed (S/1998/1096: 68–9).

Eventually, the arms embargo neither succeeded in depriving its target of political legitimacy in the region nor did it make any discernible contribution to curtailing arms flows to ALIR.

THE UN ARMS EMBARGO AGAINST EASTERN DRC, 2003–2004

A cease-fire agreement between the DRC, Rwanda, and other African states involved in the Congo conflict was signed in July 1999. These so-called Lusaka Accords called for a withdrawal of all foreign troops from the DRC. This process was to be paralleled by a "tracking down and disarming" of militia and rebel groups, including the "genocidal forces" of ALIR (Article III.22). Explicitly acknowledging the problems caused by the illicit trafficking of arms in the region (Article III.17), the intended disarmament was also supplemented by a ban on arms imports against all conflict parties "in the field" (Article I.3: d). The provisions were to be overseen and, if necessary, enforced by a proposed UN peacekeeping mission (Chapter 8.2: 2).

The Security Council authorized the deployment of military observers to the DRC in August 1999 (S/RES 1258). A year later, the UN MONUC was expanded to comprise some 5,500 personnel. Although the mandate of MONUC included some Chapter VII enforcement powers, it lacked an authorization to coercively disarm militia members as originally envisioned by the Lusaka agreement (S/RES 1291). This watering-down of robustness, as witnessed in the translation of a peacekeeping mandate from a regional agreement into a Security Council Resolution, bore a striking resemblance to Resolution 872 and the establishment of UNAMIR following the Arusha Accords in 1993. Whereas Resolution 872 had, however, not specifically incorporated the Arusha arms ban into the wording of UNAMIR's mandate, Resolution 1291 unmistakably asked MONUC to "monitor compliance with the provision of the Ceasefire Agreement on the supply of ammunition, weaponry and other war-related materiel to the field, including to all armed groups referred to in Annex A, Chapter 9.1."

Interestingly, Chapter 9.1 of the Lusaka Accords explicitly included the "ex-FAR and *Interahamwe* forces" (i.e., ALIR). Since the arms embargo against these rebel groups, imposed by Resolution 1011, was still in place, Resolution 1291 had, technically at least, provided for precisely those military observers that UNICOI had recommended three years earlier to no avail. Although the Sanctions Committee established pursuant to Resolution 918 stated in two reports, published in January and December 2002, respectively (S/2002/49 and S/2002/1406), that a "specific monitoring mechanism to ensure the effective implementation of the arms embargo" was missing, it seems to have gone somewhat unnoticed that exactly such a mechanism had in fact been put into place by the wording of Resolution 1291. Only, it would seem that within the UN bureaucracy, the creation of MONUC and the arms embargo against ALIR – although clearly overlapping – were treated as two completely separate things. Resolution 1291 did not contain a single reference to Resolution 1011. Indeed, although MONUC was tasked to monitor arms deliveries to conflict parties, the entire question of imposing an international arms embargo against them, thereby effectively expanding Resolution 1011, appears as strangely absent from Resolution 1291.

The reactivated UNICOI had been severely circumscribed by its inability to visit the DRC due to the ongoing war at the time. Yet, its conclusions had drawn a rather worrisome picture with regard to the status of ALIR and the general trend of massive arms deliveries into the troubled region. MONUC, on the contrary, maintained a physical presence in the DRC. Monitoring compliance with Resolution 1011 would not only have been fully consistent with its mandate but also could have taken the work begun by UNICOI further. Unfortunately, this opportunity was missed. The arms embargo was simply overlooked or at least not deemed to be of particular importance. A series of reports on MONUC by the UN Secretary-General, in the period between 2000 and 2003, reflected this overall lack of interest, as the issue of arms imports, let alone deliveries to the embargoed ALIR, received hardly any mention. A report from 2000 (S/2000/888) briefly alluded to "extensive military preparations by the parties," which included "the procurement of large quantities of weapons and military equipment," (III.21) and, in fact, identified ALIR as a major recipient (III.27). However, it failed to either point out that this constituted an embargo violation or to promise to investigate the matter further.

All in all, it looks as if ALIR continued to receive arms and ammunition from the government of the DRC as well as particular rebel groups in the region – at least on a sporadic basis – even after the conclusion of the Lusaka agreement. A UN report from 2001 (S/2001/128: III.25) touched upon "persistent reports" indicating that the *Forces armées congolaises* (FAC) remained a major arms supplier to ALIR.

Fueled by arms deliveries, fighting between the RPA/RCD and ALIR continued in the Kivu region of eastern Congo throughout 2000 and 2001. Under these circumstances, a voluntary disarmament of militia groups could not be expected. Thus, Rwanda had a good excuse to prolong its withdrawal, not least since it was profiting from its military presence in the DRC by exploiting the coltan mines in the mineral-rich Kivu area (S/2001/357: 104, 110–4, 126–34). The situation remained more or less unchanged until late 2001 when the military balance shifted in favor of the RPF. According to a UN report from April 2002, the morale of ALIR fighters eventually hit rock bottom (S/2002/341: 24). Reduced to a mere fifth of its estimated strength in 1998 (S/1998/1096), ALIR split into two groups of approximately 5,000 troops (S/2002/341: 22). "Sporadic attacks" were mostly carried out simply "for the sake of survival" (S/2001/1072: 141). Had the reactivated UNICOI still considered ALIR a "significant component" of the Congo war, four years later, it was believed "to be seriously weakened and to no longer pose a serious threat, many of its troops having

been captured and placed in a rehabilitation camp in Rwanda"
(S/2001/1072: 141).

The weapons deliveries to the Rwandan rebels by the FAC were probably
cut back in late 2001 and early 2002, not least as a consequence of Joseph
Kabila assuming power in January 2001 following the assassination of his
father. Unlike Laurent Kabila's war mongering, his son pursued a more
moderate policy geared toward national reconciliation and a stronger
commitment to the Lusaka Accords (McCullum, 2001). The extent to which
this change of policy in Kinshasa was conducive to the military setback of
ALIR is difficult to verify. In fact, clandestine arms shipments from the
FAC to ALIR reportedly continued on an irregular basis right up to
October 2003 (S/2004/551: 87). The impact of MONUC, on the other side,
cannot have been more than minimal, since its activities did not include a
monitoring or enforcing of the UN arms embargo as spelt out in Resolution
1011.

Finally, alarmed by the ongoing violence in eastern Congo, on July 28,
2003, Security Council Resolution 1493 imposed an arms embargo against,
on the one hand, "all foreign and Congolese armed groups and militias"
operating in the eastern provinces of the DRC and, on the other hand,
against those armed groups not party to a power-sharing agreement, which
had been signed on December 17, 2002. Since ALIR forces continued to be
active in precisely the territories referred to in this resolution, they were
placed under a second arms embargo, which effectively supplanted the one
established under Resolution 1011.

Arms Embargoes and the War in Eastern Zaire

The reasons as to why the embargo was established three years into the
deployment of MONUC in 1999/2000 are not conclusively known. It can
only be speculated that – at the time – the issue of arms imports had simply
not been conceived of as a particular priority on the diplomatic agenda at
UN headquarters in New York. This suspicion is further nourished by the
apparent lack of interest in formulating the original mandate of MONUC in
reference to the provisions of Resolution 918/1011.

Considering that MONUC had been in the DRC since 1999/2000, with
violent activity continuing unabated especially in the eastern part of the
country, the eventual arms embargo of July 2003 came far too late. To this
extent, it was the same story as with UNAMIR and the belated embargo
established pursuant to Resolution 918. Nevertheless, Resolution 1493

actually took on board two central recommendations, which had been put forward by the first UNICOI team in 1997. That is, unlike Resolution 918 of 1994, the 2003 embargo, first, broadened the scope of the embargo to include both direct and – crucially – indirect financial assistance to the target groups (S/RES 1493: 18). Second, it tasked the UN peacekeeping force deployed on the ground in the target region to specifically monitor embargo violations (S/RES 1493: 19). However, as an UN-commissioned expert group later noted, "MONUC was given the task of monitoring the arms embargo at a time when it lacked both the human resources and the technical assets to face its own operational priorities and deployment constraints, [...]. Under those conditions, the Mission's limited arms-monitoring capability was stretched to the limit, although MONUC fully appreciated the importance of the task" (S/2004/551: 24).

Furthermore, between August 2003 and March 2004, MONUC was repeatedly denied "access to inspect aircraft, military facilities or other areas where weapons and arms caches were allegedly stockpiled" (S/2004/251: 43).

In response to these remaining operative problems, the mechanisms for ensuring effective embargo implementation were further improved in Resolution 1533 of March 12, 2004, which took account of a "three-tiered" approach recommended by the UN Secretary-General in a report from November 2003 (S/2003/1098: 72). First, embargo effectiveness was to be augmented by military observers and peacekeepers situated on the ground in the target area. Initially MONUC – just as UNAMIR – had been denied any unilateral enforcement powers, but it was authorized under Chapter VII of the UN Charter "to seize or collect [...] the arms [...] whose presence in the [DRC] violates [the embargo] and to dispose of such arms [...] as appropriate" (S/RES 1533: 4). For this purpose, it was requested to "use all means [...] to inspect, without notice as it deems necessary, the cargo of aircraft and of any transport vehicle using the ports, airports, airfields, military bases and border crossings" (S/RES 1533: 3). Complementing this robust monitoring mandate assigned to MONUC, an independent and mobile group of three to four technical experts would examine and analyze the available information on arms flows to embargoed entities (S/RES 1533: 10). This, in turn, would be reported to a sanctions committee installed at the UN Security Council. Based on the expert report, the committee would develop recommendations for improving embargo effectiveness and, to this end, exert its political leverage on member states (S/RES 1533: 8; S/2003/1098: 72).

Following Resolution 1533, the embargo was, at least on paper, endowed with an enforcement, monitoring and reporting mechanism far more advanced than the ones accompanying earlier arms embargoes in Central Africa. Six years after its final report, UNICOI's recommendations were – at last – seriously considered.

REFERENCES

Adelman, H. (1998). *The role of non-African states in the Rwandan genocide*. Addis Ababa: OAU.

Adelman, H., & Suhrke, A. (1996). Early warning and conflict management: Genocide in Rwanda. In: D. Millwood (Ed.), *The international response to conflict and genocide: Lessons from the Rwanda experience*. Copenhagen, Denmark: Steering Committee of the Joint Evaluation of Emergency Assistance to Rwanda.

Africa Watch. (1993). *Beyond the rhetoric: Continuing human rights abuses in Rwanda*. Report No. 7, June.

Amnesty International. (1992). Rwanda: Persecution of Tutsi minority and repression of government critics, 1990–1992. AI Index AFR 47/02/92.

Austin, K. (1998). *Security issues, arms flows, and violence in Rwanda*. Testimony to the Subcommittee on International Operations and Human Rights, 5 May.

Austin, K. (1999). Light weapons and conflict in the great lakes region of Africa. In: J. Boutwell & M. T. Klare (Eds), *Light weapons and civil conflict*. Lanham, MD: Rowman and Littlefield.

Austin, K. (2002). Illicit arms brokers: Aiding and abetting atrocities. *Brown Journal for World Affairs*, 9, 204–216.

Berman, E. G. (2001). Sanctions against the *genocidaires:* Experiences of the 1998 UN International Commission of Inquiry. In: M. Brzoska (Ed.), *Smart sanctions: The next steps*. Baden-Baden: Nomos.

Bondi, L. (2001). Arms embargoes. In: M. Brzoska (Ed.), *Smart sanctions: The next steps*. Baden-Baden: Nomos.

Braeckman, C. (1994). *Génocide au Rwanda*. Paris: Fayart.

Caplan, G. (2004).*Rwanda ten years after the genocide: Some reminders of the international response to the crisis*. Pambazuka News 142, February, Available at http://www.pambazuka. org/index.php?issue = 142

Chossudovsky, M. (1994). Les fruits empoisonnés de l'ajustement structurel. *Le Monde Diplomatique*, November.

Chossudovsky, M. (1999). Human security and economic genocide in Rwanda. In: C. Thomas & P. Wilkin (Eds), *Globalization, human security and the African experience*. London: Lynne Rienner.

Chossudovsky, M., & Galand, P. (1996). The use of Rwanda's external debt (1990–1994) – The responsibility of donors and creditors for the 1994 Rwandan genocide. Centre for Research on Globalization, Ottawa and Brussels, November. Available at http:// globalresearch.ca/articles/CHO403E.html

Clapham, C. (1996). *Africa and the international system: The politics of state survival*. New York: Cambridge University Press.

Debiel, T. (2003). *UN-Friedensoperationen in Afrika: Weltinnenpolitik und die Realität von Bürgerkriegen*. Bonn: Dietz.

DesForges, A. L. (1999). *Leave none to tell the story: Genocide in Rwanda*. New York: Human Rights Watch. Available at http://www.hrw.org/reports/1999/rwanda/

Elliott, C., & Norton-Taylor, R. (1996). Arms sales to Rwanda questioned. *The Guardian*, 19 November.

Glaser, A., & Stephen Smith, S. (1994). *L'Afrique sans Africains*. Paris: Stock.

Goose, S. D., & Smyth, F. (1994). Arming genocide in Rwanda. *Foreign Affairs*, *73*, 86–96.

Hiltermann, J. (1997). Post-mortem on the International Commission of Inquiry. *Association of Concerned African Scholars Bulletin*, *48/49*(Fall), 19–23.

Human Rights Watch (HRW). (1995). *Rwanda/Zaire: Rearming with impunity – International support for the perpetrators of the Rwandan Genocide*. HRW Arms Project, May, Available at http://www.hrw.org/reports/1995/Rwanda1.htm

Klare, M. T. (1999). The international trade in light weapons: What have we learned? In: J. Boutwell & M. T. Klare (Eds), *Light weapons and civil conflict*. Lanham, MD: Rowman and Littlefield.

Lumpe, L. (2004). *Small arms and light weapons: Issues and options*. UN Foundation, Spring.

Maton, J. (1994). *Developpement Economique et Social au Rwanda entre 1980 et 1993: Le Dixieme Decile en Face de L'Apocalypse*. Ghent: Université de Gand, Faculté des Sciences Economiques.

McCullum, H. (2001). *Joseph Kabila begins painful pursuit of peace*. Afrol News, Available at http://www.afrol.com/html/Countries/DRC/backgr_j_kabila_peace.htm

McNulty, M. (2000). French arms, war and genocide in Rwanda. *Crime, Law & Social Change*, *33*, 105–129.

Melvern, L. (2000). *A people betrayed: The role of the west in Rwanda's genocide*. London and New York: Zed Books.

Omaar, R., & de Waal, A. (1994). *Rwanda: Death, despair and defiance*. London: African Rights.

Otunno, O. (1999). An historical analysis of the invasion by the Rwanda Patriotic Army (RPA). In: H. Adelman & A. Suhrke (Eds), *The path of a genocide: The Rwanda crisis from Uganda to Zaire*. New Jersey: Transaction Publishers.

Oxfam. (1998). *Out of control – The loopholes in UK controls of the arms trade*. London, December.

Pottier, J. (1996). Relief and repatriation: Views by Rwandan refugees; lessons for humanitarian aid workers. *African Affairs*, *95*, 403–429.

Prunier, G. (1995). *The Rwanda crisis: History of a Genocide*. London: Hurst & Company.

Sellström, T., & Wohlgemuth, L. (1996). Historical perspective: Some explanatory factors. In: D. Millwood (Ed.), *The international response to conflict and genocide: Lessons from the Rwanda experience*. Copenhagen, Denmark: Steering Committee of the Joint Evaluation of Emergency Assistance to Rwanda. Available at http://www.reliefweb.int/library/nordic/book5/pb025c.html

Stockholm International Peace Research Institute (SIPRI). (2001). Military expenditure and arms production. In: *SIPRI Yearbook 2001*. Oxford: Oxford University Press.

UNDP. (2001). *Supplement: UNDP/donor mission to DRC/GLR: Defining UNDP's role in disarmament, demobilization and durable solutions (D3)*. United Nations Development Programme, New York, 6 August–13 September.

Uvin, P. (1998). *Aiding violence: The development enterprise in Rwanda.* West Hartfort: Kumarian Press.

Wood, B., & Peleman, J. (1999). *The arms fixers – Controlling the brokers and shipping agents.* Oslo: The Norwegian Initiative on Small Arms Transfers (NISAT).

World Bank. (1994). *Rwanda: Poverty reduction and sustainable growth.* Washington, DC: Population and Human Resources Division, South Central and Indian Ocean Department, Africa Region.

CHAPTER 8

ARMS EMBARGOES AGAINST ERITREA AND ETHIOPIA

Marc von Boemcken

It is difficult to measure the effectiveness of the United Nations (UN) arms embargo against Eritrea and Ethiopia in terms of achieving its stated policy objectives. The war it sought to end was brought to a decisive, if brutal, conclusion only two weeks after the imposition of sanctions on May 17, 2000. Henceforth, the embargo served as a minor bargaining factor in the post-conflict negotiation rounds rather than as a meaningful deterrent of resource-related military considerations. Given its outdated objective as well as its comparatively low international importance, it hardly comes as a surprise that the embargo lacked an on-site UN monitoring mechanism. Instead, the responsible Security Council Committee solely relied on the provision of second-hand information from national governments. Its final report of May 9, 2001, amounted to no more than one and a half pages (United Nations, 2001).

The following inquiry will begin by assessing the massive arms deliveries to Eritrea and Ethiopia that preceded the imposition of the sanctions regime. Up to May 2000, an almost unobstructed mobilization of both countries' armed forces curtailed any possibility of short-term effectiveness the eventual embargo might have had with regard to meaningfully altering the behavior of its targets. Indeed, despite a mandatory weapons ban of the United States and, later, the European Union (EU), as well as a voluntary UN embargo, the international environment was remarkably conducive to

Putting Teeth in the Tiger: Improving the Effectiveness of Arms Embargoes
Contributions to Conflict Management, Peace Economics and Development, Volume 10, 189–203
Copyright © 2009 by Emerald Group Publishing Limited
All rights of reproduction in any form reserved
ISSN: 1572-8323/doi:10.1108/S1572-8323(2009)0000010012

Eritrean and Ethiopian efforts at rearmament throughout the latter part of
the 1990s. Weapons procurement benefited from two circumstances. First,
there was a dangerous misperception informing US strategic objectives in
the region, which overlooked growing tensions between the two countries.
Second, and more importantly, the commercial interest within Eastern
Europe and Russia to sell large amounts of surplus weaponry flourished in
the absence of effective mechanisms of international control. Indeed, the
failure of the UN to agree upon a timely and mandatory arms embargo can
be largely attributed to the opposition of Russia in the Security Council.

This is not, however, an exercise to simply dismiss the belated arms
embargo as an extraneous and inconsequential bauble of international
policy. For although it did not verifiably impact politico-military decisions
during the conflict, it was nevertheless effective in three key areas. First, it
effectively limited the actual imports of weaponry into Eritrea and Ethiopia
for the time of its one-year installment. Second, it served an implicit sender-
state objective not explicitly articulated in the resolution. That is, the arms
embargo provided for the necessary legal environment wherein relief efforts
in response to the Ethiopian famine of 2000–2001 could be conducted in a
both morally responsible and operationally effective manner. Third, it is
argued that the embargo had the symbolic effect of highlighting the
potentially disastrous consequences, which the large-scale export of
weaponry had on regional stability in the Horn of Africa. It is worth
examining how international consensus building managed to accommodate
these ethical considerations vis-à-vis the economic interests of former Soviet
states. To this effect, it may well be suggested that the embargo, despite its
obvious flaws, indeed displayed a limited degree of effectiveness.

PREPARING FOR WAR

Only two days before the UN imposed a mandatory arms embargo on
Eritrea and Ethiopia, the German Minister for Development, Heidemarie
Wieczorek-Zeul, issued a communiqué wherein she described the ongoing
absence of international export restrictions against the warring countries as
nothing less than a "scandal" (*Agence France Press*, May 15, 2000). Indeed,
the war between Eritrea and Ethiopia had pre-dated the embargo by two
years.

In mid-May 1998, an Eritrean mechanized tank brigade had moved into a
remote and mountainous territory of 160 square miles located in the region
bordering Ethiopia. According to the government in Asmara, the deployment

of troops had been a reaction to a series of transgressions by Tigray militia into its territory. The Ethiopian government, on the contrary, claimed that the region had been an Ethiopian-administered district all along. Only a year later, however, it seemed as if Eritrea and Ethiopia were no longer fighting over petty landmarks, but rather for their very survival as nations. Meles Zenawi, the Prime Minister of Ethiopia, would later refer to the border incident as "Sarajevo 1914. It was an accident waiting to happen" (*Economist*, 11 May, 1999). Eritrean President Isaias Afwerki said, in July 1998, that that the war was in fact "not a matter of boundaries but of national pride and territorial integrity" (*British Broadcasting Corporation*, February 11, 2000).

By May 2000, combat-related deaths were roughly estimated to lie at 100,000 (Seybolt, 2001, p. 29), and an additional half a million people had been internally displaced (*Guardian*, May 26, 2000). The most intense fighting occurred in February 1999. According to *The Economist* (May 13, 1999), in only four days of combat, up to 40,000 soldiers on both sides were killed or wounded. Such figures prompted the Office of the UN High Commissioner for Refugees to refer to the conflict in the Horn of Africa as the "world's largest war" in 1999 (*Refugees Magazine*, September, 1999).

Against this background, it seems appropriate to ask why the embargo was not imposed earlier. As is true for most African tragedies, the war received little attention in both the international media and policy-making organs. The coincident Kosovo conflict served to deflect the strategic priorities of most major powers. A second factor is the simplistic Western perception of the conflict realities in the Horn of Africa. In fact, the sudden outbreak of war between Eritrea and Ethiopia took the international community by complete surprise. It simply did not fit the established image of mutual friendship attributed to the two countries, which dated back to the final phase of the Ethiopian civil war in the late 1980s (Gilkes & Plaut, 2000). As the first border skirmishes erupted in early 1998, no one expected the conflict to mushroom into mass mobilization and what would eventually amount to full-scale warfare. It was not least this perception, which had facilitated massive arms exports to the region throughout the 1990s.

Militarization and Arms Transfers before 1998

Weapons shipments to Ethiopia have a long history. During the 1950s and 1960s, the United States, eager to contain communist ambitions in the region, appeared as a staunch supporter of the autocratic and conservative regime of Ethiopian monarch Haile Selassie. Although Ethiopia's unlawful annexation of quasi-autonomous Eritrea in 1962 sparked a 30-year indepen- dence struggle that would eventually stand as the longest African war of the 20th century, the United States supported Selassie with massive weapons deliveries and established a large US military intelligence base in Ethiopian- controlled Asmara.

Relations between the United States and Ethiopia deteriorated with the military coup of 1974. Although US arms sales to Ethiopia still amounted to an impressive US $180 million between 1974 and 1977 (*Johannesburg Mail & Guardian*, December 3, 1999), military dictator Mengistu Haile Mariam turned to the Soviet Union as ally. Until his defeat in 1991, he received an estimated US $13 billion worth of military assistance from Moscow (Ofcansky & LaVerle, 1993). The new governments in Addis Ababa and Asmara thus inherited a dangerous legacy of massive stocks of US and Soviet weaponry. In fact, in mid-1991, Ethiopia possessed the largest combined military and paramilitary forces in sub-Saharan Africa (Ofcansky & LaVerle, 1993). Still, the overall development in the first part of the 1990s seemed to initially suggest an atmosphere of relaxation. The demilitarization and reintegration process in the aftermath of the war was fairly successful (Kingma & Sayers, 1995). Also, Ethiopian military expenditure experienced a significant decrease. According to a SIPRI study conducted by Paul George (1997, p. 14), defense-related spending as a share of total govern- ment expenditure fell from approximately 60 percent in FY 1989–1990 to 30 percent in FY 1992–1993.

However, it is important to point out that from the mid-1990s onwards, and paralleling the rise of economic tension between Ethiopia and Eritrea, demobilization began to give way to renewed efforts at remobilization. While Ethiopia only budgeted US $106 million for military purposes in 1995, that figure had doubled by 1997 to US $211 million. It steadily rose to US $349 million in 1998 and reached a staggering US $730 million at the height of the war in early 2000, when the mandatory UN arms embargo was imposed. Eritrea, for its part, started to increase investment into its armed forces almost immediately after gaining formal independence in 1993. Eritrean military expenditure grew from an annual US $74.1 million in 1994 to US $137 million in 1996 and US $197 million in 1998.[1]

At least from 1996 onwards, the trend toward remobilization is apparent in both countries. It is rather ironic that the EU was at the time funding numerous demobilization programs in the region, while its member states seem to have simultaneously exported large military supplies to both Eritrea and Ethiopia. As William Benson notes, Finland, Germany, Italy, and the

United Kingdom provided Eritrea with military transport and jet trainer aircraft in the mid-1990s (Benson, 1997). During the same period, the SIPRI Arms Transfers Project reports that Eritrea purchased further weapons, such as combat helicopters, from China and Russia. As the crisis intensified in 1997, Ethiopia, on the contrary, apparently imported military transport aircraft as well as communications equipment from the United States, combat helicopters from Hungary, and jet trainer aircraft from the Czech Republic.[2]

On the eve of war, in early 1998, both Eritrea and Ethiopia were in the process of successfully completing a modernization of their military forces, especially the air force. Also, additional military personnel was being recruited at an accelerated pace. Between 1997 and 1999, the Ethiopian army signed up roughly 200,000 new soldiers. Meanwhile, Eritrea conscripted 150,000 combatants, which was effectively a fourfold increase of the original size of its army in 1994.

Arms Transfers, Early 1998 to February 1999

During a visit to Ethiopia in 1997, US Secretary of State Madeleine Albright was asked by a female schoolteacher to comment on an apparent "contradiction" pervading the international community. On the one hand, it entertained a popular rhetoric of peace, yet on the other hand, it continued to allow massive arms deliveries to Africa. Whilst acknowledging to have been asked a "very, very difficult question," Secretary of State Albright responded that states needed to defend themselves against "neighbors who are trying to subvert it" (*US Department or State News*, December 9, 1997). This statement was a reflection of US strategy at the time, which sought to consolidate and strengthen the axis Eritrea-Ethiopia-Uganda so as to contain the National Islamic Front government in the Sudan, considered a "terrorist" state. However, it seriously de-emphasized the growing tensions between Ethiopia and Eritrea. The Sudanese government would later openly rejoice that "the weapons which Ethiopia and Eritrea acquired from the US to fight Sudan are now being used to kill each other" (Klein, 1998).

The military build-up of Eritrea and Ethiopia accelerated after the border incident in May 1998. Yet, the first UN Resolution of June 1998, whilst condemning the use of force and demanding a cessation of hostilities, did not mention the continuing arms exports to the region. Rather, one of the first countries to address this issue and to become involved in the mediation process was the United States, who had rather quickly realized the resultant danger to its foreign policy objectives in the region. Not only did US Assistant Secretary of State Susan Rice manage to broker a moratorium on air strikes in July 1998, the Clinton administration also imposed a unilateral arms embargo against the warring countries.[3] However, the US embargo had neither a substantial impact on the amount of weapons exported into the region nor did it alter the behavior of the main actors in Addis Ababa and Asmara (*New York Times*, July 23, 1998).

Significantly, the United States did not exert much pressure on other countries to follow suit and refrain from arms deliveries to the region. In September 1998, Israeli Prime Minister Benjamin Netanjahu could thus reportedly give permission to the Israeli firm *Elbit* to sell 10 upgraded MiG-21 Lancer fighters to Ethiopia (*Israel's Business Arena*, September 7, 1998). Most likely, this deal was not simply a commercial enterprise but also had a strategic background. Just before the outbreak of war, Eritrea had signaled interest in joining the Arab League. It was already receiving considerable funds from Libya. No doubt, an Arabic Eritrea would have been a setback for both Israeli and US strategic interests in the Red Sea. Hence, it is conceivable that, to some extent, the prospect of weakening Eritrea initially served to compromise the importance that the United States attributed to a total termination of arms deliveries by third parties, particularly to Ethiopia.

In any case, both governments could rely on a steady influx of weaponry, emanating mainly from surplus stocks in Eastern Europe and Russia. According to a BBC report, in July 1998, about 20 Ukrainian transport planes loaded with Bulgarian-made AK 47 assault rifles as well as ammunition for the BM 21 rocket launcher arrived in Eritrea (Gilkes, 1999). *Reuters* (December 15, 1998) reported that in December 1998, Eritrea bought 6–10 MiG 29 fighter jets from Russia, worth an estimated US $25 million each.

Similarly, it is reported that Ethiopia received 50 T-55M tanks from Bulgaria and 40 from Belarus. The Czech Republic seems to have delivered two jet trainer aircraft. And Russia reportedly supplied Ethiopia, in December 1998, with 8 SU 27 fighters, 12 MI-24 and MI-17 as well as 2 Mi-8T combat helicopters, 10–12 152-mm artillery guns, and other military equipment in a deal worth about US $150 million.[4] In addition, Ethiopia signed a major contract for the delivery of ammunitions from China in 1998 (Gilkes, 1999).

Notwithstanding the outbreak of open fighting, Western European countries also appear to have at least attempted to maintain a fair share of the arms trade to Eritrea and Ethiopia. Reports suggest that Eritrea continued to obtain several attack helicopters from Italy (Gilkes, 1999). Also, according to *Agence France Press* (August 21, 1998), in August 1998, the French state-owned company *Thomson-CSF* sought to export five tons of military communications equipment to Ethiopia. Similarly, in January 1999, the British company *JMT Charlesworth Ltd.* apparently attempted to ship 91 containers of T-54 and T-55 tank engines, UNIMOG trucks, and thermal imaging devices to Eritrea (*Independent*, February 10, 1999). However, both cargoes lacked a transit license through Belgium. Since Belgian law prohibits unlicensed arms exports to countries currently at war, local authorities seized them.

Fighting between Eritrea and Ethiopia escalated in February 1999, thereby shattering all hopes that the war would not exceed the level of low-intensity and sporadic border skirmishes. Reminiscent of World War I tactics, Ethiopia sent waves of infantry against fortified Eritrean trench lines, resulting in tens of thousands of casualties on both sides. Eritrea in particular found itself caught up in a war that threatened its very sovereignty as nation. "Ethiopia has not expended an estimated US $300 million on arms since last June simply to retake a desolate patch of rocks," Eritrea's Ambassador to the UN remarked grimly on February 11, 1999 (cited in Gilkes, 1999).

Arms Transfers, February 1999 to May 2000

Responding to the thus far unprecedented intensity of violence in the conflict, as well as a successive series of failed peace negotiations, the UN Security Council adopted Resolution 1227 in February 1999. It included the by now well-rehearsed demand for "an immediate end to the hostilities." In acknowledgment of the disastrous consequence of massive arms deliveries to the warring states, especially over the past 12 months, it also "strongly urg[ed] states to end immediately all sales of arms and munitions to Ethiopia and Eritrea." Such a statement fell short of a mandatory arms embargo comparable to those imposed on other African countries at the time. Russia and China, both permanent members of the Security Council, had just signed major contracts for arms sales to Ethiopia. It can be assumed that they did not wish to sacrifice egotistic economic interests to a strong international commitment to promoting peace in the region. Resolution 1227 thus appeared as nothing more than a meager call for self-restraint.

The EU, on the contrary, issued a mandatory arms embargo against Eritrea and Ethiopia only one month after the voluntary UN embargo. There is no evidence to suggest that EU member states thereafter continued to export arms to the war zone. However, despite an effective cut-off of arms deliveries from the United States and the EU, Eritrea and Ethiopia could easily sustain their war efforts throughout 1999.

In March and April 1999, the Romanian company *Romtehnica* reportedly exported 100,000 pieces of "explosives" weighing 5,000 tons to Eritrea (*Evenimentul Zilei (Bucharest)*, September 23, 1999). Furthermore, Eritrea is thought to have purchased 30 M-46 towed guns and 12 2S1 self-propelled guns from Bulgaria; 6 MiG 21 fighter jets from Moldova; 8 SU-25 jets from Georgia; as well as 6 MiG 29 fighter jets, 4 MI-17 combat helicopters, and 200 surface-to-air (SAM) SA-18 missiles from Russia.[5]

According to the SIPRI Arms Transfers Project, Ethiopia, for its part, received a further 100 T-55 tanks from Bulgaria as well as 1 SU-27 fighter jet, 2 Mi-24V helicopters, and 20 D-30 towed guns from Russia. Just before the imposition of the mandatory arms embargo in May 2000, Ethiopia also seems to have bought 2 Mi-24P combat helicopters from Belarus, 100 D-30 and 6 M-46 towed guns from Kazakhstan, as well as 307 D-30 guns and 4 SU-25 jets from Russia. Interestingly, the latter purchase from the Russian firm *Sukhoi* apparently also included the services of more than 250 pilots, mechanics, and ground personnel to fly and maintain the fighter jets (Singer, 2003, p. 173). In November 1999, Ethiopia and Russia announced the conclusion of a new trade agreement, which was most likely arms related. Not only did these deliveries undermine a series of failed peace negotiations in the course of the year, they also made a mockery out of the voluntary UN arms embargo.

THE UNITED NATIONS ARMS EMBARGO

Parallel to the intensification of fighting in spring 1999, a severe drought left about eight million Ethiopians threatened by what was described as the worst food shortage in nearly 20 years. However, the looming humanitarian catastrophe did not halt the arms race. On a visit to Djibouti in mid-April 2000, Catherine Bertini, the director of the World Food Programme, spotted the Bulgarian vessel *Kapitan Petko Voyvoda* unloading munitions for Ethiopia only 200 meters away from the French ship *Val*, which had arrived with 30,000 metric tons of wheat for the famine victims (*Agence France Press*, April 25, 2000). This incident epitomized some difficult questions, which were going to spark a number of discussions within the international aid community. As the *New York Times* asked in an article from April 23, 2000, "What are the obligations of outside nations to help, if Ethiopia is spending its own money fighting Eritrea? Do outside nations actually keep the conflict going, by agreeing to feed the hungry as Ethiopia continues to fight?" For example, by modernizing the port of Djibouti and repairing the road to Ethiopia, the World Food Programme also inadvertently eased Ethiopia's procurement of weapons imports (*Agence France Press*, April 25, 2000). Other sources even claimed that the authorities in Addis Ababa had in fact purchased the munitions on the *Kapitan Petko Voyvoda* with aid money provided by the EU. (*Trud*, April 27, 2000) Despite Russian reservations, such articles in the international press certainly facilitated a sense of urgency for a renewed discussion within the UN Security Council on the need for a mandatory arms embargo against Eritrea and Ethiopia. For only a termination of the ongoing arms deliveries to both countries could sustain the moral justification of humanitarian relief efforts. As long as Eritrea and Ethiopia were engaged in warfare, it seemed as if international aid could not help but become complicit to the logistical and economic support of the fighting.

Coincident with this discussion, in early May 2000, a Security Council delegation headed by the US Ambassador to the UN, Richard Holbrooke, failed to convince Eritrea and Ethiopia to return to peace talks. Instead, on May 12, Ethiopia launched another massive offensive against the Eritrean trench lines. After three days of heavy fighting, Eritrean troops were forced to give up their fortified positions and retreat, thereby opening up a corridor for Ethiopian forces to penetrate deeply into southwestern Eritrea. As a consequence, the balance along the disputed 1,000-km border dramatically tipped. The humanitarian situation in the region worsened. Adding to the approximate 350,000 people affected by the drought in Eritrea alone, about half a million people were forced to leave their homes in the wake of the Ethiopian advance (*British Broadcasting Corporation*, May 19, 2000). Repeated bombing and intense combat in direct proximity to the refugee camps further hampered relief operations and forced the UN to pull most of its staff out of Eritrea (*British Broadcasting Corporation*, 2000). Given this war-related increase in the demand for external aid assistance, the concordant need for an arms ban as a precondition for effective emergency supply became an ever more prominent agenda item within the UN Security Council.

It was in this context that the United States, as well as the EU, sought to actively "multilateralize" their respective embargoes at the UN level.

Security Council Resolution 1297, which had been proposed by the United States and the United Kingdom, was passed on May 12, 2000. It stated that unless hostilities ceased and the combatants resumed talks under the auspices of the Organization for African Unity (OAU) at the earliest possible date "without preconditions," the Security Council would "meet again within 72 hours of the adoption of this resolution to take immediate steps to ensure compliance" with its provisions. Being increasingly forced into a strategically defensive position, Eritrea was quick to accept these demands. However, Ethiopia had sensed the chance for a quick victory over its smaller neighbor and refused to halt its advance into Eritrean territory. Whereas the "immediate steps to ensure compliance" had remained unspecified in Resolution 1297, the United States, the United Kingdom, the Netherlands, and Canada thus supported a mandatory arms ban against both countries. Three days later, the United States put forward an embargo proposal that would not only prohibit the flow of both arms and non-lethal military equipment to the warring parties but also include the imposition of travel sanctions on senior government officials from, specifically, Ethiopia as the one country unwilling to accept Resolution 1297. This latter provision took into consideration that, should the embargo objective indeed be the cessation of hostilities, an arms ban alone would have little if any immediate effect on two countries, which had been stockpiling weapons for the past two to three years. Success of the arms ban was envisioned in the long term. Its initial effect was never meant to be anything more than purely symbolic. Nancy Soderberg, at the time acting US Ambassador to the UN, contended that an arms embargo would send "a very strong signal. Initially and *over time* we hope it w[ill] degrade their ability to carry on this war" (*United States Information Agency*, May 16, 2000; own emphasis). As such, the original sanctions proposal contained two important aspects: First, it called for travel sanctions, which were expected to have an immediate effect on the Ethiopian authorities. Second, it was acknowledged that the arms embargo could only be effective over time.

However, other countries in the Security Council were reluctant toward imposing such a "strong" embargo. Many countries expressed concern over a travel ban, which targeted Ethiopia only. Russia strongly opposed the US proposal and instead put forward its own suggestion, which would simply call on UN Secretary General Kofi Annan to send his personal envoy to the region. Russia's reservations coincided with economic self-interest. According to a *Time* article from May 2000, "an arms embargo won't stop the war between Ethiopia and Eritrea, but it'll be a blow to the cash flow of the arms industry in various former Soviet states." Finally, France and Namibia came up with a compromise that marked the debut of what has come to be known as the "sunset clause" in UN sanctions legislation (*Reuters*, May 17, 2000). Marred by the visible humanitarian catastrophe engendered by the indefinite sanctions regime against Iraq, Security Council members were more willing to support sanctions subject to periodic renewal of their mandate. If not re-affirmed by vote in the Security Council, the embargo would end, even if only one of the veto powers was convinced that its explicit objective had been met. When the travel ban also was dropped from the proposal, Moscow conceded.

Security Council Resolution 1298 was unanimously adopted on May 18, 2000. It banned the "sale or supply to Eritrea and Ethiopia [...] of arms and related *matériel* of all types, including weapons and ammunition, military vehicles and equipment, paramilitary equipment and spare parts" as well as any provision to the two countries of technical aid or training related to the manufacture or use of arms. Reactions in Eritrea and Ethiopia were expectedly angry. Both regarded themselves as victim of the war and therefore felt they were being unjustly penalized (*Associated Press*, "UN Enacts Ethiopia-Eritrea Arms Embargo," May 18, 2000). However, it may be argued that the final composition of the embargo was extremely weak. The two main points that had initially opened a possibility for concrete effectiveness in stabilizing the region, that is, a discriminate travel ban supplementing the arms embargo and a long-term perspective, were both missing in the final compromise. Furthermore, the sanctions regime lacked an in-built and independent monitoring mechanism. As the final report of the Sanctions Committee from May 2001 bluntly notes, "The Committee did not have any specific monitoring mechanism to ensure the effective implementation of the arms embargo and relied solely on the cooperation of States and organizations in a position to provide pertinent information. Hence, the Committee, due to the lack of such information, was constrained in the discharge of its mandate" (United Nations, 2001).

Taking these observations into account, BBC reporter and Ethiopia expert Patrick Gilkes referred to Resolution 1298 as "virtually meaningless" (*British Broadcasting Corporation*, May 19, 2000). Moreover, its stated objective quickly became obsolete. Shortly after the decision in the Security Council to impose an arms embargo, the intensity of fighting between Eritrea and Ethiopia significantly decreased. Having suffered a major defeat, Eritrea eventually acceded to "re-deploy" its forces from all positions held before May 6, 1998, thereby fulfilling Ethiopian demands.

A formal cease-fire was agreed upon in early June 2000, and in Resolution 1312 of June 31, the Security Council decided to establish the United

Nations Mission in Ethiopia and Eritrea (UNMEE). UNMEE was to monitor the cease-fire within a 25-km buffer zone in the disputed area and included "political, military, public information, mine action and administrative components" as well as a "mechanism for coordination of its activities with those of the humanitarian community."[6] By passing Resolution 1320 on September 15, 2000, the Security Council expanded UNMEE presence in the border area to a total of 4,200 military personnel.

A comprehensive Peace Agreement between Eritrea and Ethiopia, which was brokered by Algeria and the United States, was signed on December 12, 2000, in Algiers. Only two and a half weeks later, the United States pushed for a vote in the Security Council to lift the arms embargo. This initiative provoked strong objections on behalf of Canada and the Netherlands, who both had peacekeepers in the region. They pointed out that the peace process still needed "time to mature" and that the former adversaries should, at this stage, rather spend their money in other priority areas than arms. In fact, as *Reuters* (January 7, 2001) reported, the sudden proposal of the United States to end the arms ban struck many diplomatic observers as "unusual," since Washington had, after all, been the primary initiator of the embargo in the first place. However, the report goes on to suggest that "Anthony Lake and Assistant Secretary of State Susan Rice, who brokered the peace accord, had apparently promised Ethiopia to lift the UN weapons embargo once [the peace accord] was signed." In the end, the US initiative to prematurely terminate the sanctions was unsuccessful. Yet, it may nevertheless be argued that although a peace deal motivated by the outlook to continue arms procurement sheds severe doubt on the sincerity of the parties involved, the embargo still appears to have displayed some effectiveness as a bargaining instrument in the peace negotiations.

CONCLUSION

To simply dismiss the mandatory Eritrean/Ethiopian arms embargo as meaningless and thus completely ineffective unduly neglects the complexity of the subject matter. Chapter 1 of this volume points to three interrelated criteria of measuring embargo success. First, the most ambitious measure refers to the desired policy change in the target state as it is outlined in the correlate resolution (Level I). However, as fighting stopped immediately after the imposition of the mandatory arms embargo, its chances to influence decision-making on the ending of the conflict had vanished. Very limited effect on positions of the governments can be assumed during the peace process.

The second criterion describes the actual decrease of weapons imports into the target state (Level II). Analyzed in its own right, in terms of arms flows, the embargo against Eritrea and Ethiopia appears as remarkably successful. During the one-year embargo, neither official sources nor the press and the NGO community reported a single arms-related delivery to either country. The only known incident of possible sanctions busting took place on April 26, 2001, a couple of weeks before the arms embargo was scheduled to end. It concerned a Ukrainian transport plane, which was seized by Bulgarian authorities en route from the Czech Republic. It was loaded with arms, and apparently, the pilots had reported the Eritrean capital Asmara as final destination, instead of the Georgian city Aspara, to which the end-user certificate had been issued (*Integrated Regional Information Network*, May 11, 2001). Whether this was a simple mix-up or a deliberate attempt at embargo busting could never be resolved. In any case, by and large, the arms embargo seems to have had effectively curtailed the influx of weaponry from former Soviet states. This impact on self-restraint, it can be assumed, particularly benefited from the desire of Eastern European countries not to complicate the process of EU eastwards – expansion by further worsening their already bad reputation as mavericks in the international arms trade.

The third criterion for embargo effectiveness relates to the implicit objectives of initiating and supporting state actors other than those directly articulated in the UN resolution (Level III). As it was argued, with the intensification of fighting in April–May 2000, relief operations in response to the Ethiopian famine could no longer avoid the charge of inadvertently fueling the war. The arms embargo needs to be therefore perceived as embedded within a wider context of humanitarian relief efforts.

Finally, the symbolic impact of the arms embargo should not be underestimated. The much-heard allusions to the massive weapons deliveries to Eritrea and Ethiopia in the time preceding the sanctions regime are of particular importance in this context. For what seemed to convey a simple technical comment ("the embargo is unlikely to have immediate effect") simultaneously conceded to a tacit normative conclusion ("past arms deliveries were wrong"). In this way, the discussions surrounding the ban forced the industrialized countries to acknowledge their intricate complicity in the war, whilst at the same time allowing for a discursive space wherein they could assume and perform the role of morally responsible actors. However, although the arms embargo thus displayed limited effectiveness in a number of areas, subsequent developments have all but belied any long-term impact of the lessons of the 1999–2000 war in terms of restraining arms sales to the Horn of Africa. Six months after the Security Council lifted the embargo on May 18, 2001, a major arms deal was signed between Ethiopia and Russia (Defense & Security, December 7, 2001). Indeed, between 2002 and 2006, Ethiopia received US $375 million, Eritrea US $550 million worth of weapons system (SIPRI, 2007, p. 419). In both cases, the main supplier was Russia. As of 2007, the border dispute remained unresolved and tensions between the two countries mounted once again. In November 2007, the UN Secretary-General published a report in which he expressed great concern over a renewed military build-up in the border region (United Nations, 2007). It would seem that the short-lived arms embargo did not succeed in altering the overall and long-term pattern of weapons procurement in the Horn of Africa.

NOTES

1. All figures are taken from the SIPRI Military Expenditure Database. Figures from the International Institute for Strategic Studies (IISS) are even higher: according to IISS, in 1998 alone, Ethiopia spent US $380 million and Eritrea US $236 million on arms.

2. See SIPRI Arms Transfers Project (http://armstrade.sipri.org).

3. However, US military consultants from Lockheed Martin appear to have stayed in Ethiopia until March 2000; see Indian Ocean Newsletter (2000), "Ethiopia: Departure of American consultants," 11 March: "At the end of February, eight American military consultants employed by Lockheed Martin discreetly left Ethiopia, […]. In fact, their contract with the Ethiopian government signed in February 1998 had not been renewed, following the US State Department policy of refusing to continue military cooperation because of the ongoing Eritrea-Ethiopia border dispute."

4. Figures taken from SIPRI Arms Transfers Project (http://armstrade.sipri.org).

5. Figures taken from the SIPRI Arms Transfers Project (http://armstrade. sipri.org) and from the Deutsche Presse Agentur (2000) "Drought Fails to Stop Ethiopia-Eritrea Arms Race," 12 April. Other reports suggest that Eritrea also received weapons from Egypt. In April 1999, an Ethiopian newspaper accused Egypt of selling weapons to Eritrea, which were purchased with war assistance provided by Libya. Although a weakened Ethiopia may indeed serve its regional hegemonic ambitions, Egypt denied the allegations. See Pan-African News Agency (1999) "Egypt Denies Involvement in Ethiopia-Eritrea Conflict," 5 April.

6. The text of the mission's mandate can be found at http://www.un.org/Depts/ dpko/missions/unmee/

REFERENCES

Benson, W. (1997). *Undermining development: The European arms trade with the Horn of Africa and Central Africa*. London: International Action Network on Small Arms (IANSA).

George, P. (1997). *Military spending and developments in Ethiopia and Eritrea*. Stockholm: SIPRI.

Gilkes, P. (1999). Analysis: Arms pour in for border war. *British Broadcasting Corporation (BBC)* (2 March).

Gilkes, P., & Plaut, M. (2000). The war between Ethiopia and Eritrea. *Foreign Policy in Focus*, 5(August). Available at http://www.fpif.org/pdf/vol5/25IFEritEthiop.pdf

Kingma, K., & Sayers, V. (1995). Demobilization in the Horn of Africa. Brief No. 4, Bonn: BICC.

Klein, A. (1998). Politics, conflict and conflict resolution in the Horn of Africa: Eritrea, Ethiopia, Somalia and Sudan. Institute for African Alternatives. Available at http://www.ifaanet.org/ifaapr/stateo~1.htm

Ofcansky, T. D., & LaVerle, B. (Eds). (1993). *Ethiopia, a country study*. Washington: Library of Congress, Federal Research Division.

Seybolt, T. (2001). Major armed conflicts in Stockholm International Peace Research Institute. *(SIPRI) Yearbook 2001*. Oxford: Oxford University Press.

Singer, P. W. (2003). *Corporate warriors – The rise of the privatized military industry*. Ithaca: Cornell University Press.

SIPRI – Stockholm International Peace Research Institute. (2007). *SIPRI yearbook 2007, armaments, disarmament and international security*. Oxford: Oxford University Press.

United Nations. (2001). Report of the Security Council Committee established pursuant to resolution 1298 (2000) concerning the situation between Eritrea and Ethiopia. S/2001/503, New York, 18 May.

United Nations. (2007). Report of the Secretary-General on Ethiopia and Eritrea. S/2007/645, New York, 1 November.

CHAPTER 9

A QUANTITATIVE ANALYSIS OF ARMS EMBARGOES

Michael Brzoska

This chapter summarizes the results of a comparative analysis of arms embargoes to add a quantitative dimension to the analysis provided in the case studies. The analysis is guided by the same set of variables introduced in the introductory framework chapter. Although the information used in this chapter is less nuanced than the data used in the case studies, the larger number of cases included and the use of quantitative methods add important insights to the country case analyses.

The chapter confirms the observation made in most of the case studies that arms embargoes are frequently violated. At the same time, it also shows that the number of cases in which arms embargoes reduce arms imports is significant. However, even in such cases there is often little effect on the policy behavior of target states.

The chapter begins with a description of the methodology used for the comparative quantitative analysis. Subsequent sections are devoted to describing various aspects of the data and its analysis, beginning with the identification of successful cases of arms embargoes, and followed by the factors that increase the probability of effectiveness.

Putting Teeth in the Tiger: Improving the Effectiveness of Arms Embargoes
Contributions to Conflict Management, Peace Economics and Development, Volume 10, 205–241
Copyright © 2009 by Emerald Group Publishing Limited
ISSN: 1572-8323/doi:10.1108/S1572-8323(2009)0000010013

METHODOLOGY AND VARIABLES TESTED

The dependent variables for this analysis include three measures of arms embargo effectiveness, which were referred to as 'levels of effectiveness' in the Framework Chapter. These are the embargo's success in causing a targeted policy change (level I effectiveness), success in changing arms flow to the target (level II effectiveness), and a measure of effectiveness to capture the arms embargo initiators satisfaction with the operation of the embargo (level III effectiveness).

The three dependent variables are tested against seven independent variables to explore their probable importance in explaining arms embargo success. The seven independent variables are each composed of various sub-variables. A total of 19 different variables are represented in the seven-variable clusters. The seven independent variables are designed to reflect the cost-benefit calculations of targeted states; the decision-making structure in targets; the evasion capacity of targets; the multilateralization of arms embargoes; the implementation of arms embargoes; countermeasures by the targeted state; and the importance of embargo objectives for the initiators (see Appendix 1 for full list of dependent and independent variables and their specifications).

Both the dependent and independent variables have been standardized so they all have scores that range from 0 to 3.[1] Although the scoring is based on data collected for the respective cases, it is ultimately subjective due to the nature of the data available. The scoring criteria for each of the variables are provided in the list of variables in Appendix 1. Most of the variables used in this quantitative analysis are calculated by adding the values of the sub-variables that make up each of the seven independent variable clusters. The exception is the calculation of the score for level I effectiveness, which is multiplicative (score for 'policy changed' times 'cause for policy changes').[2] Only integers are allowed as scores, with the exception of the sub-variable 'cause for policy change' which is used to calculate level I effectiveness and which can attain the values 0, 0.5, and 1.

For the three dependent variables measuring the effectiveness of arms embargoes, high scores indicate embargo success. For the independent variables hypothesized to have an influence on embargo effectiveness, a high score indicates a higher probability of sanctions success. An autocratic government for instance is hypothesized to show more resistance to outside interference than a pluralistic one. Therefore, an autocratically ruled target is scored at 0, whereas one with a pluralistic decision-making process receives a score of 1.

The main reason for the simple scoring rules is the limitations of the data. Although in theory some of the dependent and independent variables could be more fine-grained, such as the variable for reduction in arms flows, such data are hard to locate. Other data are subjective to start with, such as scoring for level III effectiveness, which measures the political satisfaction an arms embargo initiator has with an embargo – there is no numerical dataset for this variable. The scoring rules are designed to combine the various types of data used in scoring on one scale so their significance can be compared easily.

The number of arms embargo cases utilized for this chapter is a simplified version of a larger list of arms embargo regimes maintained by various international organizations, the European Union and the United States (US). Independent from that list, the basic unit used here is the embargo case. Arms embargo cases are defined by initiator, target and embargo type (stand-alone arms embargo, selective targeted sanctions, comprehensive sanctions). If any of the three parameters changes, this is counted as a new arms embargo case (Appendix 3). On this basis, a total of 74 arms embargo cases active between 1990 and 2005 are used in this study. Appendix 2 provides basic background information on each case.

Selection of variables, scoring rules and scoring procedure combine to yield variable values that only allow for fairly simple quantitative analysis. Scores for variables in individual cases often can be debated. Therefore, this analysis can only supplement the more differentiated analysis in the case studies.

RESULTS: SUCCESS RATES OF ARMS EMBARGOES

The rest of this chapter explains the results of the quantitative analysis by looking at and comparing the variables in various ways. As was to be expected from the discussion in the framework chapter, the rates of success for the three measures of effectiveness, the dependent variables, differ markedly (Table 1).

On the basis of the scoring performed for this analysis, the highest rate of success for arms embargoes is found for level II effectiveness, reduction of arms imports, at 39 percent. This is followed by 31 percent success for level III effectiveness, the initiator's satisfaction with the arms embargo. Level I effectiveness (targeted policy change) is low: on average, there was only an eight percent chance of inducing policy change in the target through an arms embargo (Table 1).

Table 1.   Average Scores of Dependent and Independent Variables.

Variable	Score (0–1)	
	All arms embargoes (74)	Arms embargoes ended before 2005
Dependent variables		
Level I effectiveness (targeted policy change)	0.08	0.14
Level II effectiveness (change in arms imports)	0.39	0.60
Level III effectiveness (initiator satisfaction)	0.31	0.47
Average score for dependent variables	0.26	0.40
Independent variables		
Cost/benefit calculation by target	0.41	0.41
Political cost–benefit calculations	0.27	0.31
Evasion capacity of target	0.62	0.69
Multilateralization of arms embargo	0.51	0.63
Implementation of arms embargo	0.29	0.39
Countermeasures by target	0.40	0.52
Importance of embargo for initiators	0.64	0.69
Average score for independent variables	0.45	0.52

All Arms Embargoes in Sample

The weak results for level I effectiveness suggest that the overwhelming number of sanction regimes have little impact on target policy. For the sample of 74 arms embargo cases, no effect on target policy was recorded for 57 of them (see Table 2 for details on each case).[3]

Level II effectiveness, the success of reducing arms flows to the target, is comparatively higher than level I effectiveness. Arms transfers were completely or almost completely stopped in nine cases; there were major reductions in another 14 cases; and minor reductions in another 23 cases. No reduction of any significance was noted in 28 cases. Although the nature of the data used here does not allow for more than a preliminary interpretation, they suggest that arms embargoes did have, on average, limited but non-negligible effects on arms flows.

This is somewhat in contrast to a good part of the literature on arms embargoes mentioned in the introductory chapter, and even more so to the general perception of the ineffectiveness of arms embargoes. It demonstrates the mixed results of arms embargoes with respect to changing arms flows. The result is supportive neither of the view that arms embargoes are

Table 2. Ranking of the Most Successful Arms Embargoes.

Country	Sanction Initiator	Begin Year	End Year	Type of Sanction	Type of Target	Sanction Objective(s)
Ethiopia	UN	2000	2001	UN arms embargo	Government	End hostilities
Eritrea	UN	2000	2001	UN arms embargo	Government	End hostilities
Haiti	UN	1994	1994	Comprehensive economic sanctions	Government	Regime change
Sierra Leone	UN	1998	2002	UN arms embargo	Rebels	End civil war
Yugoslavia	UN	1992	1995	UN comprehensive sanctions	Government	End hostilities
Liberia	UN	1992		UN arms embargo	Government	End civil war
Yugoslavia	UN	1991	1996	UN arms embargo	Government	End hostilities
Sierra Leone	UN	1997	1998	UN arms embargo	Government	Regime change; end civil war
Libya	UN	1992	2003	UN arms embargo	Government	End support of terrorism
Yugoslavia	EU	1991	2001	EU arms embargo	Government	End hostilities
South Africa	UN	1997	1993	UN arms embargo	Government	Regime change

generally ineffective nor of the view that arms embargoes are a powerful instrument to reduce the flow of weaponry.

The political satisfaction of an arms embargo initiator (level III effectiveness) is also higher than much of previous research would suggest. As stated in the introductory chapter, this dependent variable has been designed to capture primarily domestic considerations, as well as those related to the interaction of countries other than the target. In many cases, initiators realized that a reduction of arms flows could not be achieved, often because the target was allied to a major arms supplier. Despite their inability to significantly mitigate a target's access to arms, these initiators nonetheless maintained an arms embargo to signal discontent with the target's policies.

Arms Embargoes that Ended by 2005

A majority of arms embargo cases included in the data set used here were still active in early 2005. It can be expected that these embargoes had not achieved the objectives desired by initiators, particularly not the one of targeted policy change. Their continuation might also indicate that they had been less effective in terms of reducing arms imports. In addition, at least some of these embargoes were still rather new in 2005. It is therefore interesting to distinguish between embargo cases closed by 2005 and those still active at that time.

The average significance of the variables for closed embargo cases are indeed about 50 percent higher than that of all arms embargoes combined. Closed arms embargoes have been more effective across the board, with respect to changes in arms import patterns, initiator satisfaction, and targeted policy change. However, even for closed arms embargoes, level I effectiveness (targeted policy change) is a relatively rare event, with an average score of about 14 percent.

In short, the partial success of arms embargoes in changing arms import flows and achieving narrow political objectives by initiators only seldom translated into targeted policy change.

Arms Embargo Success Cases

The three measures of effectiveness can be combined into one measure of overall embargo success. Of course, the three measures capture elements of arms embargoes, which may not be additive in individual cases. For instance, an initiator may be very satisfied with an embargo that has no effect on arms import patterns. In this case, the aggregation of the three measures would not make much sense. However, such cases seem to be rare. In the overwhelming number of cases, states that initiate arms embargoes are interested in policy change and arms import reduction as well as in gaining political capital from the imposition of an embargo.

On the basis of this measure of arms embargo success that aggregates the three measures of arms embargo effectiveness, a ranking of overall sanctions success cases can be established, as found in Table 2. A number of points emerge from this ranking. One is that UN arms embargoes as well as arms embargoes linked to other types of sanctions are high in the list. Another point is that arms embargoes with the objective to end hostilities or bring about regime change can be found here comparatively often. Other frequent arms embargo objectives such as ending support for terrorism or human rights concerns have lower success rates.

DIFFERENTIATING ARMS EMBARGO EFFECTIVENESS BY SANCTION CHARACTERISTICS

The objective of this section is to analyze how different sanctions characteristics impact arms embargo effectiveness. To do this, the data set is disaggregated in various ways: by type of initiator, type of target, type of embargo, embargo objectives, time periods, and the length of the embargo.

Success of Arms Embargoes Based on Type of Initiator

The first issue considered is whether there is a difference in effectiveness between arms embargoes initiated by the US, the EU, and the UN. As discussed in the introduction, broader participation in arms embargoes is generally hypothesized to lead to more effective embargo implementation. However, as shown in the Framework Chapter, it is also sometimes argued that a powerful champion of sanctions such as the US may be able to make a formally unilateral embargo effective.

The data presented in Table 3 confirm the hypothesis that a higher degree of multilateralism improved embargo effectiveness. Among the 74 arms embargo cases in our sample, 29 were initiated by the US independent of UN sanctions. Of these 29 US initiated sanction cases, only two led to minor success with respect to targeted policy change (level I effectiveness), in Libya and Indonesia. Some reductions in arms imports by the target (level II effectiveness) occurred in 15 of these 29 cases. However, most of these reductions were minor (the only case of a significant reduction was the arms embargo against Ethiopia, a special case as discussed in the country case study included in this book).

For arms embargoes initiated exclusively by the US, level II effectiveness received a score of 23 percent success. This is well below the 39 percent level II effectiveness for the entire sample of 74 cases. A similar result is obtained for level III effectiveness, where 16 percent of US arms embargoes were successful compared with 31 percent for the overall sample.

Success rates for the 15 EU-initiated sanction cases in the sample are higher than they were for solely US arms embargoes. For both level I effectiveness (targeted policy change) and level II effectiveness (arms import reductions), success rates are in the same range as for the entire sample of 74 cases, although targeted policy change is slightly below the overall rate. The

Table 3. Average Success Rates of Arms Embargoes by Initiator.

	Targeted Policy change (Level I) (%)	Change in Arms Imports (Level II) (%)	Initiator Satisfaction (Level III) (%)	Number of Sanction Cases
UN sanctions	15	57	48	27
EU sanctions	7	42	31	15
US sanctions	2	23	16	29
Other initiators				3

EU success rate for change in arms import patterns was 42 percent and includes three cases of total cessation in arms imports (Eritrea, Ethiopia, Yugoslavia), two cases of major change (Afghanistan and Iraq, with a score of two out of three) and six cases with minor change in arms imports. No change in arms imports was recorded in five cases.

UN arms embargoes have the best record in terms of effectiveness as measured in this study. Still, the success rate for level I effectiveness (targeted policy change) remains low at 15 percent. The score for level II effectiveness (reductions in arms import patterns) is much higher than for all arms embargoes combined at 57 percent. This includes eight cases of total cessation in arms imports (Eritrea, Ethiopia, two sanction cases in Haiti, Iraq and three sanction cases in Yugoslavia); eight cases of major change (Afghanistan, Angola, Liberia, Libya, South Africa, two cases in Sierra Leone and Sudan); minor changes in six cases; and no changes in five cases.

The data presented here support the hypothesis that multilateralization has made past arms embargoes more effective. US sanctions score lowest on all measures of arms embargo effectiveness, and UN arms embargoes score highest.

Success of Arms Embargoes Based on Type of Objective

Arms embargoes differ with respect to their objectives. In the data set used here, the identification has been limited to major objectives of arms embargoes as stipulated in relevant documents mandating these sanctions. Many arms embargoes are designed to serve a host of objectives, some explicit and others less obvious. However, in most cases one objective stands out.

For classification purposes, all objectives used to analyze arms embargo cases are aggregated into six groups, listed in Table 4. The sanctions objectives evaluated include human rights, end of hostilities, end support of terrorism, end of civil war, regime change, and change in nuclear policies.

There are notable differences in the effectiveness of arms embargoes when the objective of the embargo is considered, as illustrated in Table 4. Yet these variations need further analysis. For instance, there are only three examples of arms embargoes having the objective to change nuclear policies, which makes a very small sample.

One interesting discovery is that arms embargoes with the objective to end civil wars have the highest rate of success with respect to targeted policy

Table 4. Average Success Rates of Arms Embargoes
by Sanctions Objective.

	Targeted Policy Change (Level I) (%)	Change in Arms Imports (Level II) (%)	Initiator Satisfaction (Level III) (%)	Number of Sanction Cases
Human rights	6	22	28	12
End of hostilities in interstate wars	8	52	32	20
End support of terrorism	10	40	30	10
End of civil war	12	37	38	20
Regime change	4	48	30	9
Change in nuclear policies	0	11	0	3

change (level I effectiveness) – in this case the preferred policy being peace. But this rate of success is still low at 12 percent.

Among the objectives identified in Table 4, the end of hostilities in interstate wars has the highest score with respect to change in arms import patterns. The success of the various arms embargo cases associated with the war in the former Yugoslavia and between Eritrea and Ethiopia are the major causes for this result, but also illustrate that there is a weak connection, if any, between success in reducing arms inflows to a target and achieving a targeted policy change. This relative success for reducing arms imports did little to change policies in the target states. Although it is debatable whether the comprehensive sanctions against the FRY induced the government of President Milosevic to negotiate and agree to the Peace Accords of Dayton in 1995, there is no indication that the fact that these sanctions also included arms had any effect (see the country case study included in this book). In the Eritrea and Ethiopia case, both sides were well armed when the arms embargoes began to bite, and they ended the war before there were any notable shortages (see the country case study included in this book).

Success of Arms Embargoes Based on Type of Sanction

Arms embargoes in this study have been divided into four types of sanctions: voluntary embargoes, mandatory embargoes, comprehensive embargoes, and targeted embargoes.

Six of the cases analyzed were voluntary arms embargoes, with the UN and the Organization for Security and Cooperation in Europe (OSCE) as

Table 5. Average Success Rates of Arms Embargoes by Sanctions Type.

	Targeted Policy Change (Level I) (%)	Change in Arms Imports (Level II) (%)	Initiator Satisfaction (Level III) (%)	Number of Sanction Cases
Voluntary arms embargo	0	11	11	6
Mandatory arms embargo	6	38	29	45
Comprehensive sanctions	13	48	30	9
Arms embargo element in targeted sanctions package	17	50	48	14

initiators. These had very low success rates. Forty-five of the 74 cases were mandatory arms embargoes, implemented as isolated measures. These had success rates similar to the overall rate associated with all arms embargoes – this is not surprising considering that the mandatory arms embargoes constitute the majority of cases.

Comprehensive sanctions include embargoes on arms transfers because they cover all trade, whereas targeted sanctions seek to add other instruments, such as financial asset freezes to the effort to reduce arms transfers. Both types of 'stronger' sanctions have higher rates of success with respect to changes in arms import patterns, 48 and 50 percent, respectively (Table 5). Although they were definitely more likely to produce targeted policy change than the other types of sanctions, level I effectiveness remained low, with 13 and 17 percent, respectively. This again confirms the observation that targeted policy changes do not necessarily follow in cases where arms imports are significantly reduced.

Success of Arms Embargoes Based on Type of Target

Traditionally, arms embargoes have targeted governments. Increasingly however, arms embargoes have targeted rebel groups, or particularly in civil war situations, both rebels and governments.

Rebel groups were the sole targets in eight cases out of the complete sample of 74 arms embargo cases used in this study and include sanctions directed at Afghanistan, Angola, Congo DR, Rwanda, and Sierra Leone. Success rates on all three levels of effectiveness are significantly higher than average when rebel groups are the targets. This result has to be qualified, however, because of the low number of cases, and also because most of the

Table 6.   Average Success Rates of Arms Embargoes by Type of Target.

	Targeted Policy Change (Level I) (%)	Change in Arms Imports (Level II) (%)	Initiator Satisfaction (Level III) (%)	Number of Sanction Cases
Government	8	33	28	41
Rebels	15	54	46	8
All parties	6	45	31	25

cases have been fairly recent, thus falling into a period of improved arms embargo implementation, as reported later.

Arms embargoes targeting governments have had lower rates of success. This study cannot answer the question of whether low scores are caused by the fact that targets were governments – who could have stronger capabilities to evade sanctions and to ignore arms restrictions – or whether the reasons for lower scores lie elsewhere, for instance in the objectives of arms embargoes. Arms embargoes targeting governments were mostly aimed at ending hostilities in interstate wars or achieving policy change with respect to human rights in target states – both of these objectives had low success rates (Table 6).

Success of Arms Embargoes Based on Time Period

The number of arms embargoes active at any given time has grown when measured in five-year periods. From 2000–2004, 62 arms embargoes were active, compared to 56 in the period between 1995 and 1999 and 45 in the period 1990–1994. A total of 15 arms embargo cases included started before 1990 (and continued after 1990).[4]

Success rates of arms embargoes have not changed much over the four periods distinguished in Table 7. Although the scores for level II and level III effectiveness rose slightly, the increases were not large.

Success of Arms Embargoes Based on whether They Are 'Old' or 'New'

The results look somewhat different if, instead of time periods in which embargoes were active, the time periods in which arms embargoes began is analyzed (Table 8).

Table 7.   Average Success Rates of Arms Embargoes by Time Period.

	Targeted Policy Change (Level I) (%)	Change in Arms Imports (Level II) (%)	Initiator Satisfaction (Level III) (%)	Number of Sanction Cases
Before 1990	10	27	20	15
1990–1994	9	31	28	45
1995–1999	10	33	28	56
2000–2004	7	35	27	62

Table 8.   Average Success Rates of Arms Embargoes by Year of Sanction Case Began.

	Targeted Policy Change (Level I) (%)	Change in Arms Imports (Level II) (%)	Initiator Satisfaction (Level III) (%)	Number of Sanction Cases
Before 1990	8	23	21	13
1990–1994	9	33	30	31
1995–1999	11	47	35	19
2000 and later	2	61	39	11

Arms embargoes begun in more recent five-year periods have significantly higher rates of level II effectiveness than arms embargoes begun in the earlier five-year periods. However, this has not increased level I effectiveness (targeted policy change), which has actually gone down in the most recent years analyzed.

The rise in level II effectiveness and fall in level I effectiveness in the 21st century is influenced by many factors, including changes in the types of sanctions and their objectives, as well as characteristics of targets and initiators. Still, it seems safe to conclude that arms embargoes have increasingly had 'teeth' in recent years, in the sense of leading to changes in arms import patterns.

Success of Arms Embargoes Based on Length of Sanctions

These considerations lead to the question of whether long-running arms embargoes are more successful than those with shorter life spans. Data presented in Table 9 indicate that this is indeed the case for level I effectiveness, targeted policy change, but not for the other two measures of arms embargo

Table 9. Average Success Rates of Arms Embargoes by Their Duration.

Success Rates by Age (years)	Targeted Policy Change (Level I) (%)	Change in Arms Imports (Level II) (%)	Initiator Satisfaction (Level III) (%)	Number of Sanction Cases
0	0	100	100	1
1	8	53	50	10
2	0	67	22	3
3	14	78	33	6
4	17	50	67	2
5	11	56	44	3
6–10	25	50	42	4
11–15	28	56	44	3
16–20	33	50	83	2
Still active	3	22	18	40

success. Without further discussion on the causes of policy changes in targets, it is not possible to discern the importance of arms embargoes for bringing such change about. The likelihood a policy change will occur regardless of whether or not there is an arms embargo present increases with time. That is, policies are likely to change over time whether or not there is an arms embargo. Still, the results presented here support the proposition that changes in arms import patterns, which are present in a majority of closed arms embargo cases, take time to influence policy making in targeted countries.

For arms embargoes implemented for less than three years, the success rate for targeted policy change is low. Success rates are considerably higher for closed arms embargoes that ran for more than five years, with the highest rates of success noted for the longest running arms embargoes (Libya/EU 18 years, South Africa 16 years, Iraq/UN 13 years, Libya/UN 11 years).

Even for long-running arms embargoes, however, changes in targeted policies remain low, and may not even be the result of the embargoes. There are a number of arms embargo cases that have been active longer than 10 years without having any discernible impact on targeted policies. Interestingly, these are all US embargoes (North Korea, Cuba, Libya's first embargo case, Iran Vietnam, Myanmar/Burma and China) with the exception of the EU arms embargo against China.

Correlates of Arms Embargo Success

This section analyzes the seven clusters of independent variables discussed in the introductory chapter to determine the significance of their impact on

Table 10. Statistically Significant Correlation Coefficients.

Level of Effectiveness Independent variable clusters	Targeted Policy Change (Level I)	Arms Import Reduction (Level II)	Initiator Satisfaction (Level III)	Overall Effectiveness Measure (Average Levels 1–3)
Average of scores of independent variables Cost–benefit calculation in target (A)	Significant	Significant		Significant
Decision-making structure in target (B)	Significant			
Evasion capacity/ activity of target (C)				
Multilatera- lization of arms embargo (D)		Significant	Significant	Significant
Implementation of arms embargo (E)		Significant		Significant
Countermeasures by targets (F)		Significant		Significant
Importance of embargo objectives for initiators (G)		Significant		

Note: Correlation coefficients of independent variables significant at 95% level in bivariate estimation.

arms embargo effectiveness (see Appendix 1 for full list of variables). To establish the strength of association between the variables measuring arms embargo effectiveness, bivariate correlations were calculated between each independent variable and all three measures of embargo effectiveness (see Table 10 for list of statistically significant correlation coefficients and Appendix 2 for estimated coefficients).

Bivariate estimations are a relatively simple method to analyze correlations and are therefore limited in their analytical depth. For instance, they cannot establish relative weights of independent variables. However, because the data used here are limited to begin with, a more sophisticated method of data analysis seems inappropriate.

Independent Variables and Targeted Policy Change (Level I Effectiveness)

As mentioned earlier, policy change in the direction desired by the sanction initiator that is caused at least in part by an arms embargo was a rare event.

Among the seven independent variable clusters that potentially could have impacted targeted policy change, only the 'decision-making structure in target' variable is statistically significant. About 34 percent of the variance in the dependent variable is explained by the decision-making structure of a target state.

Independent Variables and Reductions in Arms Imports (Level II Effectiveness)

Although the independent variables do not robustly account for level I effectiveness (targeted policy change), some of the independent variables are powerful in explaining the scoring variance for level II effectiveness (reductions in arms imports). The highest regression coefficients are measured for the variable clusters that capture the multilateralization of arms embargoes, implementation of arms embargoes, countermeasures by targets and the importance of embargo objectives for initiators. The correlation coefficients for these four clusters of independent variables are significant at the 99 percent level.

Another variable cluster with significance above the 95-percent threshold is the one composed to reflect the decision-making structure in a target (variable cluster B). Not significant are the cost–benefit calculations of a target and the evasion capacity of a target. The independent variable clusters included in the analysis here explains almost 70 percent of variance for level II effectiveness, changes in arms import patterns. The list of independent variables used here thus appear well selected to explain the success of arms embargoes in reducing arms flows. In summary, multilateral arms embargoes that are implemented efficaciously, with limited countermeasure options for a target and objectives that are high on the agenda of the initiators, are most likely to be associated with reductions in arms flows. The capacity of the target to find alternative suppliers and the importance of arms to the target seem to have little influence on arms flows.

Looking at the actors who shape embargo success at this level, the analysis implies that the reduction of arms flows is primarily determined by factors exogenous to the target, not by the target itself. If initiators are successful in promoting the embargo to other countries, and particularly in getting others to implement the embargo, arms flows are significantly reduced. This seems to be true even in cases where targets are economically powerful.

Independent Variables and Initiator Satisfaction (Level III Effectiveness)

Only the multilaterlization of arms embargoes (independent variable cluster D) is statistically significant for explaining the level of initiator satisfaction with an embargo. Other variable clusters with significance just below the 95-percent threshold are the decision-making structure in a target (B), implementation (E) and countermeasures available to a target (F) – although these coefficients are too low to derive any firm conclusions. No statistical relationship exists between initiator satisfaction and the variable clusters that capture the cost–benefit calculations of a target (A), evasion capacity of target (C), and the importance of arms embargoes for initiators (G).

The low level of explanation for this dependent variable by the independent variables included in the analysis may be explained by a number of factors. First, the scoring for initiator satisfaction is particularly subjective and therefore the data may not be reliable. Second, the list of independent variables may not be appropriate; it is possible that additional variables are needed, although it is not obvious which additional variables to include. A third factor that may explain the low correlation between initiator satisfaction and the independent variables used is the low level of policy change induced in targets – that is, initiators may be unsatisfied with arms embargoes (low level III effectiveness) because they rarely actually lead to policy change. Multilateralization of sanctions, the only significant independent variable, may be seen as at least opening the opportunity for effective sanction implementation in the future. Apart from the multi-lateralization of sanction, much of the success in achieving initiator objectives appears to be determined by particular circumstances in initiator countries, which are difficult to capture with structural variables of the kind used here.

Independent Variables and Overall Sanctions Success

Strong associations are found for the combined index of arms embargo effectiveness and a number of the independent variable clusters. Regression coefficients are high for variable clusters that capture the multilateralization of arms embargoes and the implementation of arms embargoes, while the variable that captures countermeasures by a target is still within 95 percent significance. Cluster G (importance of embargo objectives for initiators) is close to the 95 percent level of significance. No statistically significant correlation is found for variable clusters the measure the cost–benefit calculations in a target, the decision-making structure of a target, or the evasion capacity/activity of a target.

Overall, more independent variables are significant for the average of the three indicators of sanction effectiveness than for any one of the indicators by itself. This is not surprising because the variables were chosen to catch all explanations for all three levels of sanctions effectiveness. This result indicates that the broad approach to explain sanctions chosen here yields good results. Although not significant in many cases when considering a single measure of sanction success, the explanatory power of this study's approach accumulates with the combined measure of sanctions success.

Similar to the results for level II effectiveness (arms import reductions), variables shaped by external actors are more significant than the influences internal to the target. Multilateralization and implementation of arms embargoes, as well as initiator interest in sanctions, factors linked to external actors, emerge as three of the four clusters, which have the strongest explanatory power. Cluster F (countermeasures by target) is shaped by the targeted actor but also is strongly related to the outside world, as it catches the economic and political power of targets to find alternative arms suppliers. Among the other factors primarily reflecting domestic situations in targets, cluster B (decision-making structure in target) explains a fairly high, though not statistically significant, share of variance in initiator satisfaction with an embargo. The other independent variables have very little explanatory power.

Independent Variables

We now turn to an examination of the various clusters of independent variables and their explanatory power.

Cost–benefit calculations in target (variable cluster A) attempts to measure the likelihood that a target will yield to an arms embargo. Variable cluster A includes three sub-variables: importance of sanctioned behaviour to target; general importance of arms imports to target; and relation between behaviour and arms imports. If the target places little value on the sanctioned behavior, views arms imports as important, and there is a notable relationship between the targeted behavior and arms imports, it is assumed an arms embargo will have a higher chance to succeed.

This study, however, finds no statistically significant effect of the variables collected to represent cost–benefit calculations in a target on arms embargo effectiveness.

There are a few potential reasons for this result. First, again, is the issue of data: scores for the variables in cluster A are rather subjective estimates. The second possibility is that this independent variable is inherently linked to targeted policy change through sanctions, a rather rare event. The third is that variables chosen here may not properly reflect cost–benefit relations and the corresponding decision making in target states.

The variables chosen, in addition to being subjective, may not reflect the changing dynamics of target behavior under sanctions, particularly the 'rallying round the flag' effect. As several of the case studies show and is emphasized in the sanctions literature, targets often harden targeted policies rather than change them to appease the sanctions initiator. This is because targets may have invested political capital and are afraid to 'lose face' and domestic legitimacy by standing down. In the end, the result obtained in this analysis strengthens the view that sanctions affect costs and benefits in targets in ways more complex and dynamic than can be described with the simple variables chosen here.

Decision-making structure in target (variable cluster B) attempts to capture how the internal political infrastructure of a target will affect the various measures of embargo effectiveness. It includes three sub-variables: decision-making structure of the target (autocratic or participatory); symbolic importance of an arms embargo for the target; and relations between the arms embargo and other initiator policies.

The variable cluster decision-making structure in a target is weak in explaining variance in arms embargoes, with the exception of level I effectiveness (targeted policy change). It is, as mentioned, the only statistically significant independent variable cluster for this particular dependent variable.

Evasion capacity/activity of a target (variable cluster C) attempts to explain how a target's ability to evade an embargo's ability to mitigate arms imports affects the three measures of embargo success used in this study. It includes two sub-variables: the level of domestic arms production and the lead-time before an arms embargo that would allow the target country to prepare for the embargo's effects.

The coefficients for this variable carry the expected sign in all estimations, but the explanatory power is small never coming close to statistical significance as defined here. Why this outcome? Again, as in the case of the other two independent variables already discussed, data issues, the low incidence of policy change, as well as the 'rally around the flag' effect may be important.[5]

Multilateralization of arms embargoes (variable cluster D) is a measure of both whether an embargo is multilateral and whether the initiator is a powerful state (e.g., the US and the EU). Variable cluster D has three sub-variables: power/importance of initiators; type of arms embargo (US, EU, or multilateral); and whether both the initiators and other important states share the objectives of an arms embargo. Hypothesized sanctions successes would be cases of multilateral arms embargoes initiated by powerful states where the objectives are shared by the various initiators and other important states.

The multilateralization of an arms embargo has the highest level of statistical significance for three of the four independent variables, with the exceptional case being targeted policy change. Multilateralization explains more than 50 percent of the variance in overall sanctions success and around 40 percent of variance in reductions in arms flows (level II effectiveness) and initiator satisfaction with arms embargoes (level III effectiveness).

Implementation of arms embargoes (variable cluster E) is almost as strong in explaining arms embargo success as the variable cluster representing multilateralization. This is not surprising as these two variables are somewhat complementary. Implementation measures how effectively an arms embargo is enforced by initiator states and includes three sub-variables: capability of an initiator to implement/enforce an arms embargo; the pressure placed on states that are not among the initiators to support an embargo; and the monitoring an arms embargo.

The correlation coefficient for the implementation variable is significant for level II effectiveness (reductions of arms flows) as well as the overall measure of sanctions success and comes close to 95-percent significance for level III effectiveness (initiator satisfaction). Even for level I effectiveness (policy change), the implementation of arms embargoes is not completely irrelevant, explaining about 17 percent of variance.

Countermeasures by targets (variable cluster F) aims to capture the financial and political means available to the target to evade arms embargoes. Variable cluster F includes two sub-variables: the economic power/financial means of a target and the political power/influence of a target states' allies who are non-participants in an embargo.

Countermeasures by targets explain much of the variance in level II effectiveness (reductions in arms imports) as well as overall sanctions success. This variable cluster corresponds to both variable clusters D (multilaterializaton) and E (implementation) in valuing the political alliances of targets, while also addressing the economic power of targets that allows them to evade embargoes. Is explanatory power, however, is lower than that of the variable clusters D (multilateralization) and E (implementation). Again, data issues may influence this outcome. Alternatively, this could be the result of a general conclusion that can be drawn from the entire analysis: factors that are influenced by sanction initiators are more important than those influenced by targets in the analysis of level II effectiveness (reductions of arms flows).

Importance of embargo objectives for initiators (independent variable cluster G) measures initiator-related issues that potentially impact arms embargo effectiveness. It includes three sub-variables: strength of the domestic lobby in support of an arms embargo in the initiator state; significance of the arms embargo for an initiator's foreign policy; and prominence of the initiator as an arms supplier.

The importance of embargo objectives for initiators only yields statistically significant correlation coefficients for level II effectiveness (reductions of arms flows). It does not provide much explanation for level III effectiveness, the measure of arms embargo success it was designed to capture.

It is possible that the data used for this variable cluster are too unreliable, and the variable therefore fails to capture the relevant influences. In addition, the explanation given for the overall weak results for level III effectiveness (initiator satisfaction) seems to be convincing: satisfaction appears to result primarily from policy change, which is not often the result of arms embargoes – because arms embargoes rarely lead to targeted policy change (low level I effectiveness), initiators are seldom satisfied with an arms embargo (causing low level III effectiveness). The high rates of success for effectiveness level II (reductions in arms imports) seem to matter less.

CONCLUSION

This quantitative analysis of a sample of 74 arms embargo cases strengthens and differentiates some of the results obtained in the case studies. Among the most important results are that arms embargoes have had, on average, notable effects on arms import patterns. Although no arms embargo has been 100 percent effective, the majority of arms embargoes induced at least some reduction in arms imports, with a good number having significant effects. This fact tends to get lost in many arms embargo case studies where an excessively high standard of embargo success is set, such as the total cessation of all of arms and ammunition imports.

However, changes in arms import patterns, whether major or minor, have on average had rather little impact on targeted policies. Targeted states and groups have most often continued to pursue the policies the initiators aimed to alter, and when targets did change policies, it was often for reasons other than external manipulation through arms embargoes.

This study makes it clear that the link between arms supplies and targeted policy change is weak. Although the analysis in this chapter does not thoroughly explain why arms embargoes often fail to induce targeted policy change, the case studies provide ample insight why this is so: targets adopt their military forces and styles of war to the level of arms and ammunition available. Targeted states and groups will also often stock up weapons and ammunition before a sanctions period. Several of the case studies indicate that embargoes often come very late in the game and that more timely reactions might increase the likelihood that sanctions have some effect on policy change.

At the same time, case studies and data analysis indicate that the relationship between arms embargoes and targeted policy change becomes closer over time. Although the contribution of arms embargoes to such policy change is often hard to discern, it is plausible to assume that the reduction of arms flows requires time to take hold and thus have an influence on targeted policy change. As stocks of arms and ammunition are depleted, concerns over decreases in firepower grow and with them, at least in a number of cases, the willingness to change targeted policies. Compared to effects on arms import patterns, however, even the success rates for changing targeted policies with long-running arms embargoes remain low.

The data confirm the hypothesis that multilateral arms embargoes are more successful than unilateral ones. Multilateralization increases supplier satisfaction with an embargo, raises the likelihood of significant changes in arms import patterns, and increases the hope by the initiators that a policy change will take place in the target (although such policy change is most often not realized).

Related to multilateralization is arms embargo implementation, a higher rate of participation among countries and a stronger effort at implementation by participants increases the effectiveness of arms embargoes with respect to reducing arms imports by targets.

Arms embargo implementation has improved over time, at least with respect to changing arms import patterns, because initiators have become smarter in terms of multilateralization and improving implementation. There has not, however, been a corresponding improvement in the success rate of targeted policy change.

From this study we can conclude that the success of arms embargoes ultimately remains limited, particularly when policy change is the ultimate objective. However, policy change does not seem to be the primary goal by initiators in all, or even most cases; instead, multilateralization of national restrictions and success in significantly changing arms import patterns also seem to be valued by embargo initiators.

Variables designed to capture the expected efforts of targets to counter arms embargoes have little explanatory power. Neither the importance of a particular policy to a target, availability of countermeasures nor the decision-making structure in the target can explain much variance in the effectiveness of sanctions. In combination, all these factors have some effect, but it is not very strong.

Arms embargoes are clearly more effective when they are consistently embedded with other measures. This becomes clear from the case studies and is confirmed in the data analysis presented here. Arms embargoes that are part of a larger sanctions package have a higher rate of success, including with respect to targeted policy change. In addition, longer-running arms embargoes are in general more successful than short-lived ones.

This may then be the most important policy lesson from this exercise: arms embargoes in and of themselves will seldom lead to policy change by targeted elites or groups. Arms embargoes are instead most effective when utilized as an element of larger policy packages. In addition, there needs to be a long time period allotted for implementation of an embargo so as to increase the possibilities for success. Arms embargoes very seldom have had effects on targeted policies before their fifth year of implementation. Arms embargoes appear to need time to develop 'teeth'; however, not all arms embargoes will grow sufficiently sharp teeth.

NOTES

1. Both independent and dependent variables are summed for various analytical purposes. In addition, for much of the data presentation later, scores for independent and dependent variables are recalculated as percentages, thus ranging from 0 to 100.

2. This resembles the procedure of measuring success in Economic Sanctions Reconsidered by Gary C. Hufbauer, Jeffrey J. Schott and Kimberly A. Elliott, International Institute for Economics, Washington DC, 1990.

3. The 17 cases where an arms embargo had some effect on target policies range from strong effects in Angola (UN sanctions 1993–2003) to some effects in Haiti (UN sanctions in 1994), Burundi (Regional sanctions 1996 1999), Sierra Leone (UN sanctions 1998–2002), Liberia (UN from 1992), Sierra Leone (UN 1997–1998), Libya (UN 1992–2003), South Africa (UN 1977–1993), DR Congo (regionally limited; UN from 2003) and minor effects in Yugoslavia (UN 1992, 1995), Iraq (UN 1990 2003), Sudan (UN from 2004), Indonesia (EU sanctions 1999, 2000), and Indonesia (US sanctions from 1999).

4. The US mandated numerous arms embargoes before 1990 which are not included here as they were not active after 1990. The UN also mandated a number of

voluntary and one mandatory arms embargo (within the Rhodesia sanctions of 1963) which are excluded for the same reason.

5. The rally around the flag effect was discussed in the introduction chapter of this book, and signals the "us" versus "them" mentality that is often fostered by sanctions in targets (similar to wars).

APPENDIX 1. LIST OF DEPENDENT
AND INDEPENDENT VARIABLES

Dependent Variables:

EL I: Level I Effectiveness:
Targeted policy change
    0 no detectable change with respect to targeted policy
    1 some change with respect to targeted policy
    2 major change with respect to targeted policy
    3 targeted change occurring within reasonable period of time

Causes of targeted policy change (multiply with factor for targeted policy change)
    0 no relation to arms embargo
    0.5 some relation to arms embargo
    1 arms embargo major factor in policy change

EL II: Level II Effectiveness:
Arms supplies to target
    1 some, but minor, reduction in arms imports by target, some change in supplier composition, some increase in price of weapons, some change in military behavior necessary because of reduced arms imports
    2 major reductions in arms imports by target, major change in supplier composition, major increase in price of weapons, major change in military behavior necessary because of reduced arms imports
    3 no significant arms imports post arms embargo

EL III: Level III Effectiveness:
Satisfaction of arms embargo initiator(s)
    0 None of objectives of initiator(s) met
    1 Some of objectives of initiator(s) met, some initiator(s) satisfied
    2 Objectives of initiator(s) mostly reached
    3 Objectives of initiator(s) fully reached

Independent Variables

A: Cost-Benefit Calculations in Target (Variables 1–3 Additive)

1. Importance of sanctioned behavior to target
    0 Importance high
    1 Importance low

2. General importance of arms imports to target
    0 Importance low
    1 importance high

3. Relation between behavior and arms imports
    0 no relation
    1 notable relation

B: Decision-Making Structure in Target (Variables 4–6 Additive)

4. Decision-making structure
    0 autocratic decision-making
    1 participatory decision-making

5. Symbolic importance of arms embargo for target
    0 low symbolic importance of arms embargoes
    1 high symbolic importance of arms embargoes

6. "Embeddedness" of arms embargo in other initiator policies
    0 little relation between arms embargoes and other policies
    1 arms embargoes consistent with other initiator policies/additional
       (targeted) sanctions in place

C: Evasion Capacity/Activity of Target (Variables 7 and 8 Additive)

7. Domestic arms production
    0 major and growing arms production
    1 some domestic arms production
    2 no significant domestic arms production

8. Lead-time to arms production/length of preparation prior to arms
    embargo
    0 long lead-time
    1 insignificant lead-time

D: Multilateralization of Arms Embargo (Variables 9–11 Additive)

9. Power/importance of initiator(s)
    0 less important state(s)
    1 major power(s)

10. Type of arms embargo
    0 US or EU, voluntary multilateral
    1 multilateral (UN)

11. Objectives of arms embargo shared by initiator(s) and additional important state(s)?
    0 differing, or unclear, objectives
    1 common objectives

E: Implementation of Arms Embargo (Variables 12–14 Additive)
12. Capability of initiator(s) to implement/enforce arms embargo
    0 low capabilities in some important countries (neighbors, arms suppliers)
    1 overall good capability

13. Pressure on/support for non-initiator(s)
    0 little pressure, support for non-initiator(s)
    1 strong pressure, support for non-initiator(s)

14. Effectiveness of monitoring of arms embargo
    0 no effective monitoring
    1 effective international monitoring

F: Countermeasures by Target (Variables 15, 16 Additive)
15. Economic power/financial means of target
    0 target able to muster substantial finance for arms importation
    1 target limited in its financial means
    2 target seriously financially constrained

16. Power/influence of non-participants
    0 target with strong and important allies
    1 target widely isolated or without major allies

G: Importance of Embargo Objectives for Initiator(s) (Variable 17–19 Additive)
17. Domestic constituency in initiating state(s)
    0 weak domestic constituency, lobbying groups
    1 strong domestic lobby

18. Foreign policy importance of arms embargo objectives for initiator(s)
    0 importance low
    1 importance high

19. (Dominant) initiator(s) type of arms supplier
    0 "restraint" supplier
    1 economic or hegemonic supplier

APPENDIX 2. CORRELATION TABLES FOR CLUSTERS OF INDEPENDENT VARIABLES

Dependent Variables: Levels of Effectiveness

Average of Scores of Independent Variable		A	B	C	D	E	F	G
Average of three levels of effectives								
Correlation coefficient	0.890	0.095	0.266	0.230	0.495	0.355	0.340	0.320
r-square	0.555	0.011	0.120	0.080	0.511	0.363	0.291	0.172
Standard error	0.136	0.203	0.192	0.196	0.143	0.163	0.172	0.186
F-test	0.131	0.429	0.025	0.083	0.002	0.000	0.000	0.027
Level I effectiveness (targeted policy change)								
Correlation coefficient	0.499	0.126	0.351	0.048	0.213	0.233	0.071	0.197
r-square	0.284	0.031	0.341	0.006	0.154	0.255	0.021	0.106
Standard error	0.136	0.158	0.130	0.160	0.147	0.138	0.158	0.151
F-test	0.579	0.005	0.000	0.000	0.000	0.000	0.000	0.000
Level II effectiveness (arms import reduction)								
Correlation coefficient	1.514	0.037	0.405	0.363	0.782	0.624	0.653	0.638
r-square	0.513	0.001	0.089	0.063	0.408	0.358	0.342	0.219
Standard error	0.252	0.361	0.345	0.350	0.278	0.290	0.293	0.320
F-test	0.000	0.000	0.010	0.002	0.085	0.721	0.349	0.009
Level III effectiveness (initiator satisfaction)								
Correlation coefficient	1.155	0.248	0.391	0.328	0.702	0.441	0.368	0.321
r-square	0.357	0.028	0.100	0.062	0.394	0.215	0.130	0.066
Standard error	0.265	0.325	0.313	0.320	0.257	0.293	0.308	0.319
F-test	0.000	0.001	0.068	0.019	0.339	0.678	0.868	0.062

Note: Italic, correlation coefficient significant at 95 percent level.

APPENDIX 3. ARMS EMBARGO CASES

To better inform our analysis, this section contains brief descriptions of the arms embargoes listed in Table A1. The short descriptions that follow are summaries of arms embargo regimes listed by targeted country.

Afghanistan: The various arms embargoes against forces in Afghanistan did not have notable effects on the policies of the targets. Although the 1996 voluntary arms embargo did not reduce arms flows to forces in Afghanistan, later embargoes against the Taliban resulted in lower levels of arms inflows. The major remaining provider continued to be Pakistan. Efforts by states supporting the arms embargoes to convince Pakistani leaders to enforce the arms embargo more strictly met with only limited success. Evasion capacity of the targets was small and so was the availability of countermeasures, but sanctioned policies were of overriding importance to the targets. Despite the lack of effect on the ground, sanctions served signaling purposes, particular after the end of Taliban rule in 2001.

Angola: The sanctions against the União Nacional para la Independência Total de Angola (UNITA) rebels were ultimately successful in ending the civil war. Government forces were victorious, partly because of the highly imbalanced supply of arms. The arms supply to UNITA decreased over the lifetime of the embargo, while government forces continued to be well armed. Another element that crippled UNITA was targeted financial sanctions that deprived UNITA of critical funding and thus the capacity to counter the arms embargo. It took the main initiators of the sanctions, Portugal, other EU states, Canada and the US, considerable time to build a strong implementation regime for the embargo, which used partly new measures such as the first effective UN expert group report.

Armenia/Azerbaijan: During the war between the two countries, both the OSCE and the UN asked all supplier countries to abstain from arms deliveries to the warring parties. However, these voluntary arms embargoes, while observed by both the EU and the US, were not adhered to by a number of major supporters of the two countries, particularly Russia (Armenia) and Turkey (Azerbaijan). A tighter arms embargo may have had the potential to influence decision making in both countries, as the importance of arms imports was high and evasion capacities were low. However, with the war being of great importance to both countries, and no strong political backing of the arms embargoes by the initiators, the effect of the arms embargo remained very limited.

Belarus: The US arms embargo had no effect except to reinforce other signals of US disapproval of Belarussian domestic politics. The armed forces in Belarus were well equipped, and the country had major arms production facilities. Furthermore, Russia remained a supplier despite US protests.

Burundi: The arms embargo, as part of a comprehensive trade sanctions regime, was not initiated by major arms suppliers, but rather by neighboring countries. Still, it led to a marked decline in arms imports and an increase in the cost of weapons imported. Major arms suppliers supported the policies of neighboring countries; and neighboring countries had some capacity to control borders and thus limit arms flows. Even though weapons continued to come to Burundi, the military activities of both the government and the opposition were hampered. This also decreased their capacity for counter-measures. However, the embargo was successful primarily because the sanctioned policies were highly contentious within the political groupings in Burundi. Even the comparatively limited effect of the arms embargo thus contributed to policy change.

China: The EU and the US were notable arms suppliers to China before the arms embargoes of 1989. However, China was largely self-sufficient in arms production. Chinese evasion capacity further increased in the early 1990s due to growing Russian willingness to supply modern military equipment. The arms embargoes were thus largely symbolic and could have little real impact unless the US and the EU placed significant political pressure on Russia to also ban the supply of weapons to China.

Cuba: Although the US embargo was upheld by many other countries and Cuba had little evasion capacity, the embargo regime had little effect because the Soviet Union supplied most of the weapons the Cuban government asked for free of charge during the Cold War. After the end of the Cold War, the US was more successful in limiting flows of arms to Cuba, including from Russia. However, even though the sanctions regime has not led to policy change, the impact of US policies on Cuban rulers has been influential due to the growing military obsolescence of Cuban arms.

Cyprus: The US arms embargo had little effect in a situation where other suppliers could be found. It was aimed as a signal toward the Cyrus government, without much ambition by the US government to get other suppliers involved.

Eritrea/Ethiopia: The EU, US, and UN voluntary arms embargoes early in the conflict between the two countries did little to decrease arms flows because other suppliers continued to deliver weapons. In fact, arms imports from countries such as Russia increased. A mandatory UN arms embargo was possible only shortly before the end of the conflict. This embargo led to an end to almost all deliveries; however, because of the previous high level of arms imports, it is unlikely that the mandatory arms embargo had any effect on decision making in either of Eritrea or Ethiopia.

Georgia: A voluntary UN arms embargo against the warring parties in Georgia in 1993 had no effect on arms flows and no effect on decision making by the parties involved in the country's civil war.

Haiti: After the military overthrow of the elected government of President Aristide, successive types of embargoes, first by the US and then by the UN, led to increasing isolation of the country. Arms imports, which had been low already, quickly came to a halt. Still, the military junta only gave in when the arms embargo turned into comprehensive economic sanctions and the US threatened military invasion. In the case of Haiti, the direct effects of the arms embargo are particularly difficult to disentangle from the effects of the comprehensive economic sanctions and the threat of invasion, policy measures with which the arms embargo was close aligned.

India: A US arms embargo between 1998 and 2001 was hardly more than a symbolic measure as the main suppliers to the Indian armed forces were Russia and European countries. Although some of the European suppliers such as Germany reduced arms supplies in the wake of the Indian nuclear test of May 1998, the Indian armed forces nonetheless had little difficulty importing the military equipment they desired.

Indonesia: Massive human rights violations before independence of Timor Leste in 1999 led to EU and US arms embargoes. Indonesian arms imports plummeted, but it is not clear to what extent this was due to the embargoes. European countries and the US had been important suppliers to the Indonesian armed forces, but the country was also in deep economic crisis during this period and, after the end of the Suharto-regime, the allocation of resources to the military was intensely debated. Although seen as a strong political signal, the arms embargoes had little effect on the capabilities of the Indonesian armed forces, which had large stocks of weapons and ammunition and could also rely on domestic production for the first years of the new decade. The EU embargo was also quickly lifted, leading to some substitution of early US supplies.

Iran: Although only the US has maintained a formal arms embargo against the Islamic Republic of Iran, other suppliers have also operated with some restraint since the beginning of the 1990s due largely to pressure from the US. It is not likely, however, that the US arms embargo had any influence on Iranian human rights or foreign policies.

Iraq: Imports of weapons by Iraq came to a virtual halt after August 1990. As one element of the overall sanctions regime imposed after the end of the Gulf War of 1990/1991, the arms embargo contributed to the package of measures designed to force Iraq to cooperate with the international community. Although the record of Iraqi compliance is debated, it seems clear that it led to containment and disarmament, and thus reached the originally postulated goals. It is not possible to single out the specific effects of the provisions on arms within the overall sanctions package.

Liberia: The UN arms embargo against Liberia was long seen as the epitome of sanctions success, along with the Angolan case. Although it took longer than in the Angolan case, and never was as biting, the Liberia arms embargo regime also went through various stages and became increasingly effective. In the end, it seems to have contributed decisively in limiting the military capabilities of the government forces and thus to a negotiated settlement that brought an end to the conflict.

Libya: Libya was a major arms importer in the 1970s and 1980s, with most of the weapons coming from European countries and Russia. When the EU instituted an arms embargo, Russia became an even more important supplier. When the UN finally decided on an arms embargo, Libyan arsenals were already well stocked. However, beginning in the 1990s, the lack of spare parts became noticeable, particularly in the air force (there was also a parallel flight ban with major impacts on Libyan air traffic). After a long embargo period Libyan military equipment had seriously deteriorated, a factor that seems to have contributed to changes in Libyan policies, both with respect to international terrorism and non-proliferation.

Myanmar/Burma: Human rights policies of the ruling junta in Burma have not changed over the periods in which the EU and US operated arms embargoes. Neither of the embargo senders had been an important supplier of arms to Burma. China, on the other hand, the main supplier, continued to sell without regard to the US and EU embargoes.

Nigeria: The EU supplemented a number of policy measures designed to signal discontent to the ruling Nigerian military regime about their human and civil rights policies with an arms embargo. European countries had been the major suppliers to the Nigerian military before the embargo. However, it was fairly simple for the Nigerian military to substitute the EU with other suppliers. It can still be surmised that the arms embargo had some effect in finally bringing the military regime down, as one element within the overall strategies of the EU, the US and the Commonwealth countries.

North Korea: North Korea's large domestic defense industry is by far the most important supplier to the North Korean military. Although military technology imports played a role in modernizing production and products until the early 1990s, nearly complete autarky marks North Korean procurement since that time.

Pakistan: The US was Pakistan's main arms supplier during the 1960s and 1970s. Later other suppliers, particularly China, became important. Arms transfer relations between Pakistan and the US have been up and down since the 1960s. Although Pakistani dependence on US arms imports has been high, Pakistani arms supplies have not faced long-term disruption by US arms embargoes since they have been quickly lifted due to deference to US strategic interests.

Rwanda: Arms embargoes against Rwanda have had very little effect. The UN arms embargo came very late in the civil war of 1994, and only after the genocide. It was soon lifted against the government and shifted to the Hutu militia's operation in eastern District Republic of the Congo (DRC). Government forces thus could legally re-supply quickly, while in the DRC arms transfer control was very limited.

Sierra Leone: The arms embargoes on Sierra Leone, first against an illegitimate government and later against opposition forces, became more effective over time when combined with other sanctions. In the end, the embargo helped to bring the warring parties to the negotiating table, and thus end the civil war.

Somalia: The Somali arms embargo has been ineffective in changing the country's chaotic situation. Arms inflows decreased; however, this was largely due to reduced demand by various armed groups in the country. In addition, Somalia continued to be a transit for weapons into the region. Most of the supply consists of small arms that come in small consignments from Arab countries. Despite some measures to improve arms embargo implementation post-September 11, 2001, the Somali arms embargo continues to be marked by low levels of enforcement.

South Africa: The mandatory UN arms embargo of 1977 had a long gestation period during which South Africa built up a capable domestic arms industry. This industry continued to benefit from technology inflows that were only partially and belatedly sanctioned. However, with the arms embargo getting tighter over time, the South African arms industry increasingly lost its ability to produce modern weapons. This was one, albeit a minor one, of the factors shifting the balance in the ruling white South African elite toward negotiations with the representatives of the black majority.

Sudan: Sudan has seen various periods of sanctions, including arms embargoes, primarily aimed as a response to human rights violations. However, at least until 2004, these sanctions had little effect on the targeted Sudanese government. They also did not affect arms flows that predominantly came from China and Eastern European countries, which did not participate in the arms embargoes. The UN arms embargo of 2004, however, was accompanied by reduced arms inflows and a greater willingness of the Sudanese government to negotiate with the international community. Nonetheless, there was little change in Sudan's actual behavior over the Darfur crisis, which triggered this particular embargo.

Syria: Only the US has placed official arms embargoes against Syria, based on accusations of Syrian human rights violations and support for international terrorism. In addition, European countries, which had earlier supplied weapons to Syria, stopped most deliveries beginning in the 1980s. As long as Syria had the resources to pay, Russia and other Eastern European suppliers stepped in, so that there was no direct effect of the Western restrictions on the level of Syrian arms imports. It is debatable whether Syria changed policies with respect to human rights and support of international terrorism over time, but it also is not very convincing to argue that the US arms embargo had much influence on these policies.

Vietnam: The US arms embargo, accompanied by more subtle restrictions from other Western suppliers similar to an embargo, had little effect on the level of Vietnamese arms imports because Russia was and continues to provide arms. Still, one can argue that as part of a package of Western restrictive measures, the arms embargo helped contribute to some major policy changes in Vietnam, particularly with respect to economic and human rights policies. At best, however, this contribution was minor.

Yemen: Neither the US nor the voluntary UN arms embargo of 1994 did much to change arms flows to Yemen. Although the conflict between North and South Yemen ceased and the country reunited while the arms embargoes were in place, it is far fetched to argue that the arms embargoes more than marginally contributed to the peace process. It could be argued that the UN arms embargo sent a signal of discontent, which included traditional suppliers such as Russia. However, this is easily discredited by the fact that it was not possible for the UN Security Council to agree on a mandatory arms embargo, which instead sent a signal that UN opposition was not very strong.

Yugoslavia: The Yugoslavia arms embargoes have at best a mixed implementation record but still had some major effects on policies in and around the region. The embargo proved ineffective against Croatia and Bosnia, largely because of more or less open embargo evasion by minor suppliers clandestinely supported by the US. Serbia, whose arms imports were largely reduced and whose domestic arms industry suffered from the lack of input components, lost some of its initial advantages on the battlefield. This arguably helped to bring the Serb government to the negotiating table and thus contributed to peace in 1995. Later sanctions in the wake of the Kosovo crisis were again asymmetric on the ground in that they were fairly effective against the better-armed Serbia but did not stop deliveries to the Kosovo Liberation Army. The outcome of the crisis, which the arms embargo did not help to prevent, was an escalation of the crisis, contrary to the intentions of the embargo senders.

Zaire: Arms embargoes against Zaire were largely ineffective, both on the ground and in relation to targeted human rights policies. The main difficulties for embargo implementation were twofold: first, neighboring countries, with the help of Eastern European suppliers, substituted earlier arms and technology flows from Western Europe and the US; second, the porous borders of the nation allowed commercial dealers to evade arms embargoes.

Zimbabwe: The EU arms embargo led to a partial shift of arms supplies toward China and Eastern European countries. Overall, there was no reduction in arms imports. There was also no change in the direction desired by sanction senders of the incriminated policies of the government.

Table A1. List of Arms Embargo Cases.

Country	Sanctions by	Begin Year	End Year	Type of Sanctions	Target*	Sanctions Objective
Afghanistan	UN	1996		Voluntary UN arms embargo	All parties	End of civil war; human rights
Afghanistan	UN	2000		UN arms embargo	Taliban	End of support for terrorism; extradition of Usama bin Laden
Afghanistan	EU	1996	2001	EU arms embargo	All parties	End of civil war
Afghanistan	EU	2001		EU arms embargo	Taliban	End of support for terrorism
Afghanistan	US	1996	2001	US arms embargo	All parties	End of civil war
Afghanistan	US	2001		US arms embargo	All non-government groups	End of support for terrorism
Angola	UN	1993	2003	UN arms embargo	UNITA	End of civil war
Armenia	OSCE	1992		Voluntary OSCE arms embargo		End of hostilities
Armenia	UN	1993		Voluntary UN arms embargo		End of hostilities
Armenia	US	1993		US arms embargo		End of hostilities
Azerbeijan	OSCE	1992		Voluntary OSCE arms embargo		End of hostilities
Azerbeijan	UN	1993		Voluntary UN arms embargo		End of hostilities
Azerbeijan	US	1993		US arms embargo		End of hostilities
Belarus	US	1993		US arms embargo		Regime change
Burundi	Regional	1996	1999	Comprehensive economic sanctions		End of civil war

Country	Sender	Year imposed	Year lifted	Type	Region	Objective
China PR	EU	1999		EU arms embargo		Human rights
China PR	US	1999		US arms embargo		Human rights
Congo DR	UN	2003		UN arms embargo	Ituri and Southern Kivu	End of civil war
Cuba	US	1958		US arms embargo		Regime change
Cuba	US	1962		US comprehensive sanctions		Regime change
Cyprus	US	1992		US arms embargo		End of hostilities
Eritrea	EU	1999	2001	EU arms embargo		End of hostilities
Eritrea	UN	1999	2000	Voluntary UN arms embargo		End of hostilities
Eritrea	UN	2000	2001	UN arms embargo		End of hostilities
Ethiopia	US	1998	2001	US arms embargo		End of hostilities
Ethiopia	EU	1999	2001	EU arms embargo		End of hostilities
Ethiopia	UN	1999	2000	Voluntary UN arms embargo		End of hostilities
Ethiopia	UN	2000	2001	UN arms embargo		End of hostilities
Georgia	UN	1993		Voluntary UN arms embargo		End of hostilities
Haiti	US	1991	1994	US arms embargo		Regime change
Haiti	UN	1993	1994	UN arms embargo		Regime change
Haiti	UN	1994	1994	Comprehensive economic sanctions		Regime change
India	US	1998	2001	US arms embargo		Change in nuclear policies
Indonesia	EU	1999	2000	EU arms embargo		Human rights
Indonesia	US	1999		US arms embargo		Human rights
Iran	US	1984		US arms embargo		End support of terrorism
Iran	US	1995		US comprehensive sanctions		End support of terrorism, change nuclear policies

Table A1. (*Continued*)

Country	Sanctions by	Begin Year	End Year	Type of Sanctions	Target*	Sanctions Objective
Iraq	UN	1990	2003	UN comprehensive sanctions		End of occupation of Kuwait, verification of WMD disarmament
Iraq	EU	2003	2004	EU arms embargo		Containment of hostilities
Liberia	UN	1992		UN arms embargo		End of civil war
Libya	UN	1992	2003	UN arms embargo		End support of terrorism
Libya	EU	1986	2004	EU arms embargo		End support of terrorism
Libya	US	1978		US arms embargo		End support of terrorism
Myanmar/Burma	EU	1991		EU arms embargo		Human rights
Myanmar/Burma	US	1988		US arms embargo		Human rights
Nigeria	EU	1995	1999	EU arms embargo		Human rights
North Korea	US	1950		US comprehensive sanctions		Regime change
Pakistan	US	1979	1981	US arms embargo		Change in nuclear policies
Pakistan	US	1990	2001	US arms embargo		Change in nuclear policies
Rwanda	UN	1994	1995	UN arms embargo		End civil war, stop human rights violations
Rwanda	UN	1995		UN arms embargo	Hutu groups	End hostilities
Rwanda	US	1994	2003	US arms embargo	Non-governmental forces	End hostilities
Rwanda	US	2003	2004	US arms embargo		End hostilities

Country	Sender	Start	End	Type	Target*	Objective
Sierra Leone	UN	1997	1998	UN arms embargo		Regime change; end of civil war
Sierra Leone	UN	1998	2002	UN arms embargo	Rebels	End of civil war
Somalia	UN	1992		UN arms embargo		End of civil war
South Africa	UN	1977	1993	UN arms embargo		Regime change
Sudan	UN	2004		UN arms embargo		Human rights, end of civil war
Sudan	EU	1994		EU arms embargo		Human rights, end of civil war
Sudan	US	1992		US arms embargo		Human rights, end of civil war
Sudan	US	1997		US comprehensive sanctions		Human rights, end of civil war
Syria	EU	1986	1994	EU arms embargo		End support of terrorism
Syria	US	1991		US arms embargo		End support of terrorism
Vietnam	US	1984		US arms embargo		Regime change
Yemen	UN	1994		UN voluntary arms embargo		End of hostilities
Yemen	US	1992		US arms embargo		End of hostilities
Yugoslavia	UN	1991	1996	UN arms embargo		End of hostilities
Yugoslavia	UN	1992	1995	UN comprehensive sanctions		End of hostilities
Yugoslavia	UN	1998	2001	UN arms embargo		End of hostilities
Yugoslavia	EU	1991	2001	EU arms embargo		End of hostilities
Zaire	US	1993		US arms embargo		Human rights
Zaire	EU	1993		EU arms embargo		Human rights
Zimbabwe	EU	2002		EU arms embargo		Human rights
Zimbabwe	US	2002		US arms embargo		Human rights

*Unless government.

CHAPTER 10

PUTTING TEETH IN THE TIGER: POLICY CONCLUSIONS FOR EFFECTIVE ARMS EMBARGOES

Michael Brzoska and George A. Lopez

The case studies presented in this book, as well as in the quantitative analysis, illustrate the difficulties that the general public, as well as decision-makers, have with arms embargoes: These measures hardly ever achieve the ending of internal war or a complete change in the behavior of the targeted states or group. Arms and supplies have been getting through to violent actors in most cases and combating forces seldom seem to need to stop fighting for lack of supplies.

The case studies also demonstrate, however, that in a good number of cases arms embargoes do have noticeable effects on arms supply patterns. There is also strong evidence that the implementation of arms embargoes has improved since the mid-1990s. Arms embargoes are increasingly having effects. These effects can primarily be seen in arms supply patterns. Generally, UN and other multilateral arms embargoes lead to some, and in some cases substantial reductions in arms imports by targeted states and groups. Arms supply shifts from established arms exports to new sources, generally supplying less modern and less advanced type of weapons. Open trade is supplanted by clandestine and circuitous re-supply.

The changes in arms-import patterns also influence warfare on the ground. Forces tend to shift to fighting with less-advanced weapons and in

Putting Teeth in the Tiger: Improving the Effectiveness of Arms Embargoes
Contributions to Conflict Management, Peace Economics and Development, Volume 10, 243–254
Copyright © 2009 by Emerald Group Publishing Limited
All rights of reproduction in any form reserved
ISSN: 1572-8323/doi:10.1108/S1572-8323(2009)0000010014

sporadic, short battles. Increasingly, civilians are targeted. Arms embargoes thus demonstrate similar effects to those found in 'new wars' (Kaldor, 1999). On the one hand, we are not surprised that many of the cases of 'new wars', such as those in former Yugoslavia, Angola, Sierra Leone and Liberia, occur under arms embargoes. On the other hand, arms embargoes are only one element leading to the shifts in warfare marking 'new wars', such as the dominance of small arms and light weapons, sporadic fighting and the large ratio of civilian victims of warfare. In some of the archetypal 'new wars', such as in the Congo, multilateral arms embargoes only came about after many years of 'dirty fighting'. And with lucrative contraband trade in commodities fueling the cycle of arms and violence, targeted commodity sanctions may be as essential, if not more powerful, than an arms embargo to produce an end to war-making.

The shift towards such fighting lessens the dependence on external arms supplies. But as in particular the case of the sanctions against UNITA in Angola proves, it does not eliminate the needs for re-supply, particularly with ammunitions. Fighting forces can reduce demand for arms substantially and still continue to fight, but they cannot go on forever. Thus, the question of whether arms embargoes are able to cut off weapon supplies remains relevant – but the likelihood that fighting will actually cease drops with the adoption of strategies of low-intensity war fighting.

What then to make of arms embargoes? Do they serve a purpose when their main effects are to change arms supplies and war-fighting patterns, but very seldom have the desired political effects of ending wars or changing a target's policies? How can arms embargoes be improved in a way that has the effects desired by those deciding to impose such arms embargoes?

This chapter will review some of the suggestions made in the earlier and more recent literature on arms embargoes in light of the analysis presented in this book. The discussion follows the distinction between various levels of effectiveness laid out in the introductory framework chapter, but starting with the third level of sender satisfaction and working back to the first level of changing target policies.

ACHIEVING THE POLITICAL OBJECTIVES OF ARMS EMBARGOES

Arms embargoes in themselves are not able to achieve political goals. At least in the past, they neither stopped wars, nor did they change the political behavior of the targeted states or groups.

In none of the cases studied in this book did restrictions on arms supplies stop a war. It is more debatable, for instance in the cases of Angola, Liberia and Sierra Leone, whether arms embargoes made wars shorter or reduced violence. However, and probably more significant, these arms embargoes were embedded in broader policy measures, including additional sanctions. The wars in Angola, Liberia and Sierra Leone were shortened by packages of international policies in which arms embargoes had an important place. The prime reaction to arms embargoes, however, was first an expansion of efforts to obtain arms, and, when arms embargoes became to be better enforced and financial sanctions were added, changes in war-fighting with the goal to reduce the dependence on external weapons supplies.

Major lessons can be learned from the few cases where the imposition of arms embargoes was correlated with the attainment of political objectives:

- Arms embargoes had a greater chance of correlation with the achievement of policy objectives when combined with other sanctions. Arms embargoes should be part of larger packages of policy measures, aiming to achieve the desired policy objectives. Stand-alone arms embargoes have very little chance of achieving policy outcomes.
- Reductions in arms flows are important. They are one element in decision-making over the continuation of the targeted behavior. However, decision-making needs to be influenced on more scores than the difficulties to receive weapons. International policies aimed at changing the behavior of states or groups therefore cannot rely on arms embargoes, but rather needs to be supplemented with other measures.
- Combinations of sanctions are one instrument that can enhance the effectiveness of arms embargoes. Packages of 'smart' sanctions, including financial sanctions, travel bans, other commodity bans, and, in the case of Liberia, 'secondary sanctions', contributed to the achievement of policy objectives in Angola, Liberia and Sierra Leone. Comprehensive economic sanctions, including arms embargoes, also had effects in the desired directions in the cases of Yugoslavia before the Dayton Peace Agreement and Iraq.
- Arms embargoes were more likely to contribute to the achievement of the desired policy outcome, when they were applied asymmetrical, that is, when only one side in a conflict was embargoed, whereas the other side was allowed to receive weapons. Sanctioned groups were increasingly put at a military disadvantage in Angola, Liberia and Sierra Leone. Furthermore, prior sanctions make subsequent external military action more likely to be quickly successful. The government of Saddam Hussein

in Iraq and the Taliban in Afghanistan came to a quick end, partly, because troops were not well armed when attacked. In the Kosovo war of 1999, Serbian troops, after many years of arms embargoes, also were not well armed.

Recent studies by SIPRI and the sanctions project at Uppsala substantiate a number of these 'findings' but also add a dimension that is substantially new: that in cases of Sierra Leone and Liberia, when UN peacekeepers and other regional actors were involved in monitoring and enforcing the arms restrictions, their success and political relevance increased substantially (Fruchart, Holtom, Wezeman, Strandow, & Wallensteen, 2007).

STOPPING ARMS FLOWS

Arms embargoes are supposed to work through strictly limiting the availability of weapons to targeted states or groups. But targets react. One of the usual effects of arms embargoes, therefore, is an increase in the level of resources devoted to arms purchases if additional resources in the targeted state are available. Fundamental microeconomic theory implies that increased demand and reduced supply will lead to a higher price for weapons and a reduction in the quantities exchanges, with exact quantities depending on the shifts in demand and supply curves as well as their slopes. The case studies provide some evidence, though no solid data on rises in the prices of weapons for targeted states and groups. What is well documented, is that arms suppliers of various sorts are attracted by the opportunities to make money though illicit deliveries provided by arms embargoes.

The change in arms supplies is most noticeable for UN arms embargoes. Embargoes by the EU and the US also had some effects – weapons from these embargoing entities were greatly reduced in all relevant cases – however, the 'ripple' effects stopped short of making unilateral arms embargoes similar to multilateral ones. Among 'embargo breakers' notice-able in the cases studied in this book, three groups stand out:

- *Governments allied to the target.* Most embargoed states or groups had friends willing to, at least covertly, supply arms, act as transshipment state or help in some other way. Examples include Pakistan for the Afghanistan embargo, Burkina Faso for the Liberia sanctions and China for the Burma embargo. Governments have very seldom admitted to behavior in violation of arms embargoes. This was not because they had to fear actions by the UN Security Council or other initiators of arms embargoes.

So far, only one government, Liberia in 2002, was reprimanded by the Security Council for violation of a UN arms embargo or lack of national implementation of a UN arms embargo. For instance, although an expert committee that investigated the arms embargo against Angola (UNITA) named a number of governments such as Burkina Faso, Ivory Coast and Rwanda, no secondary sanctions followed. Judging by its past record, chances are low that the Security Council will actually reprimand a government because of the violation of an embargo. What governments fear most is public exposure for arms embargo violations. A number of governments have experienced the 'shaming power' of international NGOs and the media. Arms embargo violations are material for headlines and can influence international perception of a government's behavior in international affairs.

- *Private arms dealers and brokers.* The business of arms embargo breaking is predominantly done by small-scale arms dealers. Some of these such as Victor Bout gained prominence during the 1990s. He was involved in shipping and selling arms to several of the embargoed groups and states in Africa. Although private persons and small companies have predominantly been the sanction violators, they have benefited from a lack of government oversight and control, and, in some cases, direct government support. Skepticism is warranted toward official statements that governments were not aware of any violations of arms embargoes affected by private persons, but it is true that oversight and enforcement capabilities are poor in many countries.
- *Arms-producing states without proper export control.* Most of the weapons supplied in defiance of arms embargoes during the 1990s came from East European states such as Bulgaria, Serbia and Ukraine. The arms were then shipped to embargoed states and groups by private dealers. The lack of control often begins at the weapon stocks under the control of armed forces, extends to production facilities and goes on to border controls. Not all countries have put much emphasis in enforcing UN arms embargoes. Violations seem more likely to originate from countries where the economic pressure to export weapons is especially strong. Bulgaria and Ukraine, both with sizeable arms industries but in difficult economic circumstances, were quite often alleged to be sources of weapons that reach targeted states or groups. In fact, loopholes in national laws, weak enforcement of the law, gaps in border patrol, etc. have been major problems of implementation of all arms embargoes. Because data are limited, it cannot be said with certainty, whether targeted states and group are spending more on arms imports when embargoed. UNITA in Angola

is one case where expenditures for arms seem to have increased considerably over time. In other cases, however, such as Burma or Afghanistan, this does not seem to have been so.

A potential mitigating factor for the effectiveness of arms embargoes are domestic weapon production capabilities. Few of the countries studied in this book had the option to shift from imports to domestic production. Even in these cases such as Serbia and Iraq, there is no strong evidence that this made a difference. It seems that in both cases, domestic arms industries were capable of producing some items but not the spectrum of equipment needed by the armed forces. At least, both armed forces were badly equipped after several years of sanctions, as witnessed during the Kosovo and the Second Iraq war.

Both the case studies and the quantitative analysis indicate that the implementation of arms embargoes has improved in the new century. One reason is that states owning or producing arms have improved their export controls. Although there are still sources of weapons for private arms dealers, these are not as abundant as they were in the late 1990s. Private arms dealers are also under stronger supervision than they were a few years ago, in most countries. Another reason is that the monitoring of arms embargoes by the UN has had growing importance in raising international awareness over sanction busting, mainly through the work of active sanction committees and special investigative missions. These are now a regular feature of UN arms embargoes. A watershed in international attention to sanctions compliance seems to have been the UN Secretary General's report on conflicts in Africa (S/1998/318). But the UN's monitoring capacity remain hampered by the unwillingness of governments to provide much information, especially intelligence information, a lack of resources available and rules of procedure such as unanimity in committees established by the Security Council.

Arms embargoes have been least effective in Africa in the 1990s. Small arms were widely available on black markets in various parts of the continent and neighboring countries had very limited means to stop trade, even if they were prepared to do so. African arms embargoes lacked enforcement on the ground, especially in the African cases of the 1990s. The realities of the markets for small arms and surplus major weapons would have required a much stronger investment into enforcement capabilities in many countries, ranging from preventing corrupt officials from signing false end-user certificates to more effective border control.

Numerous proposals have been made to improve the effectiveness of arms embargoes. Obviously, the first issue that needs to be addressed is commitment to arms embargoes. Most proposals for reform assume that governments actually want arms embargoes to be effective. If that was not the case, as in the example of Yugoslavia from 1992 or unilateral arms embargoes, improvements in effectiveness will be difficult to achieve, as the crucial actors to make them more effective, national governments have no, or limited, interests in doing so. The best proposals for reform are worthless if they do not have the political support of governments which are the only actors capable of regulating the trade in arms and related goods.

Sometimes the view is expressed that political will is all that is lacking, that it would be sufficient if governments efficiently used the instruments available. However, this view underestimates the complexities of multilateral arms transfer restraints as well as the practical problems of implementation. Governments need to be able to be clear about what the embargo covers, with respect to goods and destinations. No government with a sizeable arms industry will voluntarily impede more export business than the minimum required by an embargo. Governments also need to be capable of implementing an embargo, in legal terms, as well as with respect to practical means of implementation, such as border controls. Proposals for reform cannot substitute lacking political will, but they can help increase effectiveness of arms embargoes which have been agreed upon in the Security Council.

Laws and regulations need to be properly enforced, and many governments, for instance in Africa, lack these capabilities. And, as Lamb (2007) notes, outside the European Union there is little national legislative coordination with regional or UN actors in a way that would both enhance enforcement and increase the political priority of making sanctions work. The threat of the law, even where it exists in authoritative print, becomes empty if there is no enforcement of proper licensing procedures for arms sales, no consistent checks of end-user certificates, loose border controls, unguarded international airports and so on.

Improved law enforcement has limited value if it does not result in high costs for violators. This concerns violators in the neighborhood of targeted states, but often also arms dealers, brokers and financiers in countries far away from the targeted state. A first requirement that unfortunately is not met in all states is that the violation of arms embargoes carries severe punishments. To be able to convict, courts need to have sufficient evidence. Especially in cases that involve actors in several countries, it is often difficult and time consuming to collect and accumulate the evidence. International cooperation in prosecution of violators of arms embargoes, for instance through Interpol, has so far been limited mostly to the industrialized countries. A more concerted effort to coordinate prosecution might help raise the probability that violators are actually punished. This is the purview of police forces and other crime prevention units; however, their work might benefit from closer cooperation with organizations concerned with monitoring arms embargoes.

As law enforcement and prosecution are far from perfect, monitoring of arms embargoes is essential to assess the impacts and effectiveness of an arms embargo but also to improve adherence through the exposure of suspected violators. Fear of exposure will deter sanctions breaking by both states and private actors, especially if it becomes the basis for punitive action.

A number of suggestions have been made to further strengthen the UN's capabilities to monitor arms embargoes, but there has been no agreement on how this would best be done. Proposals range from establishing a new UN body in charge of verifying various multilateral arms-related agreements and provisions to placing UN sanction monitors at crucial transit points, to strengthening the number and expertise of the UN Secretariat's professional staff, which is in charge of supporting the Security Council's work on embargoes (Knight, 1998; Brzoska, 2001; Bondi, 2001; Wallensteen, Staibano, & Eriksson, 2002).

In addition to some improvement in monitoring at the UN, there has been an increased interest and capacity by NGOs to improve compliance with arms embargoes. As several of the case studies show, NGOs, such as Human Rights Watch, International Alert, Global Witness and International Crisis Group, are a major source for information about sanctions busting. There are limits to the information-gathering activities of NGOs. They have limited resources and capacities. Also, they have agendas in addition to monitoring an embargo, which may influence the direction of their research efforts. As embargo violations do have potential 'shame power', the media has also been interested in investigating and publishing allegations.

IMPROVING SENDER SATISFACTION

Sender satisfaction with arms embargoes is closely related to success both with respect to achieving substantial reductions in arms flows to the targeted state or group and the achievement of policy objectives.

The frequent use of arms embargoes in the early 1990s undermined rather than reinforced the trust in arms embargoes as 'smart sanctions'. It was frequently questioned whether arms embargoes ever had, and even can have under current circumstances, the desired effect of reducing the targeted state's or group's ability to threaten or break the peace, or perform acts of aggression (Tierney, 2005).

The improvement in arms embargo implementation since the late 1990s that was documented both in a number of case studies and the quantitative chapter has not led to a reassessment of arms embargoes. Arms embargoes continue to be seen primarily as a very public form of self-restraint with little effect on targets.

Although this is true for many arms embargoes, it is not true for all. As argued earlier, arms embargoes that are part of larger policy measures and are well-implemented do have effects in the desired direction. Solitary arms embargoes, particularly if not multilateral but mandated by one country only, however, are largely symbolical measures, even when they are mandated by powerful entities such as the United States or the European Union. The embargoes against Burma and Rwanda are cases in point.

The political commitment to a UN arms embargo can only come about through the interplay of national political debates and international diplomatic negotiations. These debates benefit from a clearer understanding of what the objectives and likely effects of an arms embargo under discussion are. The list of objectives of arms embargoes has been expanded beyond a narrow interpretation of the maintenance and restoration of international peace and security in Chapter VII of the UN Charter and includes, for instance, the fight against international terrorism and against severe violations of human rights in the case of Rwanda. This is in line with the international reassessment of the foundations of peace and security and the role of the UN. However, there has been no parallel reassessment of what arms embargoes can actually achieve in cases where the fighting power of military forces is not a major issue. Correspondingly, observers find a long list of functions that arms embargoes have actually had to fulfill, ranging from punishment of sanctioned behavior to domestic symbolism in targeting countries. Arms embargoes that are primarily perceived as a politically motivated substitute to more stringent actions are not likely to become effective.

In addition to clearer understanding of the objectives of an arms embargo under discussion, as the basis for agreement on its imposition, more effort into the analysis of the likely effects might help to improve arms embargoes. In fact, objectives and likely effects need to be seen together, as part of the larger assessment of costs and benefits of arms embargoes mentioned earlier. Net costs for the targeted and targeting states, including likely adaptive action by targets and opportunity costs for inaction, or more stringent action by targeting states, need to be analyzed together to make sure that the embargo is 'smart'.

The cost argument makes it clear that commitment not only has a political side, it also has an economic one. Costs are higher to some states than others. Arms embargoes are especially costly to states that do not have much to export besides weapons, and those with weak governments, including weak laws, law enforcement capabilities and border controls.

CONCLUSIONS

The obvious deficits in arms embargo implementation have led the Security Council and other relevant actors since the mid-1990s to adopt a few measures designed to improve the effectiveness of arms embargoes, such as changes in the work of sanction committees, and the authorization of special missions. However, they have been slow in implementing more far reaching proposals, some of which were presented earlier, even when they came from bodies instituted by the Security Council, such as the International Commission on Inquiry on Rwanda, or as part of a package with a wider scope, such as its resolution on the promotion of durable peace and sustainable development in Africa (UN Sec Res 1196/1998).

There is a long list of measures that would put more teeth into arms embargoes, such as more commitment, common understanding of resolutions, better national implementation, closing of loopholes in national laws, strengthening of legal and administrative authority in supplier and neighboring countries, improved border monitoring, better information gathering and accumulation at the UN, better coordination with similar activities by NGOs, at the state level and by regional organizations and the use of investigative missions to uncover and report on violations of arms embargoes. The scope of reforms deemed necessary may differ among experts, but the direction is clear: more commitment by states, more government oversight, more resources at the UN, especially of a creative kind as has been manifest in the case of Liberia.

Our general acknowledgement of the poor effectiveness of arms embargoes and measures necessary for reform will not automatically lead to the necessary changes. Reforms will only come about if there is sufficient political pressure to implement them. NGOs have been very successful in highlighting the deficits of arms embargoes and have had some success in making arms embargo more effective, for instance through instigating special missions. Some governments have also pushed for reform, for instance in sanction committees. The UN Secretariat itself has lobbied for many improvements (United Nations Sanctions Secretariat, 1999). But many governments remain unwilling to support reforms, for many reasons, ranging from disinterest in the matter to unwillingness to give the UN more resources in this field.

Initiatives not directly aimed at arms embargoes but at certain aspects of the arms trade - for instance on illegal arms trade, small arms and practical disarmament - have had an important bearing on the effectiveness of embargoes through their goal to stem the flow of arms which are difficult to control. It is also a good sign that a number of regional organizations and groups of states have shown an increased interest in matters of arms transfer control. Especially promising in this respect is the example of the small arms moratorium of a number of West African states. In general, 'practical disarmament' that aims at the collection and elimination of weapons, especially small arms, enhances the chances for sanction success in neighboring countries. It can also serve as an incentive to third countries to participate in arms embargoes.

Arms embargoes remain a potentially potent tool of the international community to help in efforts to prevent, deescalate and stop wars, when sanctions are taken seriously. The embargoes against Yugoslavia and Iraq are cases in point. Arms embargoes attained an image of being largely cosmetic because of poor implementation and enforcement, in a number of cases, but also changes in the way many wars were fought and resupplied. Some improvement is discernable on both fronts: implementation and enforcement is taken more seriously than before and the trade in small arms and light weapons is getting much international attention. More needs to be done, however, to substantially increase the chances that all arms embargoes are effective, including better arms export controls in many supplier countries, improved border control in states neighboring targeted states, more effective monitoring and a greater linkage to other UN actions such as the deployment of peace-keepers in conflict zones.

REFERENCES

Bondi, L. (2001). Arms embargoes: In name only. In: M. Brzoska (Ed.), *Smart sanctions: The next steps-the debate on arms embargoes and travel sanctions within the 'Bonn-Berlin-Process'*. Baden-Baden: Nomos Verlagsgesellschaft.

Brzoska, M. (Ed.) (2001). *Smart sanctions: The next steps-the debate on arms embargoes and travel sanctions within the 'Bonn-Berlin-Process'*. Baden-Baden: Nomos Verlagsgesellschaft.

Fruchart, D., Holtom, P., Wezeman, S. T., Strandow, D., & Wallensteen, P. (2007). *United Nations arms embargoes: Their impact on flows and target behaviour.* Stockholm and Uppsala: SIPRI and Department of Peace and Conflict Studies.

Kaldor, M. (1999). *Old and new wars.* London: Polity Press.

Knight, W. A. (1998). *The United Nations and arms embargo verification.* Lewiston, Queenston, Lampeter: The Edwin Mellen Press.

Lamb, G. (2007). Beyond 'shadow boxing' and 'lip service': The enforcement of arms embargoes in Africa. ISS Paper 135. 15pp.

Tierney, D. (2005). Irrelevant or malevolent? UN arms embargoes in civil wars. *Review of International Studies, 31*(4), 645–664.

United Nations Sanctions Secretariat. Department of Political Affairs. (1999). The experience of the United Nations in administering arms embargoes and travel sanctions. An Informal Background Paper. Paper prepared for First Expert Seminar on Smart Sanctions, The Next Step: Arms Embargoes and Travel Sanctions, Bonn, November 21–23, 1999. Available at http://www.bicc.de

Wallensteen, P., Staibano, C., & Eriksson, M. (Eds). (2002). *Making targeted sanctions effective: Guidelines for the implementation of UN policy options.* Uppsala: Department of Peace and Conflict Studies.

ABOUT THE AUTHORS

Marc von Boemcken is a senior researcher at the Bonn International Center for Conversion, Germany. His areas of expertise include the international arms trade as well as the privatization of security provision.

Michael Brzoska is professor in the Department of Political Science and Director of the Institute for Peace Research and Security Studies at the University of Hamburg, Germany. He formerly was with the Bonn International Center of Conversion, Germany, and the Stockholm International Peace Research Institute, Sweden. He has published widely on economic aspects of war and peace, including the international arms trade.

Oldrich Bures is senior lecturer, Department of International Relations and European Studies Metropolitan University Prague, The Czech Republic. He has written on United Nations peacekeeping and the European Unions counter-terrorism policy.

Sami Faltas currently is the executive director of the Centre for European Security Studies, University of Groningen. He formerly was senior researcher at the Bonn International Center of Conversion, Germany, focusing his research on small arms and light weapons.

Sumita Kumar is research officer at the Institute for Defence Studies and Analyses, New Delhi, India, writing primarily on South Asian security issues. She wrote her chapter during her time as guest researcher at the Bonn International Center for Conversion, Germany.

George A. Lopez holds the Rev. Theodore M. Hesburgh, CSC, Chair of Peace Studies at the Kroc Institute for International Peace Studies at the University of Notre Dame. Working primarily with David Cortright, he has edited and written 5 books and more than 20 articles on economic sanctions.

Wolf-Christian Paes is senior researcher at the Bonn International Center for Conversion, Germany, working on issues related to small arms and light weapons, natural resources and armed conflict in Africa.

Maraike Wenzel is a freelance journalist in Cologne, Germany, specializing on international affairs. She was a research assistant at the Bonn International Center for Conversion, Germany, at the time of her contribution to this volume.